D1125967

Usefulness to Investors and Creditors of Information Provided by Financial Reporting:

A Review of Empirical Accounting Research

Paul A. Griffin

Financial Accounting Standards Board

RESEARCH REPORTS

Please turn to inside back cover for other titles and ordering information.

Usefulness to Investors and Creditors of Information Provided by Financial Reporting:

A Review of Empirical Accounting Research

Paul A. Griffin
University of California at Davis

Financial Accounting Standards Board
of the Financial Accounting Foundation
HIGH RIDGE PARK, STAMFORD, CONNECTICUT 06905

WILLIAM MADISON RANDALL LIBRARY UNC AT WILMINGTON

Copyright © 1982 by Financial Accounting Standards Board
Library of Congress Catalog Card Number: 82-71093

HF5681
.B2
.G79
1982

FOREWORD

The FASB is committed to a better understanding of how financial information can be used by decision makers. The principal objective of financial reporting as set out in FASB Concepts Statement No. 1, *Objectives of Financial Reporting by Business Enterprises,* paragraph 34, is to "provide information that is useful to present and potential investors and creditors and other users in making rational investment, credit, and similar decisions." Decision usefulness is a critical criterion for selecting among accounting policies. The process of better understanding decision usefulness should begin by gathering the results of relevant empirical research.

Empirical research has expanded at what appears to be a geometric rate since the mid-1960s. To make that research easier to assimilate, the results of the relevant research must be summarized and interpreted; moreover, if the insights available from empirical research are to influence the formation of accounting policy, key findings must be communicated to persons interested in the standard-setting process.

This study is a response to those needs. It is a comprehensive review of empirical research on the usefulness of financial information to investors and creditors. By codifying the extant research, Paul Griffin has provided an important starting point—a frame of reference—for a program of further research.

It will take many more years of research, perhaps using methodologies presently in their infancy or not yet developed, before we are comfortable that we have ascertained how investment, credit, and similar decisions are made and how financial information affects decision makers.

Stamford, Connecticut
March 1982

Michael O. Alexander
Director of Research
and Technical Activities

iii

230186

PREFACE

This Research Report identifies, organizes, and examines the evidence from empirical research in accounting. Intended for those who are interested in empirical research and its relationship to accounting and reporting policy, this report brings together what is presently known about the usefulness of financial information to investors and creditors. The report summarizes what effects such information has on investors' and creditors' behavior, both individually and collectively. The project is part of an FASB research program to learn more about how users process information and make decisions.

The studies reviewed cover research in accounting and the many disciplines that underlie accounting, such as economics, finance, psychology, and statistics. The works are classified according to whether their results pertain to (1) the environment of accounting, (2) the properties of accounting numbers, or (3) the behavior of investors or creditors as users of those numbers. Research methodology was an important consideration in assessing the quality of the materials selected—that selection was based on a broad sweep of the literature since the early 1960s.

Many people contributed to this study. I would like to express my gratitude to Michael Gibbins and Patricia Brennan of The University of British Columbia for contributing their insightful chapter on behavioral accounting research. I appreciate the helpful comments and sage advice of project advisors Victor H. Brown (Firestone Tire & Rubber Co.), John C. Burton (Columbia University), and Oscar S. Gellein (former member of the FASB). I appreciate also the efforts of the FASB staff in providing valuable consultation and criticism throughout the study. Bryan Carsberg (now at the London School of Economics), Jules M. Cassel, Terry A. Mortimer (now at Becton Dickinson Company), Reed K. Storey, and Edward P. Swanson provided helpful and detailed comments on earlier versions of the manuscript. Special thanks should be given to Michael O. Alexander for his steady support and encouragement. A. Rashad Abdel-khalik (University of Florida) also provided helpful comments. Competent editorial assistance was provided by Ellen Falk and Marianne Losch (FASB) and Heidi Roizen (Tandem Computers, Inc.). Wang Laboratories, Inc. provided technical assistance. Karen Tuozzolo typed the manuscript.

Last, but not least, I am deeply indebted to my former colleagues at the Graduate School of Business, Stanford University, especially William H. Beaver and Charles T. Horngren. Their thoughts, comments, and wisdom no doubt shaped much of my thinking in the preparation of this report. Stanford doctoral students Wayne R. Landsman and Antonio Z. Sanvicente served ably as research assistants in assembling and reviewing the materials.

Funding for this project was provided by the FASB. In addition, the Stanford Research Program in Accounting, The University of British Columbia, and the University of California at Davis provided research, secretarial, and computer support. Completion of this research study was unquestionably facilitated by that support.

Paul A. Griffin
Graduate School of Administration
University of California at Davis
March 1982

RESEARCH REPORT

Usefulness to Investors and Creditors of Information Provided by Financial Reporting: A Review of Empirical Accounting Research

CONTENTS   Page

PART I

CHAPTER 1—INTRODUCTION

A quiet revolution has taken place in accounting during the past two decades. Accounting researchers, by adopting scientific methods of inquiry, have generated a substantial body of empirically based knowledge. That knowledge concerns, primarily, the actual uses of financial information by decision makers and the effects of changes in that information on their behavior. Research examining a decision maker's use of information, and the aggregate or market effects thereof, has provided accounting policymakers and others who must select or evaluate accounting alternatives with an established body of knowledge to draw upon.

This report brings together much of that evidence. Intended for readers such as standard setters, accountants, and enterprise managers, this book presents a timely and comprehensive review of the empirical research on the uses and effects of information provided by financial reporting. To achieve this, several hundred studies have been catalogued. While the emphasis is on the more recent studies, earlier research is also examined, as it often helps to sequence material or provide a foundation for discussion of the later findings. The scope of this report is described in the second section of this chapter.

Overriding Objectives of Financial Reporting

FASB Concepts Statement No. 1, *Objectives of Financial Reporting by Business Enterprises,* states the overriding objective of general purpose financial reporting: "Financial reporting should provide information that is useful to present and potential investors and creditors and other users in making rational investment, credit, and similar decisions" (paragraph 34). The characteristics of accounting information that make it useful to investors, creditors, and others have also been defined by the Board. FASB Concepts Statement No. 2, *Qualitative Characteristics of Accounting Information,* presents a hierarchy of qualities that should be inherent in useful financial information. "Relevance" and "reliability" are of

1

primary importance in that hierarchy.[1] Those qualities are constrained, however, by two factors specific to individual users. All standards are expected to pass a cost-benefit test that weighs impact on all parties—preparers, auditors, and users. Financial information required by the FASB is also expected to be understandable to those "who have a reasonable understanding of business and economic activities and are willing to study the information with reasonable diligence" (Concepts Statement 1, paragraph 34).

The preceding objectives appear consistent with the views of the FASB constituency. A Louis Harris and Associates survey (1980), prepared at the request of the Financial Accounting Foundation, yielded strong results concerning the objectives and audience of financial reporting. With the exception of chief executive officers, respondents by roughly a two-to-one margin said that investment-oriented users should be given priority for financial reporting. The view that financial reports should provide information about management's discharge of fiduciary responsibility was accorded a lower priority.

In brief, fulfilling certain users' needs is apparently viewed as the predominant reporting objective by those in business, finance, and accounting. But it should not be surprising that the sentiment of such groups is in close harmony with the stated overriding objective of financial reporting. Extensive due process procedures of the FASB are likely to bring about general acceptance of such views. Continuous efforts by the Board and its staff to educate the public about its work should also achieve a certain consensus of opinion.

Relationship between Objectives and Empirical Evidence

But whether—and in what manner—the stated objectives are being met cannot be answered satisfactorily by either declarations of policy or opinion polling. A determination of whether account-

---

[1]*Relevant* accounting information "must be capable of making a difference in a decision by helping users to form predictions about the outcomes of past, present, and future events or to confirm or correct expectations" (Concepts Statement 2, par. 47). *Reliable* accounting information has certain measurement properties: (1) the accounting measure should correspond faithfully with the real-world phenomenon that it purports to represent, (2) the measure should be verifiable, and (3) the measure should be neutral, that is, not predisposed to a certain purpose, action, or consequence (Concepts Statement 2, pars. 58-110).

ing information is useful and serves investors and creditors depends in part on empirical research.[2] Accounting issues must be resolved positively, based on a systematic investigation of information-processing and decision-making behavior at the individual and market levels, and by the study of the consequences of such behavior, among other relevant issues.

However, empirical analysis of the use of accounting information, while having possible policy implications, makes few judgments about whether reporting objectives are being met. Further, the collection of empirical evidence does not necessarily constitute a "best" strategy for setting reporting standards. Other strategies exist and those may be better. For example, Sunder (1980) argues that a laissez-faire or market-based approach may be a more efficient way of gathering and analyzing constituents' preferences, relative to the present research-oriented system. In other words, the preferences toward accounting alternatives are inferred from current practice (i.e., the choices constituents actually make). Nonetheless, despite such other approaches, solid evidence from research accumulated over sufficiently long periods—by influencing policymakers' instincts, perceptions, and philosophical leanings—should have the potential for significant and noticeable impact on the policy process. Chapter 3 develops this view further in the context of the studies reviewed in Chapters 4-8.

Intended Beneficiaries of This Report

Those who are interested in empirical research and its bearing on the activities of the FASB are the intended beneficiaries of this report. Included are the Board and its staff, and all other groups or individuals—in the public or the private sector—who are potentially affected by the financial reporting process (e.g., managers, accountants, governmental agencies, legislators, academe, users, etc.). More than likely, the Board and its staff should benefit most directly from the material presented. Accounting and reporting standards should be logically well formulated and in accordance with the economic facts and circumstances. Failure to do so would

---

[2]*Empirical research* as used in this report refers to (1) strategies whereby the researcher experiences or originates the observations and (2) strategies whereby the researcher examines previously recorded observations. Strictly interpreted, questionnaire and survey research are excluded.

be inconsistent with the FASB's own objectives of establishing accounting and reporting standards that provide information that is relevant, reliable, and cost-effective. In short, there is an obvious and direct responsibility on the part of the Board to know more about individuals' decision processes and their uses of information.

Research and Policymakers

More specifically, the material should be helpful to the FASB in two ways. First, it should act as a check on many of the assumptions made in the policy process. Each Board member, for instance, has some notion or "model"—not necessarily well defined or even verbalized—of (1) the context in which financial information is prepared, audited, and communicated; (2) how individuals behave with respect to that information; and (3) the relative usefulness of information for predicting enterprise cash flows and other relevant inputs to decision making. A frame of reference to help reduce differences in Board and staff members' views is provided by this document.[3]

Second, assessing the economic consequences of accounting alternatives for affected parties often requires detailed empirical analysis. Controversy over the choice of one method versus another is frequently interwoven with issues of economic impact. The consequence factors must necessarily be unraveled if standards are to pass an all-inclusive cost-benefit test. Indeed, the cost-benefit constraint and the many other criteria for judging the quality of accounting information (as examined in Concepts Statement 2) practically mandate the assessment of probable impact. Sometimes this impact can be assessed by research on the alternative under consideration; in other cases, the probable impact can be inferred from research on other topics. Further assessments may be necessary after the adoption of a standard as a means of providing feedback

---

[3]Ultimately, the desire to obtain a frame of reference translates into the development of a positive theory of accounting, that is, one that would explain what accounting is, why accountants do what they do, and how accountants interact in a complex process that involves preparers, users, governments, and others—all with divergent economic interests, yet making resource allocation decisions based in part on accounting information. A strong proponent of the "positivist" view is Jensen (1976): ". . . Until we better understand the interactions of the affected parties and identify other interested groups, progress on normative accounting issues will be virtually nonexistent" (p. 13).

4

about whether the probable impacts took place. The Board may also wish to evaluate the descriptive validity of claims made by those who assert they will be, or have been, affected by an accounting standard. In fact, most research on economic consequences has been conducted after a standard has been enacted. However, not all issues of economic consequence are amenable to empirical research. Many are slight, others are hidden and cannot be isolated using present techniques, and yet others are so directly felt that there may be little benefit to the policymaker in receiving a confirmation of the self-evident.

Need for Translation

A large portion of the pertinent research is produced for academics by academics using the tools and language of academics. Doubtless, there are good reasons why this should be so. But regardless of why this occurs, one side effect is that many points of broader interest are lost on those without the means to decipher the researcher's language. A filtering or translation mechanism is therefore needed to gain wider dissemination of research results. Individual studies need to be summarized, and the cumulation of significant knowledge gained through research often needs to be organized coherently. Therefore, in bringing together much of the research, this report has a broad educational objective. It attempts to communicate not only to the FASB but also to the FASB's audience, especially those who follow the Board's activities and wish to understand the contribution of accounting researchers.

Scope of Study

Investor-Creditor Focus

This document focuses on investors and creditors and their advisors. Consistent with Concepts Statement 1, the terms *investor* and *creditor* are interpreted broadly, so the selection of the two groups should not be unduly restrictive.[4] Indeed, as many would argue

---

[4]Concepts Statement 1 states that the terms *investors* and *creditors* "include both those who deal directly with an enterprise and those who deal through intermediaries, both those who buy securities from other investors or creditors and those who buy newly issued securities from the enterprise or an underwriter, both those who commit funds for long periods and those who trade frequently, both those who desire safety of investment and those who are willing to accept risk to obtain high rates of return, both individuals and specialized institutions" (par. 35).

(e.g., American Institute of Certified Public Accountants [1973]), the informational needs of those who are not investors or creditors, broadly defined, are similar. Hence, to focus on investors and creditors is in effect to focus on other users. It should be recognized, nonetheless, that within the current scope of the FASB's conceptual framework, the priority groups for financial reporting are not managers, directors, employees, regulatory authorities, or legislators, etc., except insofar as their informational and decision-making interests coincide with those of investors and creditors.[5]

Emphasis on Basic Disciplines

The materials reviewed on investors' and creditors' uses of financial information encompass the many disciplines that underlie accounting, for example, economics, finance, psychology, and statistics. Those basic disciplines supply a means of organizing the material. A straightforward classification using three dimensions—environment, properties, and behavior—forms the basis of this organization. The environment is described mostly in rational economic terms. Economics and finance offer theory and evidence on the role of information in developed exchange economies such as the United States. Statistics provides a means of describing the properties of accounting numbers and their use in making predictions. Several outside disciplines are explored regarding information-processing and decision-making behavior. While psy-

---

[5]This may be a controversial point for some readers, particularly those who would apply some other weightings to the groups in the FASB's audience. The view has been criticized by Dopuch and Sunder (1980) as unworkable and shortsighted: "A user-primacy notion in the selection of objectives of financial accounting which ignores how firm managers are likely to adjust their behavior to the new information system (and how this adjustment in management behavior will affect the interests of so-called users) represents a very short-sighted view of the whole problem. As such, solutions derived from this simplified approach will not work" (p. 15). See also Prakash and Rappaport (1977) and Kelly-Newton (1980) for similar views on the needs to recognize management more directly. Two comments should be made. First, writers invariably overstate differences between their viewpoint and that of others (often the status quo). They have every incentive to differentiate their product. Moreover, they are often more knowledgeable about how their system will work relative to how others might perform. Second, a documentation of the research results pertaining to two groups—in this instance, investors and creditors—takes no stand on the fundamental policy issue, namely, whether it is an optimal long-run strategy for the FASB to give priority to investors and creditors to the potential detriment of others who are affected by FASB decisions.

chology emphasizes the impact on the individual, other issues are better handled by the disciplines of economics and finance. Indeed, a major limitation of much of the literature in psychology is its failure to explore the implications of theories of individual behavior at the societal or aggregate level.

Research Design Issues

Findings from research always depend on the validity of the research methodology—the explanation, justification, and application of the methods, procedures, and tools of analysis. However, no research design is ever perfect. Empirical analyses may always be improved by (1) better statement of a theoretical or logical relationship between the observed phenomena and the variables that might help explain them, (2) better assurances that untested variables have a negligible impact on the asserted relationship, and (3) better control of outside chance factors that might hamper the investigator's ability to detect a relationship if one is in fact present. All research has limitations of the preceding kind, including the studies identified in this report.

The studies reviewed were based on a broad sweep of the literature since the 1960s available to the author in libraries at the Graduate School of Business at Stanford University and the Financial Accounting Standards Board. Library resources at the University of British Columbia were also used in developing this report.

Plan of Report

The study is presented in two parts. Part I comprises this chapter and Chapters 2 and 3. Chapter 2 provides an overview of the material in each chapter. The relationship of research to the standard-setting process is discussed in Chapter 3, initially in general terms and then with emphasis on the evidence documented in the remaining chapters. The first three chapters are intended to summarize this report.

Part II, Chapters 4-8, contains a detailed review of the empirical research and is intended for the reader wishing a more comprehensive knowledge of the research to date.

REFERENCES

American Institute of Certified Public Accountants, Study Group on the Objectives of Financial Statements. *Objectives of Financial Statements.* New York: AICPA, 1973.

Dopuch, Nicholas, and Sunder, Shyam. "FASB's Statements on Objectives and Elements of Financial Accounting: A Review." *The Accounting Review,* January 1980, pp. 1-21.

Jensen, Michael C. "Reflections on the State of Accounting Research and the Regulation of Accounting." Stanford Lectures in Accounting, 1976. Stanford, Calif.: Graduate School of Business, Stanford University, May 21, 1976.

Kelly-Newton, Lauren. *Accounting Policy Formation: The Role of Corporate Management.* Reading, Mass.: Addison-Wesley Publishing Company, Inc., 1980.

Louis Harris and Associates, Inc. *A Study of the Attitudes toward and an Assessment of the Financial Accounting Standards Board.* Stamford, Conn.: Financial Accounting Foundation, 1980.

Prakash, Prem, and Rappaport, Alfred. "Information Inductance and Its Significance for Accounting." *Accounting, Organizations and Society,* no. 1 (1977), pp. 29-38.

Sunder, Shyam. "Towards a Theory of Accounting Choice: Private and Social Decisions." Research paper, 6th draft. Chicago: Graduate School of Business, University of Chicago, July 1980.

CHAPTER 2—OVERVIEW OF REPORT

The assertion that information in financial reports should be useful for economic decision making is virtually unassailable. This report identifies, classifies, and examines what empirical research has uncovered about investors' and creditors' uses of financial information, and what effects that information has on their behavior. The relationship of the evidence to the Financial Accounting Standards Board's standard-setting process is also examined. The following sections summarize and highlight points made in the remaining chapters.

Empirical Accounting Research and the Standard-Setting Process (Chapter 3)

This chapter discusses the relationship between accounting research and the process by which the FASB sets accounting and reporting standards. The following points are made:

1. Information—an economic good that assists in allocating society's resources—may be overproduced or underproduced in a free-market economy. Accounting standards affect the quality and quantity of information available. They should be chosen to satisfy the objectives of financial reporting and the criteria that those objectives imply (such as relevance and reliability). A preferred standard should be more consistent with the objectives (and criteria) than a nonpreferred standard.
2. To be capable of having a bearing on the standard-setting process, research must add to what policymakers already know. Research must possess the capacity to change or reinforce the beliefs of those who select or evaluate accounting alternatives.
3. Evidence from research (discussed in Chapters 4-8) can improve a standard setter's knowledge in various ways: by shaping perceptions of the accounting and reporting environment, by examining and assessing assertions in policies (such as ability to predict future cash flows), by providing assessments of economic consequences, by evaluating whether constituents agree on or accept the costs and benefits of extant or proposed accounting alternatives, and by identifying feasible alternatives (as a first step in setting standards).
4. While standard setters, ideally, should assess people's prefer-

ences for the economic consequences of *all* possible alternatives, for practical reasons research for accounting policy tends to emphasize evidence on the effects of and extent of satisfaction with existing standards, not standards that might have been selected or possible future standards. As such, research is used to confirm or alter standard setters' expectations, thereby assisting in evaluating and possibly justifying prior decisions.

The Accounting and Reporting Environment (Chapter 4)

Chapter 4 contains a broad description of the context in which investors and creditors make decisions and use information in securities markets. The following key features of the user's environment are summarized:

1. The objective of analysis for investors and creditors in securities markets is ultimately the assessment of prospective returns on investments and lending opportunities—the amount, timing, and uncertainty of those returns. Information must be capable of changing or confirming those probabilistic assessments.
2. In assessing returns, investors and creditors often seek the advice of analysts and other information specialists. Specialists assist in the selection and interpretation of relevant and timely information for decision making, particularly in matching an individual's needs with information that is available. Information is sometimes available from sources more timely than financial statements. The existence of more timely information, however, does not imply a lack of usefulness of information in financial reports. Accounting data provide a basis for interpreting the latest news and confirming reports based on information from other sources.
3. Portfolio principles are broadly applied by investors in practice, though the individual noninstitutional investor can be best described as only partially diversified and, hence, willing to accept additional risk that a more complete diversification would essentially eliminate. Those individual investors, apparently, accept additional risk because they believe that they are in possession of superior information relative to the information held by others.

10

4. Collectively, the information-processing and decision-making activities of investors and creditors in securities markets are reflected in the market prices of the securities they trade: How quickly and to what degree security prices respond to information indicates to what extent the market is efficient.
5. Evidence from research demonstrates that the U.S. securities markets are highly efficient processors of public information, though in certain instances research indicates that the market's reaction to new information appears to be delayed. Researchers argue that while such delayed reaction is consistent with market *in*efficiency, other explanations such as inadequate research design are equally plausible. Selected tests of market efficiency with respect to nonaccounting announcements are summarized in an appendix to Chapter 4. Evidence pertaining to accounting announcements is reviewed in Chapter 8.

Evidence on the Properties of Reported Accounting Numbers (Chapter 5)

This chapter emphasizes the statistical properties of reported accounting numbers and ratios, arguing that such properties can be critical in making forecasts of future earnings and in employing accounting ratios and other data in econometric models. Key points in this chapter include the following:

1. Investors and creditors who need to assess prospective returns on securities should find knowledge of certain properties of reported accounting data a helpful intermediate step in making those assessments.
2. The empirical research on the patterns displayed by annual earnings suggests that earnings changes behave as if they are determined primarily by random or chance factors. Further, predictions of annual earnings based on the "random walk" notion are generally better than the predictions from other simple, extrapolative models. Also, they are not significantly worse than prediction models that incorporate information about other firms (e.g., index models).
3. Improved forecasts of annual earnings can be made using earnings components such as line-of-business information and interim earnings (in addition to past annual earnings).
4. Statistical models using quarterly data are not noticeably less

accurate in predicting the next year's earnings than are published forecasts by management and analysts. The models recognize quarterly earnings from the previous year as well as the most recent change in quarterly earnings relative to one year earlier.

5. The research provides few clues for policymakers and others about the extent to which the properties of earnings (e.g., predictability, volatility) might change as a result of changes in measurement techniques or other attributes of the enterprise. Also, the research states little about how the earnings pattern of one firm might differ from the pattern of another firm due to the choice of accounting methods.

Behavioral Research and Financial Accounting Standards (Chapter 6)

Chapter 6 explores the use of financial information and the development of accounting and reporting standards from the perspective of research in psychology and other behavioral sciences. Some of the findings about behavior apply to decision making in general and not simply to decision making in an accounting or business context. The focus is on the use of information by investors, creditors, and other external users. While a systematic review was not conducted, some of the key findings about the behavior of managers, auditors, and others are referred to where relevant. The following general conclusions are drawn:

1. Behavioral research suggests that people do not behave according to analytical models that predict how they ought to behave. People in general have relatively little awareness of how they make decisions or use information. (Auditors, however, seem to have a good understanding of the factors that govern their judgments.) In forming judgments, people simplify and may distort their own environment. They may fail to recognize or fully adjust for changing aspects of the situation.

2. Some simple, weighted combinations of information and other variables (linear models) are good approximations of actual choices or judgments, and such simple models can often outperform the individuals themselves. Also, composites of people's judgments, by removing idiosyncrasies, often outperform all but the most successful individuals.

3. Behavioral research has uncovered little interest in supplementing or modifying the basic historical cost accounting model (e.g., using confidence intervals), although the work done so far is limited. Experiments that systematically observe decision making and use of information directly are few in number. However, controlled studies of the bank lending process, while they reveal that such people use accounting information, document that they seem to pay attention to only a handful of critical variables or summary indicators, such as key ratios.
4. An understanding of the environment of decision makers is essential to understanding their behavior. People construct their own explanations of the world around them, based in part on accounting information. Behavioral studies also underscore important considerations in an organization's planning and control system: Accounting information motivates, influences, and otherwise induces behavior by way of alerting the decision maker to the results of past decisions and by acting as a scorekeeper for measuring performance.
5. Behavioral research offers few insights that can be applied directly in setting accounting standards. The field of research is presently young, unfocused, and predominantly empirical in its approaches to research. As such, it has little in the way of an integrating framework that would enable results to be channeled into issues of information choice or evaluation.
6. Behavioral research is conducted predominantly at the level of the individual, with little concern for how individuals interact in organizations or society in general. Research at the individual level has limited value to standard setters who are ultimately concerned with aggregate behavior and resource allocation (an aggregate concept).

Predictive Value of Accounting Information (Chapter 7)

From the standpoint of an individual decision maker, predictive value involves the ability of accounting information to predict (1) events of interest and (2) the combination of events and actions as results, outcomes, or consequences. Recently, research describing and predicting the behavior of parties involved in the standard-setting process itself has also been conducted.

1. The research examined provides evidence that investors and creditors can use accounting information to predict several phenomena of interest. Statistical formulas developed from research are reasonably effective predictors in the following areas: (a) enterprise failure and financial distress, (b) judgments by rating agencies, (c) trade credit and lending decisions, and (d) mergers and acquisitions. Research on the ability of accounting data to assess prospective cash flows is sparse, though limited work has been done in predicting dividends.
2. In the context of competitive and efficient capital markets, predictions are made based on both formal and informal sources of publicly available data. Consequently, the result that accounting numbers are significant predictors of certain events is not necessarily evidence that those numbers, or even estimates of those numbers, are actually used. It is possible that the predictions are based on other variables correlated with accounting variables.
3. Attempts to use the predictive-ability criterion to judge accounting alternatives—such as the ability of price-level-adjusted information to predict failure relative to the ability of historical cost information—have so far not produced conclusive findings.

**Research on the Use of Information in
Capital Markets (Chapter 8)**

Studies classified and summarized in this chapter focus on three measures of association between security prices and financial information: whether at a point in time when the information was first made public there was (1) an effect, (2) an effect in the right direction, and (3) an effect in the right direction of a given order of magnitude. The major points follow:

1. As evidenced by an increase in the volatility of security returns, the market responds to earnings announcements. The market also responds in the direction of the unexpected change in earnings, though prices respond to unexpected changes in earnings by only a small fraction of the change in earnings. The research has examined the New York Stock Exchange, the American Stock Exchange, and the over-the-counter exchanges as well as the exchanges in other developed countries. These findings

mean that it is almost inconceivable that investors do not find information about earnings useful for decision making.

2. The evidence on whether—and to what extent—investors react to the annual report per se and the numbers published therein is inconclusive. Some studies suggest that line-of-business information is valuable to investors, and that users distinguish between operating and extraordinary items in assessing future returns. Other studies conclude that no noticeable stock market reactions have accompanied the issuance of accounting and reporting standards. In this regard, researchers have investigated research and development costs, foreign currency translation, leases, changing prices and inflation, sensitive foreign payments, social responsibility, SEC 8-K reports, and audit qualification. One possible exception to the overall conclusion of no noticeable reaction is in the area of oil and gas accounting—the 1977 FASB proposal to require a uniform method of "successful efforts" accounting apparently precipitated a small decline in some firms' security prices.

3. The overall conclusion—that shifts in market values have not accompanied accounting policy changes—does not mean that better research designs may not be able to detect such shifts. Current empirical work is hampered by a lack of theory to predict who should be better or worse off by accounting policy changes and which changes, if any, might induce changes in management behavior to offset the effects of an accounting policy change.

4. When accounting changes are initiated at the discretion of management, the security market's response depends on how enterprise cash flows are affected, either directly (e.g., due to tax consequences) or indirectly, because the accounting change signals something about the intentions of management. The research indicates that firms that switch to the last-in, first-out method of inventory accounting are likely to experience higher stock prices due to expected tax savings, although more recent research suggests that other factors such as earnings trends may be important in analyzing the market's response. The evidence also indicates that the market recognizes and comprehends accounting changes made to create "illusory" earnings. If anything, illusory accounting changes are likely to bring about below-normal security price performance, as if the market rec-

ognizes and discounts inappropriate or questionable accounting practices.

5. Several studies indicate that accounting data is useful in estimating and predicting the relative risk of individual securities and portfolios. Attempts to evaluate accounting alternatives in terms of their ability to improve predictions or estimates of relative risk, however, have not been conclusive.

6. Two newer methodologies involve using (a) option prices to infer when the market learns of forthcoming news (that affects the future volatility of the underlying stock price) and (b) intraday prices (e.g., second-by-second) to study relationships between earnings and stock prices at a microscopic level. The latter methodology could prove useful in designing short-term investment strategies or in developing optimal strategies for the release of information by management.

7. Much of the appeal of security price analysis for investors, policymakers, and others is its relevance to the future. For particular classes of disclosures and changes in accounting policy, the research attempts to assess the probable effects on the value of the firm as manifested in security prices.

CHAPTER 3—EMPIRICAL ACCOUNTING RESEARCH AND THE STANDARD-SETTING PROCESS

Investors' and creditors' uses of and needs for financial information are unquestionably the cornerstones of present FASB policy objectives. As such, knowledge about what information investors and creditors actually use (and might use if it were available) is critical to the Board's success. Chapters 4-8 of this report identify, classify, and examine the evidence from empirical accounting research.[1] This chapter discusses the relationship of that evidence to the FASB's standard-setting process. Board members, FASB staff, and others who must often evaluate or select accounting alternatives should, in addition to knowing the research results, understand how such results might be factored into standard setting. Only then can accounting and reporting standards be grounded in ideas and concepts supported by empirical evidence.

An exhaustive examination is not made, however, regarding whether the research identified in the remaining chapters has had any impact on specific accounting standards. To do that would be unduly conjectural, and thus not a worthwhile exercise. The issue of research impact has been comprehensively studied by others (e.g., Dyckman, Gibbins, and Swieringa [1978]; Kaplan [1978]), with largely negative findings. Still, numerous examples exist to support the contention that, by its influence of the instincts, perceptions, and viewpoints of those involved in the policy process, empirical accounting research of the past 20 years has not been systematically ignored.

This chapter comprises four sections. First, the concept of an accounting choice is discussed in the context of present FASB objectives. The second section provides a general explanation of how research can assist in selecting a preferred accounting standard. The third section offers several examples to demonstrate ways in which evidence from research has been brought into the policy process. Some concluding comments are made in the final section.

---

[1]Studies examined in this report are primarily the output of accounting academics (working independently or under sponsorship) who seek to provide explanations, predictions, and understandings of the environment of accounting and reporting, the properties of accounting numbers and other information, and the behavioral and economic effects on those who use accounting information. A brief definition of *empirical research* is stated in Chapter 1.

Financial Reporting and Accounting Choices

Information, in its most fundamental sense, is an economic good that assists in the allocation of society's resources—in the distribution of existing wealth and in the formation of productive capital. However, left alone to the invisible forces of the free marketplace, too much or too little information may be produced. This results in a less-than-satisfactory allocation of society's resources. In accounting, for example, there is a basic conflict between investors and creditors who have rights to know how their funds are being managed and enterprise managers who must have certain rights to privacy in order to operate profitably. Similar conflicts arise when interested parties (e.g., investors) have unequal access to information. In that case, there is a potential for the party with superior information to exploit the other party, who is comparatively ill-informed.

Societies use a variety of means to resolve such conflicts. Some means rely on the free market, as in the case of lenders who specify their informational needs explicitly in the loan contract. Most, however, are institutional arrangements designed to supplant or facilitate market mechanisms. They are usually established by government and its agencies. But affected parties may delegate their individual rights voluntarily to a private-sector agency whose function it is to make decisions on their behalf. The FASB is one such private agency with power to act for its constituents in matters of accounting and reporting policy. (The principal governmental agency affecting accounting and reporting is, of course, the SEC.)[2]

Quite simply, the FASB's mission is to set accounting and reporting standards (see FASB, *Rules of Procedure,* January 1978). These should be consistent with the objectives of financial reporting (as set forth in Concepts Statement 1) and the characteristics of accounting information that make it useful (as explained in Concepts Statement 2). According to Concepts Statement 1, "financial reporting should provide information that is useful to present and potential investors and creditors and other users in making rational

---

[2]FASB standards are recognized as authoritative by the American Institute of Certified Public Accountants' *Professional Standards* (vol. 2, sec. 203) and the SEC's ASR No. 150, *Statement of Policy on the Establishment and Improvement of Accounting Principles and Standards* (December 1973). The SEC's release formally endorses the FASB as the organization in the private sector to provide authority in establishing accounting principles.

investment, credit, and similar decisions" (paragraph 34). Concepts Statement 2 identifies relevance and reliability as the two primary components of information that are useful. Those qualities are subject to the constraints that the information be understandable and pass a cost-benefit test that considers the effects of a standard on all parties (e.g., users, auditors, and managers).[3]

In short, according to FASB policy, accounting standards should be chosen to satisfy the objectives of financial reporting and the criteria that those objectives imply. A preferred, or "better," standard should be more consistent with the objectives (and criteria) than a nonpreferred, or "inferior," standard.

The Role of Research

How does research help in selecting a preferred standard? Ideally, the standard setter should complete four steps in choosing a preferred standard. The task entails (1) stating all the possible accounting choices that could be made regarding the issue at hand; (2) assessing how every person would be affected if each possible choice were made; (3) evaluating people's preferences or, more simply, the degree to which every person under every possible choice would like or dislike those effects; and then (4) combining the various individuals' likes and dislikes (preferences) into a measure of the overall "usefulness" of each choice for society.

Research can help at each of the preceding stages. At the first stage, research may bring to light what accounting choices are available to the policymaker. Discovery would be based in part on a study of existing practice. At the second stage, research can aid in predicting the effects or consequences of each possible choice. Such effects depend on how people use information to make decisions and how they perceive others as using it. Research at the third stage would focus on assessing individuals' preferences for consequences. In other words, the consequential effects of accounting choices must be translated into individual costs and benefits, or indicators of individual satisfaction with the results of decisions made. To the extent that the effects of others' decisions are felt (i.e., there are side effects), these too must be incorporated into an individual's costs and benefits. At the fourth stage, research can assist in describing and evaluating relationships between individuals' preferences and

---

[3]See Chapter 1 for more detail.

measures of society's preferences (that would appropriately balance the individual interests of those affected by the standard). The objective under present FASB policy, in the broadest sense, is to choose the standard that is most useful for decision making by individuals in society, subject to cost-benefit and understandability constraints.

While the aforementioned four stages should provide a useful organizing device for relating evidence from research to the standard-setting process, policy decisions in practice are not the product of such a comprehensive—and no doubt costly—analysis (Lindblom [1959]). Accounting choices are simplified in numerous ways. For instance: (1) a small number of alternatives are usually considered, often the status quo and one proposed change; (2) the focus is generally on groups of individuals who make similar decisions (investors, creditors, etc.); and (3) the set of consequences is restricted and often oriented to how similar groups will be affected in the aggregate. Research strategies, in turn, are likely to reflect those simplifications.[4]

Standard setting is likely to be constrained in a more fundamental manner. For reasons that are set out below, accounting choices are less likely to be evaluated in terms of whether objectives are met but, instead, in terms of whether there is agreement on the alternative selected. This not only alters the focus of research but also suggests that the criteria of usefulness, relevance, and reliability may have more importance in the rhetoric of gaining acceptance than as specific evaluative criteria. The usefulness criterion and subsidiary criteria, for example, do not state whose preferences are to count and how the relative intensities of those preferences will be factored into the accounting-choice process. Nor do the criteria suggest which possible consequences of the policy choice are truly relevant. Also, it is unclear how the criteria should be applied when Board members, FASB staff, and constituents in the policy process disagree as to what the criteria are and what they mean (Dopuch and Sunder [1980]).[5]

Effective strategies for accounting policy research are likely to

---

[4]This does not imply, however, that strategies for policy research ought to reflect such simplifications. Nonetheless, cost limitations and time pressure are powerful constraints in the policymaking process.

[5]For an assessment of the opinions of the FASB's constituency regarding the objectives and audience of financial reporting, see Louis Harris and Associates (1980).

reflect the above changes in orientation. Two obvious signs are, first, that significant research effort is likely to be devoted to obtaining agreement on standards themselves (not agreement as to whether objectives are satisfied) and, second, that research on economic consequences is likely to be restricted principally to the proposed accounting choice and not to all possible choices, and then only at the margin (i.e., in terms of expected effects of differences between the proposed and the existing standard). Additionally, given an emphasis on marginal effects, accounting standard setters are likely to focus their attention on the consequences of policies already undertaken as much as or more than on future consequences. This is because success in standard setting (and in most social and economic policy) tends to be judged incrementally—relative to what was and not what might have been. FASB experience should feed back into the organization's planning and control system, just as the past results of any organization are a basis for charting its future.[6]

To summarize, an organizing framework has been described to show the relationship of research to standard setting. In broadest terms, evidence from research is *information* for standard setters and others who make accounting choices. The influence of that evidence is essentially an issue of whether those people think any differently as a result of the new knowledge derived from that information. Several modifications of that framework were identified, but they do not alter the primary role of research; they merely shift the emphasis placed on certain kinds of research (e.g., research on economic consequences).

Research and the Policy Process

In the context of the research discussed in the succeeding chapters, this section considers how research can enter the policy process. Fundamentally, to be capable of having any influence whatsoever, evidence from research must be *informative*. It must possess the capacity to alter or reinforce the beliefs of those who, individually or together, select or evaluate accounting alternatives. Policymakers' confidence in their beliefs may also be changed by evidence from research. The capacity of empirical research to alter or confirm the beliefs of policymakers should not, however, be

---

[6]For a similar viewpoint, see Alexander and Carsberg (1981).

overstated. To be sure, the limited role of research is underscored by the tentative nature of its findings. Contributions from research may also be limited due to differences in outlook between researchers (who seek to contribute to knowledge and theory) and standard setters (who make policy choices based, in part, on research).

The role of evidence is discussed under six interrelated headings:

1. Research shapes people's perceptions.
2. Research examines policymakers' assertions.
3. Research provides assessments of consequences.
4. Research records what happened.
5. Research examines the extent of agreement.
6. Research identifies accounting alternatives.

Research Shapes People's Perceptions

All decision makers are predisposed to certain viewpoints that are in large part a function of the way those persons assimilate ideas, evidence, opinions, past experience, and other input to interpret the world in which they live. Accounting policymakers are no different in this respect. In what key areas might accounting policymakers' perceptions have been influenced by findings from research? Chapter 4 discusses several examples.

Perceptions of the extent to which the market is efficient have undoubtedly been influenced by research findings. Accepting the notion of an informationally efficient securities market has fairly clear implications for standard setting.[7] Insofar as markets reflect available information promptly without overreacting or underreacting to that information, the implications may be described in the following ways: First, with market efficiency, the more substantive policy issue is likely to be how information might affect users' assessments of return rather than where or how that information is placed in the financial report. This suggests also that the lack of uniformity of accounting method, and the concomitant potential for manipulation of accounting numbers through the choice of accounting method, is not always a critical issue as far as resource

---

[7]For detailed analyses, see Beaver (1973 and 1981); Gonedes and Dopuch (1974); Lev (1974); Dyckman, Downes, and Magee (1975); and Abdel-khalik and Ajinkya (1981).

allocation is concerned (if disclosure is adequate). A second implication of market efficiency for standard setting is that accounting information should have value to users only in terms of whether their current expectations about future cash flows or earnings are confirmed or changed. Such expectations are based on past accounting information as well as on information from numerous alternative sources. A third implication of market efficiency for standard setting is that prices can be used to provide reliable and potentially helpful signals about the consequences of accounting standards.

Perceptions of how information specialists interpret and disseminate financial information can also have important ramifications for standard setting, particularly in terms of the level of detail of information provided by financial reporting. Financial information need not be geared solely to the average investor if it is assumed that specialists are available to help understand the complex data. Management, also, can be assured that its disclosures are understood by a broad audience.

Finally, of importance to standard setting are perceptions about whether investors hold just one security rather than a number of securities in a diversified portfolio. Acceptance of the diversification principle suggests that it is important for policymakers not only to consider information about securities themselves but also to consider information about securities in relation to each other. For example, this means that policymakers might wish to consider the effects of accounting alternatives on comovements between securities' returns.

Research Examines Policymakers' Assertions

Present FASB accounting and reporting objectives assert that investors and creditors find information about the amounts, timing, and uncertainty of enterprise cash flows useful for decision making. Specific standards of accounting and reporting make statements similar to this (e.g., FASB Statement No. 33, *Financial Reporting and Changing Prices*). The FASB's conceptual framework also implicitly asserts that information about revenues, expenses, and other components of income provided by accrual accounting is more useful for assessing future cash flows than other means of summarizing enterprise transactions (e.g., cash flow accounting). But to what degree are those assertions consistent with investors' and creditors' actual preferences? While it is generally impossible to test such assertions directly, various indirect tests are available and are discussed in Chapters 7 and 8. Indirect tests usually evaluate hypotheses based on assumptions that investors and creditors act as if they assess cash flows in assessing future returns. Security price research (Chapter 8), for example, makes inferences about what investors and creditors assess based on tests of relationships between security prices and financial information. However, those tests are far from sufficient to establish that users actually assess cash flows. The evidence is merely consistent with the assumptions. Other indirect tests involve conducting experiments on how individuals use information. Although preliminary at this stage, such experiments are beginning to highlight discrepancies between assumed rational behavior and actual behavior (Chapter 6).

Research Provides Assessments of Consequences

Much of the research examined in later chapters focuses on the consequences of accounting alternatives. Chapter 5 examines research on the consequences of accounting alternatives as manifested in the behavior of the reported accounting numbers. The evidence helps determine what is new information under the existing accounting policy (e.g., unexpected change in earnings) and how accounting numbers such as earnings might change in terms of predictability, volatility, etc., as a result of an alternative policy. The research in Chapter 5 gives primary emphasis to existing patterns of earnings behavior. Those patterns assist in making predictions about future earnings numbers and, as such, their determination can be viewed as an interim step in predicting enterprise cash flows or other items of interest.

Chapter 7 emphasizes the prediction of consequences either directly (e.g., as cash flows) or indirectly by predicting events and actions that together produce such consequences. Many examples of how accounting information might be used to improve users' decision processes are provided. But there is little evidence that would suggest how users' predictions would differ due to the choice of an alternative accounting procedure. Moreover, what little evidence there is (see the section on enterprise failure and financial distress in Chapter 7) is inconclusive.

A potentially valuable means of assessing consequences of

accounting alternatives is to infer those effects from investors' and creditors' beliefs, as those beliefs are reflected in security prices. The techniques outlined in Chapters 4 and 8 involve assessing security returns before and after the accounting policy is announced or disclosures under the new policy are publicly released. The issue is whether the market reacted appropriately to the announcement. In effect, the market's reaction is the basis for the policymaker's forecast of consequences. But the research on price effects of accounting policy changes has provided generally weak results. Recent FASB policy changes, for example, have not triggered noticeable and permanent shifts in firms' market values for perhaps two reasons. In most instances, the change in information available to investors and creditors is too small—relative to public and private sources of data—to be detected by existing research techniques. This is compounded by a lack of rigorous theory about what the nature of the response should be and by an inability to control adequately for other variables (e.g., offsetting effects by managers) which might also be affecting the response.

Research Records What Happened

Accounting standard setting, as argued earlier in this chapter, tends to be judged relative to past policies, not policies that might have been implemented but were not. Hence, a good deal of research can properly be devoted to understanding the ex post consequences of accounting policy decisions. Research of this nature provides the necessary feedback to evaluate whether the expected consequences actually occurred. Such evidence provides input regarding likely consequences in future policy decisions. In addition, evidence on the consequences of past policies can serve to justify prior judgments, especially if the evidence is independently generated (Watts and Zimmerman [1979]).

Based on indications to date, it would appear that much of the research either sponsored or encouraged by the FASB can be viewed as attempts to evaluate past policy. This is certainly consistent with the FASB's May 1978 sponsorship of a conference on the economic consequences of financial accounting standards; its evaluation of standards in effect at least two years (FASB Statement No. 8, *Accounting for the Translation of Foreign Currency Transactions and Foreign Currency Financial Statements,* was reconsidered partly as a result of this evaluation); its funding of research on controversial standards such as FASB Statement No. 13, *Accounting for Leases;* and its initiation of research to monitor progress on Statement 33.

Research Examines the Extent of Agreement

Because in many cases it is simply impossible to assess whether a given accounting alternative meets accounting objectives better than another alternative, the focus of standard setting is often on obtaining agreement on the standard, not on its ability to meet stated objectives. This suggests that knowledge of constituents' likes and dislikes (preferences) is likely to be critical to the FASB's success. There are several ways research can assist. Most notably, standard setters should find useful the results of surveys and questionnaires, analyses of letters of comment on specific issues, and findings from other investigations that evaluate the extent of agreement on issues. While not strictly empirical research per se, certain survey findings are discussed in Chapter 6. Research focusing on investors' and creditors' attitudes toward risk (Chapter 4) is a second area that might help assess the extent of agreement on issues. People who are highly averse to risk would probably not share the same views regarding some accounting standards (e.g., standards that increase earnings volatility) as those who were less concerned with risk and more concerned with payoff. (In the extreme, a risk-neutral person would have no desire for information about firm or security risk.) A third area pertains to research on the preferences of management as reflected in their submissions, and whether those preferences might be predictable as a function of past behavior or of economic factors. Relevant research about management submissions and the potential of that research for policy are discussed in Chapter 7.

Research Identifies Accounting Alternatives

Finally, research can assist in deciding what choices are available to the policymaker. Research of this kind is mostly deductive and nonempirical. However, sometimes a starting point for policy is an identification of what practices are currently available to business enterprises (see, for example, Jaenicke [1981]). In fact, as Sunder (1980) points out, a strategy for research based predominantly on knowledge of existing practices may be most satisfactory for accounting policy if the environment is reasonably stable. A stable environment enables all constituents' preferences (including those of users) to be reflected in the rules that managers select. In such an environment, the demand for uniform standards is likely to decrease.

Concluding Comment

This chapter has explored the use of research in standard setting—what research is needed and how it might help in accounting policy decisions—against the backdrop of empirical findings examined in later chapters. The following extract from Ijiri's (1980) dialogue between a typical doctoral student and a hypothetical member of the FASB highlights most of the issues raised. The standard setter (S) is explaining just what is needed from the researcher (R) (page 33):

R—. . . I am still not clear as to exactly what you want. . . . Can you summarize your point?

S—Number one. Facts, concepts, and theories which will provide a basis for our discussion on standard setting. These are needed as a general background. It is certainly our responsibility to keep up with research literature but researchers can also help us by calling interesting findings to our attention. Number two. For a specific decision on hand, we have to nail down all feasible alternatives and evaluate them in terms of objectives and guidelines for financial reporting, their consistency with other standards, and their possible consequences if adopted. Any research results that have a bearing on these matters will be useful, whether they are generated as part of a general research study or through a specific study tailored for the specific decision on hand. Finally, number three, once a decision is made, we need research results to persuade those who preferred alternative routes to go along with the selected one. Enormous effort has been expended in explaining why one alternative was chosen over the other as you can see from any pronouncement in recent years.

R—In other words, you need research for general background, for specific decisions, and for justification of decisions.

S—That's right.

REFERENCES

Abdel-khalik, A. Rashad, and Ajinkya, Bipin B. "Accounting Information and Efficient Markets." In *Handbook of Accounting and Auditing,* edited by John C. Burton, Russell E. Palmer, and Robert S. Kay, chap. 47. Boston: Warren, Gorham & Lamont, Inc., 1981.

Alexander, Michael, and Carsberg, Bryan. "Glory, Knock-down Arguments, and Impenetrability." In *The Impact of Accounting Research on Policy & Practice.* Paper presented at The Arthur Young Professors' Roundtable, April 2-3, 1981, at Cotode Caza, Trabuco Canyon, California.

Beaver, William H. "What Should Be the FASB's Objectives?" *Journal of Accountancy,* August 1973, pp. 49-56.

_____. *Financial Reporting: An Accounting Revolution.* Prentice-Hall Contemporary Topics in Accounting Series. Englewood Cliffs, N.J.: Prentice-Hall, Inc., 1981.

Dopuch, Nicholas, and Sunder, Shyam. "FASB's Statements on Objectives and Elements of Financial Accounting: A Review." *The Accounting Review,* January 1980, pp. 1-21.

Dyckman, Thomas R.; Downes, David H.; and Magee, Robert P. *Efficient Capital Markets and Accounting: A Critical Analysis.* Prentice-Hall Contemporary Topics in Accounting Series. Englewood Cliffs, N.J.: Prentice-Hall, Inc., 1975.

Dyckman, Thomas R.; Gibbins, Michael; and Swieringa, Robert J. "Experimental and Survey Research in Financial Accounting: A Review and Evaluation." In *The Impact of Accounting Research on Practice and Disclosure,* edited by A. Rashad Abdel-khalik and Thomas F. Keller, pp. 48-105. Durham, N.C.: Duke University Press, 1978.

Gonedes, Nicholas J., and Dopuch, Nicholas. "Capital Market Equilibrium, Information Production, and Selecting Accounting Techniques: Theoretical Framework and Review of Empirical Work." *Journal of Accounting Research.* Supplement, *Studies on Financial Accounting Objectives: 1974,* pp. 48-129.

Ijiri, Yuji. "A Dialogue on Research and Standard Setting in Accounting." In *Perspectives on Research: Proceedings of the 1980 Beyer Consortium,* edited by Raghavan D. Nair and Thomas H. Williams. Madison: Board of Regents of the University of Wisconsin System, 1980.

Jaenicke, Henry R. FASB Research Report, *Survey of Present Practices in Recognizing Revenues, Expenses, Gains, and Losses.* Stamford, Conn.: FASB, 1981.

Kaplan, Robert S. "The Information Content of Financial Accounting Numbers: A Survey of Empirical Evidence." In *The Impact of Accounting Research on Practice and Disclosure,* edited by A. Rashad Abdel-khalik and Thomas F. Keller, pp. 134-73. Durham, N.C.: Duke University Press, 1978.

Lindblom, Charles E. "The Science of 'Muddling Through'." *Public Administration Review,* no. 2 (1959), pp. 92-109.

Louis Harris and Associates, Inc. *A Study of the Attitudes toward and an Assessment of the Financial Accounting Standards Board.* Stamford, Conn.: Financial Accounting Foundation, 1980.

Sunder, Shyam. "Towards a Theory of Accounting Choice: Private and Social Decisions." Research paper, 6th draft. Chicago: Graduate School of Business, University of Chicago, July 1980.

Watts, Ross L., and Zimmerman, Jerold L. "The Demand for and Supply of Accounting Theories: The Market for Excuses." *The Accounting Review,* April 1979, pp. 273-305.

PART II

CHAPTER 4—THE ACCOUNTING AND REPORTING ENVIRONMENT

An understanding of the accounting and reporting environment is essential for analyzing the activities of investors and creditors. This chapter provides a broad picture of the economic context in which investors and creditors make decisions. Initially, the focus is on an individual decision maker who assesses prospective returns from investment or lending opportunities using financial and other information. But in a competitive economy, individual decision makers cannot be viewed in isolation. Their activities collectively determine market prices and hence the returns or payoffs that they receive. Therefore, in order to describe the accounting and reporting environment, the relationship between information and security prices must be examined. An integral aspect of that relationship is the so-called concept of an efficient market.

This chapter comprises four sections. The first section concentrates on the role of financial reporting and those factors that influence an individual's demand for financial information. Moving from the viewpoint of the individual investor or creditor to the aggregate, the second section examines the relationship between securities markets and financial information. This leads, naturally, to a discussion of the concept of market efficiency.[1] The third section discusses different approaches to testing market efficiency and evaluates those approaches in terms of the recent evidence. The final section presents some conclusions.

Financial Reporting and the Demand for Information

The Role of Financial Reporting

Accounting and financial reporting exist within a larger economic, legal, political, and social environment. In that larger

---

[1]The first and second sections also provide a general context in which to view the empirical research discussed in later chapters. Readers interested in only the actual research findings should proceed directly to Chapters 5-8.

environment, the principal role of financial reporting is to provide users with information for decision making.

The Financial Accounting Standards Board emphasizes investors, creditors, and their advisors as the groups to be given priority for financial reporting; investors and creditors are defined broadly. Present policy at the Securities and Exchange Commission, however, is somewhat narrower in focus. The SEC closely follows its jurisdiction as implied by the securities acts. That pertains to only investors, present and potential, defined as those who buy, sell, hold, or exercise voting rights associated with equity securities. Under present securities law, holders of registered public debt securities do not necessarily receive corporate reports and SEC filings. However, the growth of the bond market in recent years and the increase in bond portfolio management could well sway the SEC's priorities in the near future.[2]

Regardless of whether the primary emphasis is on both groups or investors only, the objectives of financial reporting, in the most fundamental sense, still derive from decisions to be made by users. What general kinds of information do those decisions require? Traditionally, the buy-sell-hold decision of the security holder is viewed as one based on information about the past activities of management as the steward to whom funds have been entrusted. That information should reveal management's custodial abilities as well as the effectiveness and efficiency of their performance relative to

---

[2]The SEC's Advisory Committee on Corporate Disclosure (1977) makes little reference (and no recommendations) as to whether the needs of debt holders and creditors are presently served by the Commission's statutory system of disclosure. That report states: ". . . The Commission has focused little attention on the unique informational needs of bondholders or, indeed, their right to obtain information ordinarily provided to common stockholders. This latter omission is particularly curious because debt securities represent a contractual obligation of corporations such that the interest of the holders of such securities ranks senior to the interest of common stockholders in the event of liquidation" (p. 553).

expectations, stated goals, and other evaluative criteria. This is the stewardship or feedback role of financial reporting.[3]

Investors and creditors, when making decisions, also need information of a more direct, forward-looking nature, that is, information that better enables them to assess future events, actions, or consequences. This is often termed the *decision-making* or *predictive role* of financial reporting. An emphasis on future considerations of investors and creditors translates, according to the FASB, into their needs for "assessing the amounts, timing, and uncertainty of prospective cash receipts from dividends or interest and the proceeds from the sale, redemption, or maturity of securities or loans" (Concepts Statement 1, paragraph 37). That interest in cash flow is, in turn, "affected by an enterprise's ability to generate enough cash to meet its obligations when due and its other cash operating needs, to reinvest in operations, and to pay cash dividends and may also be affected by perceptions of investors and creditors generally about that ability, which affect market prices of the enterprise's securities" (Concepts Statement 1, paragraph 37).

Other interpretations of the role of financial reporting of course exist. For instance, Ijiri (1975) and others (e.g., the Canadian Institute of Chartered Accountants [1980]) stress "accountability" as the foundation for understanding the accounting and reporting function. Existing accounting practices, in Ijiri's judgment, are better interpreted by adopting an accountability view, one that is less directly oriented to the user. Accountability, in Ijiri's terms, appears broader than stewardship but is still focused on the measurement and assessment of enterprise performance and not on the supply of quantitative input for specific user decisions. Moreover, the accountability view appears to be less prescriptive. Its central theme is

---

[3]Performance-related interpretations of the stewardship role of financial reporting are becoming increasingly popular and are often stated as a relationship between principals (e.g., equity holders) and their agents (e.g., managers). According to this "principal-agent" viewpoint, both the principal and the agent have express needs for information that helps monitor compliance with the terms, obligations, and responsibilities of their contractual, legal, and statutory duties. For instance, bondholders (principals) obtain protection from the actions of management (the agent) contrary to their (bondholders') best interests by establishing a bond indenture with covenants that require disclosure of information and prevent or restrict actions in areas such as production-investment, dividend, and financing policy. For an analysis of the kinds of covenants used to reduce possible bondholder-stockholder conflict, see Smith and Warner (1979).

not to identify priority groups such as investors and creditors, but to understand the nature and means of resolving the conflicting claims of those with rightful interests in firm-oriented information (who have a need to know) and the interests of the enterprise managers who, legitimately, can claim certain rights to privacy.[4]

Another interpretation, one based on an evaluation of empirical literature in accounting and finance, is offered by Benston (1978), among others. Stressing the preemptive or confirmatory role of information in financial reports, Benston suggests that on balance the mandated reporting and disclosure process does not supply the public with financial statements useful for investment decisions. Instead, he argues that the required standards of reporting and disclosure benefit the public, primarily "by helping the government enforce management's and insiders' implied contracts to act as fiduciaries towards stockholders. . . . Disclosure may [also] reduce the incidence of fraud, self-dealing, and poor performance by managers. . . . The [SEC's] requirements should be directed towards these goals" (page 153). The evidence, according to Benston, tends to be consistent with the statements and filings having value to investors primarily in a preemptive or confirmatory sense.[5]

Many other views of the role of financial reporting could no doubt be discussed. The essential point, however, is that to a large extent it is one's perceptions of (1) the groups in society with legitimate interests in the reporting process, (2) the accounting and reporting environment in which they interact, and (3) mechanisms[6]

---

[4]Ijiri (1975) remarks: "The contemporary, user-oriented view . . . has certainly contributed greatly to accounting theories and practice by emphasizing the usefulness of accounting information to users. However, as a result of emphasizing users, this view has failed to recognize the fact that (i) the entity's interest is closely tied to the content of the information released to the users and (ii) the entity is actively interested in seeing that the information released is in its best interest" (p. 46).

[5]Benston (1978) discusses the confirmatory "hypothesis" as an alternative explanation of the need for financial reporting. The preemptive role—to use financial statements to minimize or eliminate the opportunity for unfair advantage by managers and insiders—is discussed in Beaver (1981). Note that the preemptive role has strong ethical overtones in its justification.

[6]Society's mechanisms for resolving conflict among competing demands on the financial reporting system are numerous. It is helpful, however, to distinguish two broad kinds: (1) mechanisms that arise out of competition, freedom of choice, and the protection of private property rights (a market-based system) and (2) mechanisms to supplant or facilitate market processes that are specifically imposed by the government and its agencies (e.g., the SEC) or private-sector agencies or bodies to whom individuals have delegated individual rights or privileges (e.g., the FASB).

that would help them resolve their conflicting interests that are the keys to determining the appropriate balance among different objectives (e.g., users' decisions, stewardship, etc.). This chapter, by summarizing relevant research, is intended to clarify those perceptions.

The Demand for Financial Information

Investors and creditors are two prominent groups in society with legitimate and direct interests in the accounting and reporting process. Their needs for information about equity and debt securities are the focus of this section. Equity and debt securities differ principally in the amount, timing, and uncertainty of the cash flows they provide. Debt securities are usually the least risky in terms of the expected amount and timing of such future cash flows. To enable comparisons to be made among firms' securities, prospective cash flows are usually expressed on a periodic basis as the sum of the dividend or interest and the price change or capital gain component. For a single period, that sum is the security's *return*. Returns averaged over several periods are usually described as *yields*. The choice between returns or yields generally depends on the intended holding period of the individual. (The distinction between returns and yields is important for understanding some of the discussion that follows.)

Prospective Return Is Assessed

It is the assessment of prospective return on a security—amount, timing, and uncertainty—for a specified holding period that is the ultimate object of analysis for the investor and creditor. Information must be capable of changing or confirming an individual's probabilistic assessment of return in order to be of potential benefit to that individual. Understanding an individual's use of financial report information, consequently, implies understanding how probabilistic assessments are made and how they might change in response to input from financial reports and other sources. Not a great deal is known about such processes. Many behavioralists, for instance, argue that individual behavior tends to be instinctive, sub-

ject to massive simplification, and idiosyncratic and is thus not well
described by probability theory and statistics.[7]

Specialists Are Used

What is apparent even to the casual observer, however, is that
investors and creditors often seek the assistance of specialists.
Somehow they are cognizant of their own lack of ability to evaluate
or articulate how and what information might affect their uncertain
beliefs. A rich and diverse array of services is provided by specialists
in securities markets. Some services are informational only; others
relate more directly to the investor's or creditor's role as decision
maker. The term *information specialist* is used here to describe
those who assist the investor or creditor mainly in informational
ways. Such entities include stock and bond analysts, portfolio managers, brokers, newspapers, reference services, and all others who
gather, process, and disseminate information for the evaluation of
investment and lending opportunities. They are generally able to
ferret out more relevant, timely, and comprehensive information
than that presented in financial reports and other firm-oriented
documents.[8]

However, while more timely and useful information might well be
available elsewhere, that by no means implies a lack of usefulness of
the information in financial reports. It suggests instead some degree
of reorientation of the relationship between investor-creditor decisions and financial reporting. There is always a need for historical
data about a firm—first, as a means of interpreting the latest news
which in isolation might be largely meaningless and, second, as a
basis for those who evaluate past relationships as a primary means

---

[7]Chapters 5 and 6 discuss the available research on how probabilistic assessments are
made. Chapter 5 emphasizes the statistical properties of accounting time series such
as earnings or income; Chapter 6 focuses on certain behavioral features of the use of
information to assess relevant variables. Also, evidence on the relationship between
security returns and financial information is presented in Chapter 8. The link, however, between individuals' information processing and market behavior is not well
developed, as is evident in both Chapters 6 and 8 and, as well, in the material on
market efficiency discussed later in this chapter.

[8]See Advisory Committee on Corporate Disclosure (1977) for a detailed discussion
on the role of the analyst in the SEC's disclosure system. The data in that report generally support the extensive dependence of the analyst on informal sources of
information.

of assessing the future. In addition, the reporting process provides the necessary historical feedback to maintain the integrity of the system. This allows users to assess the "quality" of those who make predictions about accounting numbers (e.g., future reported earnings). Knowledge of superior versus inferior forecasting ability necessarily has a salutary effect on the functioning of capital markets.

Finally, in discussing the analyst's role, it should be recognized that the scrutiny of the competitive analyst community does not extend the breadth of all listed public companies. The bias appears to be toward firms with large capitalizations readily marketable in the quantities that institutional traders generally transact. Grant (1980) provides evidence consistent with this view. He found that the stock market's reaction to earnings was statistically greater for securities on the over-the-counter (OTC) market compared with securities on the New York Stock Exchange (NYSE). The implication is that *less* information from nonaccounting sources is available to investors regarding smaller, OTC-traded securities relative to NYSE-traded securities.

Having identified the investor's and creditor's basic informational need—to assess uncertain prospective security return—and having recognized that in today's environment those assessments can depend heavily on help from analysts and other specialists, the next step is to specify the choices to be made.

Investment Choices

Conceptually, the choice of an investment breaks down into two components. The first is how much to consume now versus how much to invest in securities (the savings decision). The second is selection of productive opportunities in which to place investable funds (the portfolio decision). For present purposes, the equity or debt content of the portfolio is emphasized. Of course, the portfolio concept can be, and generally is, extended to all productive efforts including human capital (e.g., education), real capital (e.g., commodities), and financial capital in the form of securities.

How much to invest and in what securities are in part a function of people's tastes and preferences. Given adequate present consumption, more wealth (future consumption) is generally preferred to less. Increases in wealth beyond a certain level, though, apparently bring about lesser amounts of satisfaction. A second characteristic of investor behavior is that, other things equal, most investors prefer less uncertainty about wealth to more uncertainty. They are thus "risk averse" in their choice behavior. They are willing to gamble on the future, but if somehow they could avoid some or all of the risk of losing their initial investment, they would (if the costs were low enough). Alternatively, if the returns more than compensated for the risk of loss, they would find the gamble an acceptable investment alternative.

A practical concept of risk aversion for security analysis purposes uses mean and variance of prospective return as investment-choice criteria. By that approach, investors' preferences can be maximized by focusing on two characteristics of the return distribution— expected return and variance of return. Risk aversion is implied if an individual is willing to trade off expected return for a lower variance of return. For the risk-averse investor, increases in variance must be compensated by higher expected return. But mean and variance may not be good choice criteria if security returns do not approximate a bell-shaped, normal distribution. This is because two parameters by themselves may not adequately describe all the payoff possibilities. Potential unusually large returns, either positive or negative, may simply not be given enough weight under the bell-shaped, normal assumption. A more encompassing choice criterion is one that concentrates on the entire distribution of returns.

Empirical Issues

The preceding discussion identifies assumptions about how persons choose investments. Those assumptions should be evaluated empirically. First, do individuals actually exhibit risk aversion? Generally, they seem to. Just as most people purchase some kind of insurance, investors generally require a higher risk premium or higher return on risky assets such as common stocks than they require on relatively risk-free government bonds or similar securities. Risk seeking, like compulsive gambling, is usually not a consciously deliberated and positively oriented behavior on the part of the investor. However, after the fact, risk aversion may not always be apparent. For example, in the presence of high rates of inflation, stock market returns have been observed to correlate negatively with rates of inflation. It is questionable whether the investor has been adequately compensated for the risks involved.[9]

---

[9]See Modigliani and Cohn (1979) for a stimulating analysis of this phenomenon.

A second empirical issue is the adequacy of the assumption that returns are distributed as a normal curve and, thus, whether investment choices based on only security return means and variances are appropriate. The evidence suggests that common stock returns, on a daily basis, do not behave as if they are selections from a normal distribution. There is a tendency for greater numbers of extreme return observations than normality would predict, as well as a greater number of observations close to the mean. Longer holding period (e.g., monthly) returns are more closely normal but are slightly skewed, with larger numbers of extreme positive returns than extreme negative returns.[10]

The normality assumption can be examined indirectly by evaluating the validity of the two-parameter (mean and variance) asset pricing model, which depends crucially on the use of mean and variance to describe uncertain security return distributions. Most studies agree that variance-based risk factors are important determinants in the pricing of securities, although newer models of capital asset pricing appear to include additional explanatory factors (e.g., firm size, Banz [1981]; earnings growth prospects, Basu [1977]; and dividend policy and tax factors, Litzenberger and Ramaswamy [1979]).

A third empirical issue involves the extent of portfolio diversification. This is important since the demand for financial information changes depending on the extent to which the primary object of analysis is portfolio return and not *individual* security return. (See Chapter 8 for a detailed explanation.) Just about every conceivable kind of portfolio strategy is pursued in today's financial markets. The derived demand for financial information is, consequently, equally varied. Financial intermediaries package and repackage common stocks, bonds, and other fixed income instruments such as closed-end funds, open-end funds, dual funds, real estate funds, hedge funds, index funds, and so on. Most are highly diversified; the remainder are partially diversified, with the diversification depending on the degree to which the fund manager believes that superior returns can be obtained by sacrificing some of the benefits of full diversification (e.g., investing disproportionately in a few stocks).

---

[10]See Fama (1976) for further discussion. Specific studies have been conducted by Blume (1968), Officer (1973), and Blattberg and Gonedes (1974).

Studies of individual investors, on the other hand, show rather limited diversification. Blume and Friend (1978), for instance, note that the median number of stocks held by a stock-owning family, exclusive of mutual funds and personal trusts, was less than four. Seventy-seven percent of families held nine stocks or less. Similar results are presented in the report of the Advisory Committee on Corporate Disclosure (1977). Fifty-one percent of individual investor respondents held 10 stocks or fewer. Sixty-seven percent, moreover, did not hold a mutual fund stock. Lease, Lewellen, and Schlarbaum (1974), however, report that about 10-15 stocks are the average holding in their individual investor sample, and mutual fund stocks were held by a majority of the subjects in that study.

Assumptions about risk aversion, normality of returns, and extent of diversification are just that—assumptions. They are never literally true for all securities or individuals. The evidence is clear on that issue. The central issue is whether they are sufficiently representative of decision making by investors to capture the essence of behavior for economic analysis and financial policy. It should be recognized that such assumptions about investor behavior do not necessarily imply that investors know about or fully comprehend those issues. What matters, particularly for economic analysis and policy based'thereon, is that investors behave *as if* they were cognizant of such assumptions. On this issue, the evidence is reasonably clear-cut. For investment institutions and for individuals (although to a lesser extent), the use of portfolio principles seems pervasive. As such, the traditional investor—naive, unaided by professionals, and unaware of the extent of risk that might remain uncompensated by a failure to diversify—is likely to be a minor participant in today's capital markets.

Choosing Bonds

For debt securities, the rational choice criterion of Markowitz (1959)—to find a set of risk-return combinations that dominates all others and from that set to choose one that maximizes the investor's desire for wealth—is more difficult to exploit directly. One can of course characterize bond funds as attempts to offer diversification services, but choice criteria based on present value and yield concepts, rather than on expected return and variance, tend to be more commonplace in the analysis of bonds. The longer anticipated holding periods and the protection given to coupon and principal in the event of default are usually in contrast to the assumptions of portfolio theory (such as the assumption that investors assess returns one period at a time). Yield to maturity (that rate of return that, when used to discount the coupon payments and principal amount, makes their present value precisely equal to the current market price of the bond) is probably the most frequently applied choice criterion for bond investment. Some bond analysts, however, use percentage change in bond price plus interest receipts (bond return) in their analysis. Bond return, in contrast to bond yield, may be more suitable in periods of high price volatility since the holding periods of bond investors are likely to be shortened considerably.

Informational Requirements

While the preceding discussion has described aspects of stock and bond investment decisions, little has been said regarding the kinds of information that those decisions require. The following section focuses on relationships between debt and equity investment decisions and the derived demand for financial information.

Debt Securities

For debt securities, the work of analysts centers on an explanation and comparison of yields, cross-sectionally and over time. Bond risk, one determinant of that yield, requires an assessment of the issuer's prospective cash flows to service the debt under adverse conditions. Useful financial information should, therefore, enable that assessment. (Chapter 7 discusses relevant empirical studies in this regard.) Naturally, some information will be unique to the firm, for example, information concerning managerial performance, leverage, and earnings variability. But as in the analysis of common stocks, a significant amount of input tends to relate to the assessment of the firm's responsiveness to industry and economic factors. The impact of outside factors in explaining bond yields shows up clearly if one measures the dependency of yield on macroeconomic indicators. However, to the extent that bonds are judged on a comparative basis, information about the determinants of yield common to all firms (e.g., default-free interest and risk premiums) takes on somewhat lesser significance than those that are company-specific.

Debt holders have a second kind of demand for information in financial reports, apart from the need to assess cash flows and future earnings. Debt holders have a contractual relationship with the firm and thus need information that would provide for the monitoring of that contract and its enforcement in the event of violation. Information in financial reports on asset protection, production-investment decisions, and financing and dividend policy forms an essential part of the bond contract. Issuers will often agree to provide financial statements, SEC filings, and other required reports to bondholders. Issuers and bondholders, to improve the quality of information pertinent to their contract, will sometimes negotiate the accounting methods and classifications to be employed in assessing indenture compliance (Leftwich [1980]).

Equity Investors

Equity investors, on the other hand, can readily take advantage of portfolio diversification. They have a direct interest not only in financial information about expected return and variability for each security, but also in information about covariations between pairs of security returns (often assessed as an association between the individual security's return and the return on a market portfolio). If investors hold diversified portfolios, variability due to company-specific factors is virtually eliminated if the number of securities is large enough. Some investors may even wish to hold a portfolio comprising all traded securities (the "market" portfolio). The need to gather information about risk factors peculiar to each security is obviously diminished in this portfolio context. However, for those investors who are not well diversified, information about company-specific risk is paramount. That kind of investor must assess how much additional return is required to compensate for the additional (company-specific) risk that others could eliminate relatively cheaply via diversification. (Chapter 8 also discusses this idea, in describing the research on estimating and predicting security relative risk.)

One of the more interesting aspects of investors' informational requirements concerns the "rationality" of the individual investor's decision. A failure to diversify fully when cheap—almost costless—sources are available, for instance, suggests either an element of irrationality or that the individual has superior information or at least believes that he or she is in possession of superior information sufficient to compensate for the higher risk. The available evidence seems consistent with the *perception* but not the *actuality* of possessing superior information. Blume and Friend (1978), for example, found that many individual stockholders earn returns well below those necessary to compensate for the risks inherent in a portfolio that is not fully diversified. A more detailed analysis is provided by Schlarbaum, Lewellen, and Lease (1978). Relative to several mutual fund and exchange indexes whose annual percentage returns ranged from 6.7 to 14 percent, the individual investor at best did no better than the lowest performing benchmark considering all round-trip trades (although over some shorter trips, up to 30 days, there was some evidence of trading success). They comment: ". . . of the round trips identified, it happens that only 52% yielded net returns in excess of the mean return available during the period on Treasury Bills" (page 323).

Summary

This section on informational requirements has discussed the stewardship and predictive roles of financial reporting and has identified factors that may influence an individual's demand for financial information. Stock and bond investors' decisions were described in order to understand the kinds of information that those decision processes imply. Common stock investment decisions appear to emphasize the need to assess means and variances of portfolio returns, whereas bond investing seems more closely connected with an analysis of yield to maturity or some similar average return measure.

Nonetheless, despite somewhat different investment criteria, both stock and bond investors require information about (1) the firm, (2) the firm in relationship with other firms, and (3) how the firm is affected by industry and market factors generally. Information about areas (2) and (3) is crucial to the diversified investor. On the other hand, a holder of a *few* stocks or bonds is vitally interested in company-unique information.

The available empirical evidence on the behavior of individual and institutional investors suggests that the principles of portfolio theory have broad application in practice. However, the individual investor can only be best described as partially diversified and therefore willing to accept additional risk that a more complete diversification would essentially eliminate.

Securities Markets and Financial Information

Investors' and creditors' decision-making and information-processing behavior cannot be viewed apart from the market in which it occurs. Securities are sold by business enterprises to stockholders and bondholders and are subsequently traded on national and regional exchanges. Such transfers of securities are the results of ever-changing supply and demand forces in the economy. The most basic of those are the individual's wealth, tastes and preferences (and, hence, attitude to risk taking), beliefs about prospective return, available information, and perception of the prevailing economic and institutional environment in which the market operates. Prices are, of course, a reflection of those basic factors only when supply and demand are in equilibrium. Changes in security prices, therefore, are a result of imbalances among those relationships. The rational investor, interested in enjoying the benefits of wealth to the fullest extent, naturally wishes to know when, in what direction, and by how much those prices will change.[11]

This section is concerned with relationships, primarily at a conceptual level, between price changes and new information. (The empirical research is reviewed in Chapter 8 and in the appendix to this chapter.) Only by understanding the nature of the association between prices and financial information, and the likely responses such information will cause when released to investors, is one able to draw valid inferences regarding possible uses of such information. An individual investor, for instance, may have little demand for specific information on a stock that is well researched and frequently traded. In this situation, such information, when it becomes public, is likely to be quickly impounded in price. A financial statement preparer's supply of information might also be altered by an understanding of the timing, direction, and magnitude of price change in response to information. For example, a manager who perceives that prices do not react blindly to accounting numbers but instead react on the basis of the underlying cash flow data

---

[11]The private return to the investor from obtaining information actually takes two forms. The valuation effect is emphasized here. This is the capital gain expected to be made by those who believe that somehow they know more than the market (or have greater luck or insight). Private returns to information also occur when investors receive information that allows those persons to obtain portfolios better suited to their personal tastes and preferences.

is likely to view certain reforms in the area of disclosure differently from a manager who believes prices react on the basis of the "bottom line" alone.

Accounting policymakers, too, are likely to be concerned with such relationships between prices and information. A policy proposal that essentially shifts control of the formatting of financial information from managers to regulators (e.g., a switch from footnote disclosure to capitalization of certain long-term leases) should have different (probably smaller) price effects from one that actually increases (or decreases) the available supply of financial information for investors and creditors (e.g., disclosure of line-of-business information).

Efficient Capital Markets

Relationships between the prices of debt and equity securities and financial information are most often discussed in terms of the efficiency of the market. The concept is not new; economists since the time of Adam Smith have been debating the benefits of the price system as a low-cost transmitter of information. Even the early American writings in finance and accounting extolled the virtues of the efficient market. Ripley (1972, originally published in 1927) discusses the salutary effects of publicity on shareholders: "Must one reiterate that the prevention of fraud, while important, is limited to a few companies; while the registration of a fair market price, consonant with the real earning power of the company, is a matter of daily and universal importance to every shareholder who may have occasion to buy or to sell securities?" (page 219). The concept of market efficiency, however, was only loosely described in the early literature.

What Does *Market Efficiency* Mean?

Intrinsic Value

The earliest definitions of market efficiency dealt with the concept in a negative sense. For investment analysis and portfolio selection, a stock or bond was said to be *in*efficiently priced if the most current price differed from a personal evaluation of what that price ought to be, either derived directly or based on the assessments of other individuals. That personal or subjective estimate of price was the asset's "intrinsic value." A security could be overpriced or underpriced relative to its intrinsic value. Others (e.g., Lorie and Hamilton [1973]) added that intrinsic value means not only what the price ought to be but also what the price would be given that other individuals possess the same information and interpretative abilities as the person making the estimate.

Intrinsic value analysis, though an often-used term and descriptive of the activities of many analysts, now seems to be losing some of its appeal, especially among textbook writers in finance and accounting. This is largely because others have offered better definitions that outline more carefully the meaning of information fully discounted in price or definitions that are more consistent with the empirical research. Those definitions also attempt to describe a mechanism whereby information becomes impounded in price.

Fama's Definition

Fama (1970), for the purposes of examining the empirical literature, identified three sets of information "available" to the market at a point in time as (1) information inherent in past sequences of prices, (2) all information available to the public, and (3) all information whether held publicly or privately by one or more individuals. A market, then, was efficient only with respect to a given set of information. If, at most, security prices fully reflected the information in past prices, the market was "weakly efficient." If, at most, prices fully reflected all public information, the market was efficient in the "semistrong" form. If, literally, all information regardless of cost was fully reflected in prices, then the market was "strongly" efficient.

Subsequently, Fama (1976) defined *fully reflect* in terms of an equality of two assessments or probability distributions of prospective returns. When the "true" assessment of prospective returns was equal to the market's assessment based on its set of available information, prices were said to fully reflect all available information. But "true" assessments were not well defined. Fama alluded to an imaginary economy in which everything that was knowable given present information was reflected in price, including not just elementary information but whatever could be predicted about the future from present knowledge. The "market's assessment," moreover, was only a metaphor. It merely summarized some undefined composite of investors' opinions.

Fama's definitions, while helpful in discussing the empirical research, said little about how information is transformed into prices.[12] The more analytical definitions of market efficiency are limited in the same way. Like Fama's, they depend on some imaginary economy wherein individuals who hold securities are assumed to know (or act as if they know) not only their own information set but everyone else's as well. One such definition states that a market is "informationally efficient" if the equilibrium prices or returns that are established when people use only their own information are identical to the equilibrium prices or returns that would be established if people, somehow, were to use their own information plus everybody else's. Another group of definitions involves statements about investor trading: a market is viewed as efficient according to this view if the securities held optimally by all investors, when based on their own information, are identical to the securities held optimally by those same investors when based on access to all information (including their own). These definitions, while they do not require some set of "true" prices (as in the Fama case), still require that prices exist in an imaginary "as if" economy and that the full set of information is available in that "as if" economy.[13]

More recent definitions of the mechanism that "aggregates" information in prices are likely to employ some form of model based on the theory of "rational expectations," namely, a model in which individuals form correct expectations on the basis of all information available to them, including prices. The most common explanation involves a set of behaviors by which the more-informed individuals reveal information to the less-informed through either their trading actions or sales of their information. But only under very restrictive conditions will all information be revealed. The rational-expectations model described in Grossman and Stiglitz (1976 and 1980), for example, generates prices that do not fully

---

[12]A process of price formation strictly consistent with the Fama view is one based on costless information with individuals holding uniform beliefs about future returns over identical time horizons. With these kinds of artificial assumptions, it is possible to view the market as assessing probability distributions and setting prices. The composite and the individual are one and the same.

[13]See Rubinstein (1975), Verrecchia (1980), and Beaver (1981) for further details.

reveal everything since, in addition to the condition for equilibrium that securities supplied equals securities demanded, a second condition is imposed, namely, that participants are indifferent to being informed versus remaining relatively uninformed. Information is sufficiently costly so that the uninformed individuals are not willing to buy all available information from the insiders. Hence, markets can never be efficient in the strongest form. Information and predictions based on that information are not available free of charge. According to the Grossman-Stiglitz view, however, a decrease in the cost of information increases the informativeness of the price system. With zero costs, though, the system breaks down since there is no return to be made by information specialists.

Beaver (1981) provides yet another explanation of the concept of market efficiency—one not directly tied to transfers of information from the more-informed to the less-informed. Beaver's view is that individuals' beliefs about prospective returns contain unsystematic or idiosyncratic personal components that are essentially independent across a group of investors. These idiosyncratic components cancel out at the market level, leaving only the nonidiosyncratic component of investors' beliefs reflected in efficiently determined market prices. Moreover, the nonidiosyncratic component represents a higher quality of knowledge than, say, the information held by an average individual in the market. This "portfolio" viewpoint is also consistent with the earlier definition of market efficiency, namely, a market in which prices are set as if each individual possesses not only his or her own information but everyone else's at the same time. Knowing everyone else's simply allows the individual to eliminate the idiosyncratic component (which is taken care of by market transactions in the ordinary as opposed to the imaginary, "as if" market). Still, Beaver's appeal to diversification principles does not describe the revelation of information in prices. Obviously, however, it assumes that information and beliefs are not uniformly held by market participants, and that at least there is some subset of all participants who think they have information that will lead to better-than-average returns.

Summary

Descriptions and explanations of the relationship between security prices and financial information generally embrace the concept of market efficiency. While the earliest definitions were mostly for purposes of classifying existing empirical research, later definitions attempted to model mechanisms that depicted supply-and-demand relationships in both the market for information and the market for securities. Such mechanisms depend on assumptions about individuals' wealth, attitudes to risk, beliefs about prospective returns, access to information, and perceptions of the prevailing environment. However, the recent explanations are still limited in their ability to explain empirical phenomena. And as the next section indicates, the empirical research on market efficiency uses statistical rather than conceptual models to explain how security prices and investors ought to behave.

Testing Market Efficiency

For empirical tests of market efficiency (i.e., the degree to which a specified set of information is fully discounted by the market), assumptions must be made concerning the way prices are set or prospective returns are assessed by investors. As explained below, researchers normally make one of the following assumptions: (1) prospective returns are assumed positive or constant in all future periods or (2) prospective returns conform to the "market model" or an asset-pricing model. This section describes tests of market efficiency based on those assumptions and highlights the evidence relating to such tests. The first set of tests is concerned with "weak form" efficiency; the second is concerned with tests of the "semi-strong" form of market efficiency.

Early Tests of Market Efficiency

Early tests of market efficiency assumed simply that expected returns are positive. If true, that implied that investors could not outperform the market by assuming that, based on the information in past prices, returns in some future periods would be negative. In other words, technical analysts who attempt to exploit short-run upward and downward price movements should not be capable of consistently outperforming those investors who use a simple buy-and-hold investment strategy. Most tests concentrated on past price sequences and whether any systematic pattern in those sequences might be exploited to earn profits over and above the buy-and-hold strategy. The evidence on this issue is consistent with market efficiency in the "weak" sense (i.e., the market reflects all information inherent in past sequences of security prices). Various statistical strategies (e.g., filter rules, runs tests) were unable to beat the buy-and-hold strategy, particularly when trading costs are considered. Notable studies are Alexander (1961), Fama (1965), and Fama and Blume (1966), which are reviewed in Fama (1976).[14]

A related set of tests by early researchers assumed that prices were set as though expected returns were constant and positive over time. The assumption that returns are constant allows the researcher to compute correlations between returns in one period and returns in another. The absence of correlation, of course, is consistent with the hypothesis of market efficiency. Correlation tests, in turn, allow certain tests of the "random walk" and "fair game" properties of past price sequences to be conducted.[15]

Like the earlier studies, the results of the studies using a correlation analysis are consistent with market efficiency in the "weak" sense.[16] But, again, data *consistent* with a world in which the market is efficient and expected returns are constant does not rule out situations in which expected returns do not in fact remain constant over time. If changes in investors' expectations are small enough, they will not invalidate the correlation analysis as an investigative tool. However, if expected returns experience wide swings over short intervals, an assumption on which correlation analysis is based will have been violated. Note, also, that all such tests have a major drawback: They make no adjustment for security risk. Changing risk at the individual security level will surely alter expectations about future returns.

Later Tests: Returns Conform to the Market Model or Asset-Pricing Model

Two other pricing assumptions have been made for purposes of testing market efficiency. These now form the basis for the bulk of

---

[14]The studies examined various holding periods; for example, a five-year period was used by Fama (1965). However, on a very short-term basis (e.g., trading hourly), it may be possible to devise schemes that beat the buy-and-hold strategy. For example, one might be able to exploit the tendency for price movements to reverse themselves over very short intervals. (See Chapter 8 for further discussion.)

[15]A fair game is played if, over a large number of plays of the game, the player (e.g., investor) wins what is expected to be won. A random walk has two essential properties: (a) successive price changes are independent and (b) the expected price change is a constant.

[16]See Fama (1965 and 1976) for a discussion of particular studies that confirm the random-walk and fair-game properties. See also Cootner (1964).

empirical analysis. The first assumes that expected returns conform to the "market model." The market model is primarily a statistical relationship between returns on securities and returns on the market portfolio, when those returns are distributed according to the normal curve. The model's importance stems from the decomposition of return into two components: (1) a component of return that correlates perfectly with the return on the market portfolio and (2) a component that is totally uncorrelated with the return on market. The uncorrelated factor is presumed to be the security's price response to information specific to the firm (and its industry) but not to market-wide factors in general. Since an efficient market assesses returns, and hence determines prices, based on all available information, only the new information known after the market has established present prices has the potential to explain differences between expected returns (which establish present prices) and the return that is actually achieved one period later (a function of today's prices and prices of one period later). If the difference between the expected market return and the actual market return is extracted, that difference can only be due to announcements, events, information, etc., that concern the firm and its industry (but not the economy as a whole). In other words, the difference between actual and expected returns—called the *market model residual*—is a measure of the effects of information released in a period relevant to the firm but not captured by the movements in the market.

Many studies use this basic idea to obtain estimates of market model residuals before, during, and after an announcement known to contain relevant information. The timing, direction, and magnitude of those residual price adjustments form the basis on which to determine whether the market is efficient with respect to a given item of information. The timing of the observable price adjustment is crucial. A noticeable lag in the adjustment of prices to new information is prima facie evidence of an inefficiency. But there is a more convincing test than one based simply on whether a lag exists. Information released today but not acted on by the market until later should be able to be exploited by someone who is cognizant of that delay, provided the costs of using the information in a trading strategy are not too high. Research that demonstrates such profitable investment opportunities is strong evidence of a market that is not informationally efficient. Competition among traders, however, serves to remove such opportunities once they are recognized, assuming they are economically viable.

An efficient market should also respond to new information without bias. In other words, the market should neither overreact nor underreact to the news. In many situations that is difficult to predict since the implications of new information in terms of, say, future cash flows to the firm may be subject to diverse interpretation. Even in the case of a straightforward earnings announcement, when the price changes promptly and in the direction predicted, it may be unclear whether an appropriate response was made in the sense that the market responded without bias. However, if one examines a broad sample of stocks known to be experiencing both good and bad news, the absence of a positive or negative drift in prices subsequent to the announcement (minus any market movement) is consistent with the property that prices are responding to information without bias.

The last of the assumed pricing mechanisms is based on asset-pricing theory. According to this view, security returns should be adjusted for differences in security risk before they are used to assess whether investors responded to the new information. The two-parameter capital-asset-pricing model, for example, posits a linear relationship between security expected return and risk. In this model, one component of return is equal to either a risk-free rate or the return on portfolio with zero risk, and the other component is the excess of expected market return over the risk-free rate multiplied by the risk factor.[17] Many variants of the two-parameter model are used in the empirical analysis, but the approach is essentially the same as the market model approach. A comparison is made between the returns of securities that have reacted to the information in question and expected returns, that is, returns that are as yet unaffected by the information and remain identical in all other factors that are determinants of expected return. Expected returns are those returns predicted by the capital-asset-pricing model just before the information's release. Expected returns could also be based on a control sample otherwise equivalent in the factors that explain expected return.

---

[17]More complicated asset-pricing models have been proposed, for example, Ross' (1976) arbitrage model and Merton's (1973) intertemporal model. These models explain return in terms of factors in addition to diversifiable risk.

Literally hundreds of studies testing market reactions to announcements and events, etc., have been published. Most of that attention has focused on corporate financial news, usually related to the numbers in financial reports. Since this evidence is highly pertinent to the issue of whether such information is apparently "useful" to investors and creditors, the discussion of those studies is left to Chapter 8. However, selected "nonaccounting" studies are identified as being representative of the market's behavior with regard to different events, and these are summarized in the appendix to this chapter. The studies tend to support the hypothesis of market efficiency in all but the strongest sense. In other words, security prices reflect available public information but do not reflect information held privately by some individuals (e.g., managers) and available to the public only at high cost. Still, researchers continue to examine the proposition of market efficiency with better data, sharper tools, and better theory to guide them in their analysis. The result: a much better understanding of why, in what contexts, and to what extent the hypothesis holds.

The appendix discusses studies in the following areas: (1) block trades (Kraus and Stoll [1972]; Scholes [1972]; Dann, Mayers, and Rabb [1977]); (2) insider trades (Jaffe [1974]; Finnerty [1976]); (3) stock splits (Fama et al. [1969]; Charest [1978]); (4) new issues (Ibbotson [1975]); and (5) mutual fund performance (Jensen [1968]; Mains [1977]; Kon and Jen [1979]).

Summary

Empirical tests of market efficiency in the "weak" sense assumed that prices are set as if expected returns are positive (implying that a buy-and-hold strategy performs about as well as a strategy based on short-term price trends) or constant (implying that an individual security's returns are uncorrelated). The empirical findings are consistent with the implications of both those assumptions.

Tests of the response of prices to public information require different assumptions. Prices are assumed to conform to either the "market model" or a model of asset pricing. The research approach is to observe differences between actual return and the return expected on the security in the periods (days, weeks, etc.) before, during, and after the news is made public. A significant delay in the market's response to the new information is prima facie evidence of an inefficiency.

However, researchers must be careful to calculate a security's expected return correctly. It may be that an alleged market inefficiency is simply the product of an incorrect statement of the model used to estimate expected return. Selected tests of the market's response to news, events, information, etc., are summarized in the appendix to this chapter. The market's response to accounting information is the subject of Chapter 8.

Concluding Comments

Understanding the results from research and developing implications of that research for accounting and reporting policy require that aspects of the accounting and reporting environment be described. For present purposes, the term *environment* refers to (1) those groups that have an interest in the reporting process, (2) the economic context in which they interact, and (3) the mechanisms that they use to satisfy their demands for information.

This chapter focuses on investors and creditors and their advisors—information specialists—whose ultimate objective is to assess prospective returns from investment or lending opportunities. Although investors and creditors alike are generally averse to risk, they differ in most other ways. Some are fully diversified, while others are willing to accept company-specific risk; some are active traders, while others tend to "buy and hold" for longer periods; and some use specialists frequently, while others make decisions essentially unaided by specialists. As a result, financial and other information is used in many different ways.

Collectively, decision-making and information-processing activities of individual investors and creditors are reflected in market prices. How quickly and to what degree information is impounded in security prices involves a discussion of market efficiency or, more generally, the relationship of prices—timing, direction, and magnitude of response—to information. In general, the evidence is consistent with market efficiency. Thus, the economic setting is one in which prices react promptly and without bias to new information. The evidence is discussed in the appendix to this chapter and in Chapter 8.

A final feature of the accounting and reporting environment is the mechanism that individuals use to attend to their informational needs. Investors and creditors satisfy their needs for information through private means (e.g., the use of information specialists) and through means designed to supplant or facilitate the use of those private means (e.g., the FASB or the SEC). Both mechanisms serve to "regulate" the quality and quantity of available information.

Appendix to Chapter 4

SELECTED EVIDENCE REGARDING MARKET EFFICIENCY

This appendix summarizes studies of the relationship between prices and events not directly related to accounting and financial reporting. The focus is on tests of the market's response to *public* information—in particular, whether abnormal gains can be made subsequent to its disclosure.

Block Trades

Studies of the price effects of large block trades include Kraus and Stoll (1972), Scholes (1972), and Dann, Mayers, and Rabb (1977). Both Kraus and Stoll and Scholes report evidence of price decreases that seemed to persist for at least a month following the block trade; the weakening in price was slight, however—approximately two percent in two weeks. Kraus and Stoll also found that prices dipped temporarily as the large block trade was made. But this appeared to be due to an imbalance between buyers and sellers more than anything else. Whether abnormal gains could be made during the posttrade recovery of prices was examined in the Dann et al. study. The authors, using intraday data, report that individuals would have had to react within five minutes or less to earn net positive returns. In reality that is probably impossible. They note further that within 10-15 minutes the prices had adjusted completely and thus were unbiased estimates of the close-of-day prices. But it is conceivable that Exchange members, particularly floor traders (who pay lower transaction costs), could gain if they were able to purchase precisely at the depressed block price before the public is notified. In short, the market is efficient with respect to public information—responding, it appears, extremely quickly. One cannot conclude, however, that there is an inefficiency in the "strong form." The existence of excess profits to Exchange members is prima facie evidence of an inefficiency, but other explanations should not be ruled out. For example, the apparent ability of traders to make excess profits acting on the basis of private information could simply be some kind of special fee that the seller of securities pays in order to obtain instant liquidity from the large parcel.

Insider Trades

Another set of studies measured the price effects of insider trades. Jaffe (1974) and Finnerty (1976) present evidence consistent with the proposition that insiders (e.g., officers of corporations) receive abnormal gains in excess of reasonable transactions costs from buying and selling their own firms' securities (even after adjustment for risk). But the potential gains or losses avoided have all but dissipated by the time of publication of the SEC's *Official Summary of Security Transactions and Holdings.* Lorie and Niederhoffer (1968), however, do observe some persistency after the publication date. They suggest that securities experiencing more insider buying than selling are likely to advance following publication and, conversely, that the securities being sold by insiders are more likely to decline. Overall, the findings tend to refute "strong form" efficiency in the sense that information about insider trades apparently is not quickly impounded in prices. Unfortunately, the extent to which trading strategies are successful, when based on public information, is not examined. One needs to know how costly it would be to obtain information about insider trades as they occur rather than waiting for the SEC's publication.

Stock Splits

The impact of stock splits on security prices provides another context in which to examine market efficiency. Typically, prices rise before a stock split and then stabilize awaiting clarification of the firm's policy regarding dividends to be paid on the new number of shares. An efficient market would provide no opportunity for abnormal gain following information about the split. In effect, this is equivalent to a market that neither overreacts nor underreacts in terms of expectations about the forthcoming change in dividend payout. Fama et al. (1969) present evidence consistent with market efficiency focusing on the date that the split is actually realized. Charest (1978) replicated and refined the Fama et al. analysis, concentrating on the dates of the split proposal, approval by stockholders, and split realization. Trading rules based on the earlier dates yielded only slim excess profits, not viable in an economic sense. Charest is led to the conclusion: "The NYSE appears reasonably efficient with respect to publicly available stock split information, but less efficient than estimated from the past literature . . ." (page 292).

57

New Issues

Another area of interest to researchers concerns the price performance of new issues of common stocks following the date the new issue takes place. Probably the most complete of a sequence of studies conducted since the early 1960s is Ibbotson (1975). Concentrating on "unseasoned" stocks on the over-the-counter market during 1960-1969, Ibbotson demonstrated that even after adjusting for the higher risks of the OTC offerings, investors on the average could gain abnormally in the short term by taking advantage of the upward price movement between the offer date and the price at the end of the month of issuance. Individual price changes, however, were skewed, showing higher probabilities of abnormal price increases rather than price decreases. From the second month on, the evidence is consistent with market efficiency. Various trading strategies, adjusted for transaction costs and higher risks associated with the new issues, were able to earn excess returns. The positive initial price performance suggests either that the new issues are purposely underpriced by the issuers (and underwriters) or that investors consistently overvalue those stocks in the initial period (making corrections later on). The latter explanation is, of course, consistent with market inefficiency. Another possible explanation is that the underpricing is a goodwill gesture or side payment to be recouped in future issues or compensated for in other ways.

Mutual Funds

For some time now, researchers have tested whether mutual fund managers are consistently able to outperform market averages. If mutual funds exhibit superior performance but do not have access to inside information, a market inefficiency probably exists since abnormal returns are obtained on the basis of analyzing public information. An analysis by Jensen (1968) casts doubt on the abilities of fund managers to outperform simple buy-and-hold strategies. Later reexamination by Mains (1977), however, shows that almost 80 percent of Jensen's funds posted gains, although after management fees and other costs, those gains were slight. Jensen's analysis covered the 1955-1964 period. Evidence relating to fund performance during 1960-1971 is presented in Kon and Jen (1979). Their evidence suggests that individual funds are seldom consistently better than normal. Nonetheless, they present findings on both sides. On the basis of some tests, the funds were able to recoup all expenses and commissions yet still report profits, although other tests led to the opposite conclusion. Mutual fund performance during the 1970s awaits comprehensive analysis.

Summary

The preceding material summarizes selected studies regarding the relationship of stock prices to certain "nonaccounting" events or disclosures. The evidence appears consistent with (1) the information inherent in past price sequences being fully reflected in prices and (2) publicly available information being fully reflected in prices but only insofar as those prices reflect information whose benefits are no less than the costs. Some studies reporting so-called inefficiencies are of little practical use since only unrealistic trading strategies are able to produce higher returns than normal.

With respect to all information, whether public or private, a limited number of studies demonstrated that the market does not react instantaneously to the information held privately by a few, obtainable at high cost and perhaps even illegally. But this too is what one would expect since equilibrium in the securities market means not only an equality of supply and demand for securities but also that the more-informed and the less-informed investors wish neither to sell nor to buy information given the costs they face. Transaction costs are critical in explaining the results of tests of market efficiency.

The major results based on financial information and disclosures about events such as rating changes, merger announcements, analysts' recommendations, and announcements of changes in accounting and reporting standards are documented in Chapter 8. The focus in that chapter, however, is on examining the response of prices to information on the *assumption* that the market is efficient rather than testing the validity of the assumption per se.

REFERENCES

Advisory Committee on Corporate Disclosure. *Report of the Advisory Committee on Corporate Disclosure to the Securities and Exchange Commission.* 2 vols. Washington, D.C.: U.S. Government Printing Office, November 3, 1977.

Alexander, Sidney S. "Price Movements in Speculative Markets: Trends or Random Walks." *Industrial Management Review,* May 1961, pp. 7-26.

Banz, Rolf W. "The Relationship between Return and Market Value of Common Stocks." *Journal of Financial Economics,* March 1981, pp. 3-18.

Basu, S. "Investment Performance of Common Stocks in Relation to Their Price-Earnings Ratios: A Test of the Efficient Market Hypothesis." *The Journal of Finance,* June 1977, pp. 663-82.

Beaver, William H. *Financial Reporting: An Accounting Revolution.* Prentice-Hall Contemporary Topics in Accounting Series. Englewood Cliffs, N.J.: Prentice-Hall, Inc., 1981.

Benston, George J. *Corporate Financial Disclosure in the UK and the USA.* Reprint. Hampshire, England: Saxon House, 1978.

Blattberg, Robert C., and Gonedes, Nicholas J. "A Comparison of the Stable and Student Distributions as Statistical Models for Stock Prices." *The Journal of Business,* April 1974, pp. 244-80.

Blume, Marshall. "The Assessment of Portfolio Performance." Ph.D. dissertation, Graduate School of Business, University of Chicago, 1968.

Blume, Marshall E., and Friend, Irwin. *The Changing Role of the Individual Investor.* A Twentieth Century Fund report and a Wiley-Interscience publication. New York: John Wiley & Sons, Inc., 1978.

Canadian Institute of Chartered Accountants, The. *Corporate Reporting: Its Future Evolution.* Research study. Toronto: CICA, 1980.

Charest, Guy. "Split Information, Stock Returns and Market Efficiency—I." *Journal of Financial Economics,* June/ September 1978, pp. 265-96.

Cootner, Paul H., ed. *The Random Character of Stock Market Prices.* Cambridge: The Massachusetts Institute of Technology, 1964.

Dann, Larry D.; Mayers, David; and Raab, Robert J., Jr. "Trading Rules, Large Blocks and the Speed of Price Adjustment." *Journal of Financial Economics,* January 1977, pp. 3-22.

Fama, Eugene F. "The Behavior of Stock-Market Prices." *The Journal of Business,* January 1965, pp. 34-105.

_____. "Efficient Capital Markets: A Review of Theory and Empirical Work." *The Journal of Finance,* May 1970, pp. 383-417.

_____. *Foundations of Finance.* New York: Basic Books, Inc., 1976.

Fama, Eugene F., and Blume, Marshall E. "Filter Rules and Stock-Market Trading." *The Journal of Business,* January 1966, pp. 226-41.

Fama, Eugene F.; Fisher, Lawrence; Jensen, Michael; and Roll, Richard. "The Adjustment of Stock Prices to New Information." *International Economic Review,* February 1969, pp. 1-21.

Finnerty, Joseph E. "Insiders and Market Efficiency." *The Journal of Finance,* September 1976, pp. 1141-48.

Grant, Edward B. "Market Implications of Differential Amounts of Interim Information." *Journal of Accounting Research,* Spring 1980, pp. 255-68.

Grossman, Sanford J., and Stiglitz, Joseph E. "Information and Competitive Price Systems." *The American Economic Review,* May 1976, pp. 246-53.

_____. "On the Impossibility of Informationally Efficient Markets." *The American Economic Review,* June 1980, pp. 393-408.

Ibbotson, Roger G. "Price Performance of Common Stock Issues." *Journal of Financial Economics,* September 1975, pp. 235-72.

Ijiri, Yuji. *Theory of Accounting Measurement.* Studies in Accounting Research, no. 10. Sarasota, Fla.: American Accounting Association, 1975.

Jaffe, Jeffrey F. "Special Information and Insider Trading." *The Journal of Business,* July 1974, pp. 410-28.

Jensen, Michael C. "The Performance of Mutual Funds in the Period 1945-1964." *The Journal of Finance,* May 1968, pp. 389-416.

Kon, Stanley J., and Jen, Frank C. "The Investment Performance of Mutual Funds: An Empirical Investigation of Timing, Selectivity, and Market Efficiency." *The Journal of Business,* April 1979, pp. 263-89.

Kraus, Alan, and Stoll, Hans R. "Price Impacts of Block Trading on the New York Stock Exchange." *The Journal of Finance,* June 1972, pp. 569-88.

Lease, Ronald C.; Lewellen, Wilbur G.; and Schlarbaum, Gary G. "The Individual Investor: Attributes and Attitudes." *The Journal of Finance,* May 1974, pp. 413-33.

Leftwich, Richard. "Private Determination of Accounting Methods in Corporate Bond Indentures." Ph.D. dissertation, Graduate School of Management, The University of Rochester, 1980.

Litzenberger, Robert H., and Ramaswamy, Krishna. "The Effect of Personal Taxes and Dividends on Capital Asset Prices: Theory and Empirical Evidence." *Journal of Financial Economics,* June 1979, pp. 163-95.

Lorie, James H., and Niederhoffer, Victor. "Predictive and Statistical Properties of Insider Trading." *Journal of Law and Economics,* April 1968, pp. 35-53.

Mains, Norman E. "Risk, the Pricing of Capital Assets, and the Evaluation of Investment Portfolios: Comment." *The Journal of Business,* July 1977, pp. 371-84.

Markowitz, Harry M. *Portfolio Selection: Efficient Diversification of Investments.* New Haven, Conn.: Yale University Press, 1959.

Merton, Robert C. "An Intertemporal Capital Asset Pricing Model." *Econometrica,* September 1973, pp. 867-87.

Modigliani, Franco, and Cohn, Richard A. "Inflation, Rational Valuation and the Market." *Financial Analysts Journal,* March/April 1979, pp. 24-44.

Officer, R. R. "The Variability of the Market Factor of the New York Stock Exchange." *The Journal of Business,* July 1973, pp. 434-53.

Ripley, William Z. *Main Street and Wall Street.* Accounting Classics Series. Lawrence, Kans.: Scholars Book Co., 1972.

Ross, Stephen A. "The Arbitrage Theory of Capital Asset Pricing." *Journal of Economic Theory,* December 1976, pp. 341-60.

Rubinstein, Mark. "Securities Market Efficiency in an Arrow-Debreu Economy." *The American Economic Review,* December 1975, pp. 812-24.

Schlarbaum, Gary G.; Lewellen, Wilbur G.; and Lease, Ronald C. "Realized Returns on Common Stock Investments: The Experience of Individual Investors." *The Journal of Business,* April 1978, pp. 299-325.

Scholes, Myron S. "The Market for Securities: Substitution versus Price Pressure and the Effects of Information on Share Prices." *The Journal of Business,* April 1972, pp. 179-211.

Smith, Clifford W., Jr., and Warner, Jerold B. "On Financial Contracting: An Analysis of Bond Covenants." *Journal of Financial Economics,* June 1979, pp. 117-61.

Verrecchia, Robert E. "Consensus Beliefs, Information Acquisition, and Market Information Efficiency." *The American Economic Review,* December 1980, pp. 874-84.

CHAPTER 5—EVIDENCE ON THE PROPERTIES OF REPORTED ACCOUNTING NUMBERS

An investor's or creditor's ultimate objective, as stated in the preceding chapter, is to assess the prospective periodic return on a firm's securities. Such assessments depend in part on the accounting information available for use by each present or potential investor or creditor. The purpose of this chapter is to develop an understanding of certain empirical and statistical properties of reported accounting information. Knowledge of those properties should enhance the investor's or lender's ability to use accounting numbers and ratios in making decisions. That knowledge should also benefit managers, standard setters, and others who often select or evaluate accounting alternatives.

For the most part, the literature in accounting and finance documents the properties of reported accounting numbers in terms of the methods by which those numbers are produced—methods that are based on generally accepted accounting principles or other standards of reporting, rather than on the empirical and statistical properties of the numbers. Relevance and reliability, and subsidiary criteria such as consistency and comparability, currently guide the accounting profession, the FASB, and others who choose accounting alternatives.[1] But such "accounting criteria" can be ambiguous and are often not precisely defined.

This chapter, in describing certain empirical and statistical properties of accounting numbers, does not use so-called accounting criteria. Still, the material may be helpful in clarifying some of the contemporary criteria now defined in Concepts Statement 2 on qualitative characteristics (although to bridge the gap between accounting and statistical concepts would go well beyond the scope of this inquiry). For instance, an understanding of statistical patterns of earnings is potentially useful for assessing enterprise cash flows and thus evaluating "predictive ability." Statistical considerations are also pertinent to whether accounting numbers confirm or deny expectations; in other words, whether the numbers have "feedback value." What this chapter does, primarily, is explore properties of accounting numbers—mainly income numbers—using criteria developed from statistics. The emphasis is on

---

[1]See Concepts Statement 2.

describing reasonably concisely the behavior of reported accounting earnings. Combinations of accounting numbers as accounting
ratios are also examined.

The material is presented in three major sections. First, some
statistical concepts and tools that help recognize random or chance
factors in reported numbers are discussed. Chance factors are
defined in that section. Second, the literature on the time-series
properties of accounting numbers is reviewed. That literature is
classified on the basis of (1) whether the work focuses on annual or
quarterly series and (2) whether the analysis emphasizes predictive
or descriptive qualities of those series. Predictive value is defined in
this chapter as the ability to forecast future reported values of the
accounting numbers under consideration. (Research on the predictive ability of financial information is examined more generally in
Chapter 7.) Third, certain properties of accounting ratios are
described, primarily in a cross-sectional sense—that is, by looking
at differences and similarities across firms (within an industry, for
example) at a given point in time. Approaches to aggregating ratios
are also addressed.

Recognizing Chance Factors in Reported Accounting Numbers

It has long been acknowledged that reported accounting numbers
are imperfect representations of the economic phenomena they purport to represent and that, consequently, firms experiencing similar
economic events are unlikely to report equivalent measures of performance or financial position. A primary reason for this is that
managers and others select and apply different accounting
methods. Accounting numbers, therefore, contain an element of
noise, sometimes called *measurement uncertainty.* Chance factors
due to events external to the firms also create a certain amount of
noise in reported accounting numbers. Estimates of uncertain
events often underlie accounting measurements. Depreciation
expense, for example, is typically based on useful life and residual
value estimates. Such events or factors are uncertain. Uncertainty
of this kind (a function of unknown future events) is sometimes
referred to as *real uncertainty.*

Random Character of Accounting Numbers

Chance or random factors under conventional criteria (e.g., generally accepted accounting principles) are recognized in a number of

ways. Accountants have typically given attention to the decomposition of earnings or income into what is "regular" and what is "irregular." The FASB Discussion Memorandum, *Reporting Earnings* (July 31, 1979), for example, suggests that the assessment of regular versus irregular revenues and expenses is a basic need of financial statement users, especially those users interested in estimating future sustainable earnings. Others have called for disclosure of confidence intervals and ranges to describe the overall effects of earnings uncertainty. Forecasts of future earnings by management and analysts often reflect such uncertainty by reporting a range of values rather than a single point estimate.

Both views regarding the recognition of chance factors are consistent with the idea that accounting numbers can be represented as "random variables," that is, variables whose values are governed in part by the laws of chance. What one observes as accounting numbers, then, are specific values of the variable "drawn" from a probability distribution. The probability distribution, which is unobservable, dictates the range and frequency of the values that might be reported.

A fair coin, for instance, has a 50-50 chance of turning up heads (or tails). That is, only two values can be observed, each with an equal likelihood of occurrence. Uncertainty surrounding reported accounting numbers can be described similarly. Consider a company whose reported earnings per share is $5. This number is an estimate of the underlying economic earnings activity. Based on a statistical analysis of the uncertainties involved, one might suppose that chance factors could have produced earnings per share of anywhere from $3 to $7. However, earnings of $3, $5, or $7 (or, for that matter, any monetary amount between $3 and $7) may not occur with equal certainty. The analysis requires an empirical assessment of the probability distribution of earnings per share for that firm. Probability distributions are usually described by parameters that capture the distribution's central tendency (e.g., mean), dispersion (e.g., variance), extent of skewness and peakedness, etc. While the distributional properties of security returns are reasonably well known (see Chapter 4 for evidence on whether returns are bell-shaped), the distributional properties of reported accounting numbers are not. Some of those properties are detailed in the next section.

Accounting numbers are seldom analyzed without consideration of either the numbers for other firms or sequences of past numbers for the firm in question. A model describing the structure of a sequence or series of observations governed in part by chance is called a *probability* (or *stochastic*) *process*. An underlying theme of this chapter is that users assess such models whenever forecasting future values of a series. They may not always be aware of actually doing that, but their actions certainly appear to be consistent with the notion of assessing probability processes. It is not obvious, though, whether individuals make assessments that are strictly "correct" in terms of the statistical criteria.

The following example should make this clear. Consider an investment in a venture whose $1 profit or $1 loss each period is determined by uncertain economic events that can be *represented* by the flip of a fair coin. In other words, there is a 50-50 chance of winning (or losing) a dollar each period. Over time, the venture's accumulated winnings at the end of each period if profits are *always* made would be $1, $2, $3, $4, and so on. Another sequence might be that profits and losses alternate over time. At the end of each period, the accumulated winnings associated with this sequence would then be $1, $0, $1, $0, etc. Obviously, a large number of possible sequences exist. Naive extrapolation of the exhibited patterns in the data suggests in both cases that profit of $1 will be made in period 5. Yet, both forecasters have been misled. They are clearly incorrect given knowledge of the "true" probability model generating each period's winnings (or losses). Expected winnings next period (period 5) and in all future periods are actually zero, because the $1 profit and $1 loss are equally uncertain results.

Similar, though more complicated, issues arise in the analysis of accounting numbers. In other words, some firms' earnings that appear to follow a steady growth trend may upon further inspection be better modeled as if they are generated randomly. This could be troublesome when anticipating the possible effect of a change in accounting method on the volatility of reported earnings. Fortunately, statistical tools are available to infer the underlying behavior from the observed values. The central idea is to exploit any regularities in the series, such as the level of the series, its extent of growth, and any seasonal or cyclical patterns that might persist in future periods. The time-series properties of accounting earnings have been analyzed extensively in that manner. Evidence on those properties forms the bulk of this chapter. In addition, some properties of accounting ratios are discussed. Ratio analysis is probably the most widely used tool for understanding the economic activities portrayed by financial reports.

Summary

Accounting variables reflect chance factors due to, for example, choice of accounting methods and use of estimates in those methods and, hence, can be described as random variables. This allows the evaluator of information or the researcher to adopt the concepts and techniques of statistics in describing and predicting the behavior of financial information. A statistical and probabilistic perspective should allow a more scientific and precise evaluation of the qualities of accounting information heretofore based exclusively on accounting criteria.

Time-Series Behavior of Reported Earnings

A primary emphasis in financial reporting is the provision of information about earnings and its components. A firm's reported earnings are generally presumed to provide information relevant for assessing prospective cash flows. But such cash flow information is not always apparent, even to the experienced decision maker. One possible source of knowledge about future cash flows derives from an understanding of the nature and extent of the relationship between past and present values of reported earnings.[2]

This section summarizes what is known about the complex patterns exhibited by firms' reported earnings, in statistical terminology called *probability* (or *stochastic*) *processes*. Such processes, as noted, are probabilistic models that compactly describe whatever systematic properties (regularities) and chance factors the

---

[2]The accounting profession and standard-setting bodies such as the FASB have only recently officially adopted the view that current and past earnings are useful as predictors of future enterprise cash flows. Concepts Statement 1, for instance, reflects this emphasis: "Investors, creditors, and others often use reported earnings and information about the components of earnings . . . in assessing their prospects for cash flows from investments in or loans to an enterprise. For example, they may use earnings information to help them (a) evaluate management's performance, (b) estimate 'earning power' . . . , (c) predict future earnings . . ." (par. 47).

series of numbers possesses. Whether one is developing an earnings forecast, assessing if an earnings report is considered "good" or "bad" news, or even deciding which discretionary components to adjust to remove unwanted volatility[3] in the income number series, little progress can be made without knowledge of the manner in which reported earnings evolve over time. The material is discussed in terms of: (1) research on the behavior of reported annual earnings, (2) research on models that describe quarterly earnings, (3) using components of earnings for prediction, (4) predictive ability of analysts' and managements' forecasts, and (5) using information about other firms in generating forecasts.

Annual Income Numbers

Systematic study of the behavior of reported earnings dates back to the work of the English economist Little (1962). Rayner and Little (1966) extended that work, which concluded that successive changes in corporate incomes in the United Kingdom are independent. The major implication of that result is that earnings changes (or growth rates) are largely a matter of chance. Hence, as a general rule, they are not predictable by simple extrapolation of past trends or growth rates. Lintner and Glauber (1967) and Brealey (1968 and 1969) examined and in essence confirmed that conclusion in the U.S. context. Brealey (1969), for example, computed correlation coefficients between percentage of earnings changes in adjacent years (between 1951 and 1964) for approximately 700 companies. The correlations were generally small, ranging from -0.26 to 0.17 (page 91). Moreover, the number of companies experiencing successive good or bad years was about the same as if those good or bad years had been classified by the flip of a fair coin.

Understanding and describing the time-series properties of accounting earnings has received considerable attention by researchers in accounting since those early studies. So-called time-series research now occupies a central position in the empirical accounting literature.

---

[3] The term *unwanted volatility* is a more neutral expression to depict income smoothing. Whether earnings are smoothed and, if so, due to what kinds of incentives are issues not addressed in this report. An extensive literature exists, however. For a review, see Ronen, Sadan, and Snow (1977).

Three Descriptions of Annual Earnings

To gain an appreciation for the literature, presented here are three characterizations of the process generating annual earnings. The first is a "random walk" process. Earnings changes that appear as if they have been generated by the flip of a fair coin have the random-walk property. Each earnings change is independent of all past earnings changes, and the best guess of next period's earnings is reported earnings for the present period. Past earnings changes, therefore, are of no help in predicting the future. It is as if the "black box" generating earnings changes has no memory beyond the most recent observation. A strict random-walk process also generates earnings changes that have constant volatility over time. However, the random walk does not apply literally to all firms. Researchers argue that inflation and the reinvestment of earnings imply that there will most likely be a tendency for earnings to drift upward over time. And as the evidence suggests, the volatility and other properties of an earnings series may be influenced by the selection of accounting methods and changes therein.

At the other extreme of possible descriptions, earnings may be viewed as the output of a process with a "constant mean." Over time, earnings appear as if they fluctuate randomly about some unwavering level. A related process is one that has a steady trend line. The trend is usually determined as a function of time. For the "constant mean" process, any deviation of reported earnings from the historical trend is presumed to be totally determined by chance factors. Moreover, the best expectation of earnings next period is developed using all past reported values. This view of earnings behavior apparently has widespread recognition in practice. Indeed, investors and creditors seem well accustomed to developing projections based on historical averages or trends determined by a line of best fit. However, most earnings series are not well described by a model that assumes a firm's earnings are a constant value. Nevertheless, certain ratios involving earnings (e.g., earnings to price) and other ratios exhibit some characteristics of a process with a constant mean value, although the series usually takes several years to move toward its mean value.

Most series can be described by models between the two extremes. These models combine the persistency characteristic of a constant-mean model with the unpredictable behavior of a random-walk model. One subclass of models displays a tendency to revert to some mean level over long periods, although, in the short run, the series could bounce around in an unpredictable fashion, thus camouflaging any tendency to revert to a long-run mean. Academics call these models *autoregressive processes.* Another subclass contains models that smooth out the most recent chance factors to provide a best guess of earnings next period. These models are called *moving average processes.*

The most primitive autoregressive model states that the expected deviation of next period's earnings from the long-run mean (e.g., an industry average) is some fraction (between zero and one) of the deviation of this period's earnings from the long-run mean. Earnings are expected to converge to the mean, but chance factors obstruct immediate convergence. If that fraction is close to one, convergence will occur only over very long periods. The series will appear to be random on first inspection. However, if the fraction is small, the series will resemble a constant-mean process. Deviations from the mean are mostly transitory and thus unrelated to deviations in future periods. According to this idea, then, earnings may be viewed as containing both permanent and transitory (chance) components; the emphasis on permanent versus transitory components depends on whether the fraction is close to one or to zero.

The simplest form of the moving-average model states that the best expectation of next period's earnings is this period's earnings adjusted downward (or upward) by some fraction (between zero and one) of last period's positive (or negative) forecast error. As in the autoregressive process, this adjustment serves to remove a portion of the transitory-error component that would otherwise affect the forecast for next period. Stated another way, it acts as a smoothing coefficient. However, if the smoothing coefficent is close to zero, most of the error component is carried over to future values. The best guess of next period's earnings thus approaches earnings reported for this period. A moving-average process with a near-zero smoothing coefficient, consequently, approximates a random walk.

More complicated models of the process generating earnings employ the methods and procedures outlined in Box and Jenkins (1970). Advanced autoregressive models not only incorporate adjustments based on last period's deviation from the mean, but also incorporate adjustments for deviations in any number of preceding periods. Likewise, more complicated moving-average models smooth the series not only for last period's error but also for error in the two, three, or more preceding periods. Any number of earlier periods can be added. Cyclical and seasonal adjustments can also be made.

Although more complex models are available, the three "primitive" models—the random-walk, the constant-mean, and the autoregressive (moving-average) models—are useful for analysis. They (1) capture an entire spectrum of possible behavior and (2) are extremely compact descriptions (i.e., they involve only a small number of parameters to be estimated). And as the evidence below suggests, certain models have been found to be relatively accurate in predicting future values of reported earnings.

What Are the Main Findings?

All three general descriptions of annual earnings have received research attention. The prominent descriptive studies are by Beaver (1970), Watts (1970), Ball and Watts (1972), Lookabill (1976), and Watts and Leftwich (1977). The Watts study provides preliminary evidence that the series "earnings available for common" behaves as a random walk. Applying the Box and Jenkins time-series modeling techniques to 32 firms in 3 industries in the 1927-1964 period, Watts tested the random-walk model against a variety of alternative behaviors. The random-walk model could not be rejected for 22 out of 32 firms (at conventional levels of statistical significance). In one-year-ahead predictive tests, moreover, the more detailed alternative models only very slightly outperformed the random-walk model. More extensive tests of Watts (1970) are reported in Watts and Leftwich (1977). The conclusion in this later study is even more favorable to the random-walk hypothesis, especially with regard to predicting earnings one year ahead.

Beaver, Ball and Watts, and Lookabill, in exploring the time-series behavior of the "average" firm in a broad sample of American companies, however, provide only partial corroboration of the random-walk result. While Ball and Watts essentially confirm the fact that earnings changes are independent, their analysis using statistical "smoothing" models suggests that a representative model of the average firm's earnings contains a small moving-average component. Hence, the optimal next-period forecast is not simply earnings for this period (as the random-walk model would predict). Instead, the optimal forecast is this period's earnings adjusted by a small fraction of last period's forecast error (since a fraction of the forecast error is considered transitory). Ball and Watts also note that the moving-average effect was more pronounced for a deflated earnings measure (earnings to common equity) than for undeflated earnings or earnings per share.

Beaver and Lookabill provide additional evidence that reported annual earnings behavior is not a strict random walk. Beaver studied time series of earnings to price, earnings to common equity, and "earnings available for common" for 57 firms during the 1949-1968 period. Observing that the deflated earnings numbers (e.g., earnings to common equity) drifted slowly toward the average return of later periods when stratified into high and low categories, Beaver concluded that measures of accounting return exhibit a tendency to converge to a long-run value. Such convergence is, in Beaver's words, "consistent with these measurements coming from a moving average model" (page 86). Beaver's results regarding undeflated earnings (earnings available for common), however, are reasonably consistent with the random-walk process. (For further discussion, see Jensen [1970].) Lookabill extended Beaver's research and studied 65 firms in 3 industries. His conclusion: that the moving-average model is a reasonable description of accounting rates of return for the average firm. This confirmed Beaver's findings, although Lookabill provided no evidence on the behavior of undeflated earnings.

The aforementioned studies thus favor the random-walk model for reported annual earnings (e.g., available for common) and models that closely resemble a random walk (moving-average or mean-reverting processes) for annual earnings if deflated by size. Equally significant is that those models are extremely simple. Complex Box and Jenkins models using several values of past earnings values are apparently neither more descriptive of the statistical process describing earnings nor more accurate for predictive purposes.

Other Research on Annual Earnings

Numerous limitations and unresolved methodological issues render the preceding results little more than broad approximations of the patterns exhibited by reported earnings. They may be sufficient for large-scale macroeconomic research, but they should not be applied unconditionally in investment or lending situations. Issues in need of further study include the impact of industry variables, dividend policy (i.e., extent of reinvestment of earnings), and

74

increased rates of unexpected inflation on the time-series properties of accounting earnings.[4]

One area in particular need of additional research, and of potential interest to policymakers, concerns the effect of accounting policy changes on probabilistic models of earnings behavior. Several of the FASB's rulings (e.g., accounting for research and development costs, accounting for contingencies, accounting for foreign exchange gains and losses) have allegedly had significant effects on firms' earnings patterns—at least, according to the critics. But have the parameters of descriptive and predictive models been noticeably affected by such policy changes? If statistically valid models remain basically unchanged in structure and parameters, then, this is prima facie evidence that the accounting changes would have little impact on investors' and creditors' use of information. In other words, their expectations about earnings would remain unchanged.

Dopuch and Watts (1972) tested the hypothesis of whether a respecification of the accounting system would "cause" a change in the model describing earnings. They examined various accounting series of 11 firms that voluntarily switched from straight-line to accelerated depreciation in the 1947-1956 period. The statistical tests indicated that the earnings behavior of 8 out of the 11 firms changed during the period. The cause-and-effect linkage between change in earnings behavior and change in accounting method was not well specified, however. Accounting changes could be related to other events that are either reinforcing or offsetting in their impact on earnings behavior, and separating the various explanatory factors is difficult.

Behavior of Price-Earnings Ratios

The time-series properties of the price-earnings ratio or its reciprocal should be of interest to investors and creditors. Beaver (1970)

---

[4]A related issue, but beyond the scope of the present discussion, is whether security prices behave as if earnings are being generated by a random-walk process, even though it is generally known that market expectations about future earnings are based on a much broader information set. Beaver, Lambert, and Morse (1980) report that earnings models that include price data give more satisfactory assessments of market expectations of earnings than does the random-walk model (or, for that matter, other models based exclusively on past earnings values).

suggested that the ratio of accounting earnings to price converges to a long-run value (e.g., an economy average). The average of the portfolio containing high earnings-to-price firms was roughly equal to the average of the low earnings-to-price firms within three to four years after the initial stratification was made. In other words, high earnings yields and low earnings yields are reasonably short-term phenomena. Similar results are reported in Beaver and Morse (1978), with the exception that the convergence was not fully complete until about 13 to 14 years after the initial stratification. The initial convergence is attributed largely to the existence of transitory components in earnings (that are independent over time). Differences in growth, risk, and use of accounting method were given as reasons for the longer term persistence, though growth and risk turned out to be negligible in other tests.[5]

Quarterly Time-Series Models

So far, this chapter has emphasized the descriptive properties of *annual* accounting earnings. A similar, though later, tradition emerged with regard to the properties of interim earnings. The focus on quarterly earnings provides the model builder with more observations within a given time period, thus improving estimates of certain parameters that might describe the behavior of earnings. Alternatively, if the researcher thinks that the earnings process is changing over time, the quarterly approach can be applied over shorter time intervals relative to an analysis based on annual observations.

The initial step in modeling quarterly earnings is to assume that the four-period difference in quarterly earnings (earnings this quarter less earnings for the same quarter one year ago) behaves according to the random-walk model. The basic property of the quarterly-earnings process, then, is that successive changes in four-period differences are independent of each other. This means that earnings next quarter are expected to be earnings for the same quarter last year plus the difference between earnings this quarter and earnings for the same quarter one year ago.

Watts (1975), Foster (1977), and Griffin (1977) extended this random-walk view by adding "smoothing" adjustments. Such

---

[5]Convergence of price-earnings ratios over time was also reported in Basu (1977 and 1978).

adjustments remove a portion of transitory error from past changes in quarterly earnings that would otherwise affect forecasts of future quarters' earnings. Foster argued that a single autoregressive parameter is the appropriate adjustment. Both Griffin and Watts posited the inclusion of two moving-average parameters; the first removed an element of error from the most recently observed four-period difference and the second eliminated error from the four-period difference of one year ago. As such, the model used by Griffin and Watts smoothed both the seasonal component and the latest quarterly data for forecasting purposes.

Briefly, the descriptive research on quarterly earnings offers two principal results. First, the quarterly-earnings process is not totally random in character. Second, despite differences in the ways much of the randomness in quarterly earnings is smoothed out, all authors agree that models of quarterly earnings based on past earnings alone should recognize two major patterns in quarterly data. One reflects the change in quarterly earnings between any two adjacent quarters. The other reflects the seasonal pattern, namely, the change in quarterly earnings relative to one year ago.

Predicting Future Accounting Earnings

The ability of past earnings numbers to forecast future earnings numbers is one determinant of their informational content. Predictive ability is usually defined as a function of the distribution of earnings-forecast error (or some parameter describing that distribution, e.g., average error or dispersion of error). The focus in this section is on the prediction of next period's earnings based on models employing (1) past annual earnings, (2) past annual and past quarterly earnings, and (3) various components of earnings. Those models are then compared with forecasts made by analysts and corporate management which, presumably, are based on a much richer information set.

Use of Past Annual Earnings

There have been several studies on the use of past annual earnings to predict future earnings. The major contributions in this area are by Ball and Watts (1972), Albrecht, Lookabill, and McKeown (1977), and Watts and Leftwich (1977). The studies restrict themselves to a comparison of statistical models. The major result is

77

that, relative to sophisticated autoregressive (or moving-average) processes developed using Box and Jenkins' procedures, the random-walk model does not appear to be dominated in terms of an ability to predict next year's earnings. Statistically sophisticated extrapolation models, in other words, do not appear to forecast significantly better. However, researchers such as Brooks and Buckmaster (1976) and Salamon and Smith (1977) question the random-walk hypothesis. Salamon and Smith, for instance, suggest that a bias is present in the prior analysis (because only firms with long histories were studied) and this favors the random-walk hypothesis in that earnings are unlikely to decrease as often as increase. They also warn against generalizing to all firms when the analysis is based on a representative "average" firm. However, the results of Watts and Leftwich (1977) in support of the random-walk model are based on an analysis of individual firms. Moreover, Ball and Watts (1977), in their reply to Salamon and Smith, suggest that the survivorship issue is of little practical importance.

Brooks and Buckmaster also question the overall applicability of the random-walk result. Stratifying their firms on the basis of several measures of income variability, they demonstrated that the random-walk model is not descriptive of a large number of the firms examined. But this is not surprising; the random-walk result uses only a limited set of information—past annual earnings. When additional information is used there is no obvious reason that the random walk should remain the "best" statistical model.

Addition of Past Quarterly Earnings

A number of studies that appeared in the 1960s evaluated whether past quarterly and annual earnings yielded superior forecasts of earnings compared with past annual earnings alone. The early studies were by Green and Segall (1966 and 1967) and Brown and Niederhoffer (1968). Coates (1972) and Reilly, Morgenson, and West (1972) extended that work. By the mid-1970s, better models of the quarterly earnings process were available[6] and, consequently, the predictive power of quarterly earnings could be addressed more thoroughly than in the earlier studies. Those later studies included Foster (1977), Brown and Rozeff (1979), Lorek (1979), and Collins and Hopwood (1980).

---

[6]See the discussion on quarterly time-series models earlier in this chapter.

The major result was that quarterly time-series models are able to predict annual earnings more accurately than are models based on only past annual data. The research procedure is to compare forecasting success, namely, to posit different models and then compare certain properties of the distribution of forecast errors. The candidates given most attention were those derived from the Box and Jenkins techniques, including the straightforward models offered by Foster, Griffin-Watts, and Brown-Rozeff. Foster (1977) examined forecasts of quarterly earnings 1 quarter ahead for 69 firms in the years 1962-1974 and found that a simple autoregressive model (of 4-period differences) outperformed other contenders. Brown and Rozeff (1979) examined their proposed quarterly model, which contained autoregressive and moving-average parameters, relative to the Foster and Griffin-Watts models. Based on 23 firms and 1-, 5-, and 9-quarter forecast intervals, Brown and Rozeff concluded that their model was the best single model of the quarterly earnings process. The authors note, however, that their model performs as well as the Griffin-Watts model for the shorter forecast horizons. Lorek examined forecasts of quarterly earnings 1 to 4 quarters ahead for 30 firms during 1971-1973. The Griffin-Watts model provided the most accurate predictions across all forecast intervals. But the authors caution that to label any model as "best" is probably not a valuable exercise. Indeed, Collins and Hopwood (1980), extending the previous tests, demonstrated "superior" predictive ability for the Brown-Rozeff model (but only at low levels of confidence).

To summarize, compact models of quarterly earnings do well against annual models and the more comprehensive Box and Jenkins "individually identified" models. But, no single quarterly model shows clear-cut superior performance. Still, the straightforward models are rigorous in a statistical sense and have some economic justification insofar as they include mean-reversion and moving-average components (Van Breda [1980]). Their use may offer a low-cost alternative to the relatively expensive structural approaches to forecasting. At a minimum, they supply benchmarks useful for judging the quality of publicly available predictions by analysts and management.

Use of Earnings Components

The research on this topic is rather limited. Studies by Kinney (1971) and Collins (1976) compared the accuracy of forecasting models using segment income and sales data with the accuracy of models using only consolidated figures. Based on 1968-1969 predictions of annual earnings for 24 companies that voluntarily provided segment data, Kinney found that the use of the disaggregated sales and earnings data permitted significantly better forecasts than the use of consolidated data alone. However, according to Collins in similar but more extensive tests, there was considerable overlap in the segment sales and profit data. The main advantage of segment data appears to accrue from segment revenue disclosure, since predictive ability was enhanced only nominally when "segment profit data [were used] in addition to segment revenue data" (page 169). Segment data, thus, appear useful in a predictive context, although it should be noted that such "usefulness" is not obtained without incurring cost, due to competitive disadvantage, additional information processing, etc.

A different approach was taken by Manegold (1981), who compared the predictive ability of models based on components such as interest expense, depreciation expense, operating income before depreciation, and interest expense with models based on aggregate earnings only. The hypothesized "superiority" of a component-based predictive model could not be demonstrated.[7]

Are Analysts' or Managements' Forecasts of Earnings Superior to Statistical Models?

Analysts' Forecasts

Since analysts and managers use more information, their forecasts should have greater predictive accuracy. However, managers and analysts may exhibit unintentional biases in the processing of information. (Chapter 6 reviews the psychological literature.) A

---

[7]Possible misspecification of the statistical and economic relationships involved is no doubt a partial explanation. Issues of specification arise in all such studies. In segment-based forecasting, for instance, little is known about the relationships between the properties of segment earnings and their aggregated counterparts. What segment-earnings process, for example, is consistent with the random-walk property for annual consolidated earnings? Similar explanations of the behavior of earnings components (e.g., depreciation) that are consistent with aggregate earnings are equally unresearched in an accounting context. A more structural approach to earnings forecasting is needed. Accounting research, however, has shown little interest in such modeling efforts.

related issue is that while managers and analysts may predict more accurately than the statistical models, the difference may be marginal. And, if the cost of preparing the forecasts is considered, the development of such data may not be worthwhile.

Evidence that analysts pay attention to quarterly earnings in revising published forecasts is provided by Abdel-khalik and Espejo (1978). They used a regression model to explain the accuracy of Value Line's 1976 annual earnings forecasts in terms of error in the prediction of quarterly earnings. The findings are consistent with the proposition that Value Line revised its forecasts of the predicted portion of annual earnings in the same direction as the quarterly forecast error in all three quarters. Brown et al. (1980) confirmed the result using quarterly forecast data for 50 firms during 1972-1976. Analysts also appear to pay attention to changes in accounting methods. Brown (1981), examining the accuracy of analysts' predictions of earnings in 1974-1979, concluded that there was little difference in Value Line's forecasting ability before and after selected voluntary and mandated accounting changes.

But the above finding that analysts seem to use quarterly numbers and recognize accounting changes for forecasting purposes does not answer the basic question of whether persons with access to public and private information can outpredict extrapolative models, especially those of the kind discussed earlier. Numerous "model comparison" studies have been performed in the last decade or so. Cragg and Malkiel (1968) reported only limited success by participating investment firms in predicting the 5-year earnings growth of 185 companies relative to a regression model based on past growth rates. And results by Elton and Gruber (1972) indicated that analysts' forecasts did not significantly outperform those based on statistical techniques (specifically, an exponential smoothing model), although the exponential smoothing model was marginally superior. However, if sufficient numbers of statistical models are evaluated, chance factors alone might produce a better performance.

Industry variables seem to make a "difference" in forecasting ability. Gray's (1974) analysis of 10 years of brokerage house earnings estimates by industry shows wide variation in the absolute error forecast criterion. Utility company forecasts, for example, were about four times as accurate as forecasts for firms in the automobile industry. Gray's main conclusion: The analyst appears to do significantly better than naive models in industries with more volatile earnings. In the less volatile industries, the naive models seemed to perform only slightly below the accuracy of the analysts. But analysts were better able to predict "turning points" regardless of industrial classification.

More recent studies comparing analysts with mechanical forecasts are by Crichfield, Dyckman, and Lakonishok (1978) and by Brown and Rozeff (1979). Crichfield et al. examined 46 firms that appeared in Standard & Poor's *Earnings Forecaster* in 1967-1976. Thirteen monthly predictions of each firm in each of the 10 years were compared with predictions from naive models using past annual and quarterly data. Three principal findings are reported. First, the analysts' predictions became relatively more accurate as the end of the year for which the forecast is made was approached. Second, analysts were not inclined systematically to overpredict or underpredict future reported earnings. Third, differences among analysts' forecasts did not appear to decrease as the date of actual earnings was approached. The last result contradicted the authors' expectations.

Results from research favorable to the superiority of analysts' forecasts vis-à-vis benchmark models are also reported by Brown and Rozeff. Using 50 firms and forecasts from 1 to 5 quarters ahead in the 1972-1975 period, they reported that (1) Value Line estimates were significantly more accurate than mechanical models based on Box and Jenkins' techniques and (2) such Box and Jenkins models outperformed other naive models employing past quarterly earnings. However, their results are probably overstated, given their strong emphasis on the significant 1972 results and not on other years. (See Abdel-khalik and Thompson [1977-1978] for further discussion.)

Managements' Forecasts

Numerous studies have evaluated managements' forecasts against statistical benchmarks. Copeland and Marioni (1972) compared 50 management earnings-per-share forecasts (published in 1968 only) with 6 naive models. They found that the executives were better forecasters. An extension of the Copeland and Marioni test is reported in Lorek, McDonald, and Patz (1976). In that study, the superiority of management forecasts was explored using sophisticated Box and Jenkins modeling techniques. Lorek et al. concluded that, for the 40 forecasts examined, there is no significant difference in the magnitude of prediction error between firm-specific Box and Jenkins forecasts and those voluntarily disclosed by a firm's management. Nonetheless, when management's prediction error was greater than 10 percent, the mechanical models were superior 18 times out of 20.

Managements' forecasts of earnings have also been compared with those produced by financial analysts. Basi, Carey, and Twark (1976) and Ruland (1978) report generally consistent results: Management forecasts and analyst forecasts were roughly equivalent in their ability to predict future earnings. Imhoff (1978) and Imhoff and Paré (1980) also report that there is no significant difference in managements' versus the analysts' forecasting performance. One study was located, however, that supports the proposition that managements' forecasts are better predictors of earnings. Jaggi (1980) reported that Value Line's estimates of earnings were significantly less accurate relative to managements' estimates.

To summarize, the tentative conclusion is that managements' and analysts' forecasts of earnings are not decidedly better than models of earnings based on a statistical analysis of the patterns in historical annual and quarterly earnings. However, a few studies indicate slightly better performance by analysts and managers. Additionally, in interpreting the results, three principal caveats should be mentioned. First, the results are typically based on an "average" firm or a firm at the median position in a cross section. Such average results may have little application in specific contexts. Second, analysis by industry, size, risk, and other possible explanatory variables has received only scant attention so far in developing statistical models. Third, most studies use rather naive models and thus do not recognize recent research on the properties of accounting earnings. This suggests that they are potentially biased in favor of the superiority of the published forecasts.

Finally, the finding that managers and analysts have about the same degree of forecasting success is probably not unreasonable given the present institutional setting. Company investor-relations programs and analysts' periodic meetings with management suggest that, insofar as the earnings forecast is concerned, the overlap of information accessible to management and analysts is considerable.

Index Models: Use of Information about Other Firms

The essence of an index model is to employ information about other firms using an economy- or industry-wide index of corporate earnings in order to (1) develop better forecasts of earnings or (2) improve one's understanding of the process that generates earnings. A single index model partitions a firm's earnings change into two factors: one sensitive to changes in the earnings of other firms, the other statistically uncorrelated with the earnings of other firms. Changes in the earnings of other firms are represented by an index. A firm's responsiveness to changes in economy-wide earnings is called its accounting "beta." Accounting beta is a direct analog of market beta, that is, security relative risk.[8] That portion of the earnings change uncorrelated with other firms is considered "specific" to the firm itself. And if the random-walk hypothesis holds, it is also unrelated to past earnings changes. Thus, this variable is an important indicator of a change in earnings that is unique to the firm and is essentially unanticipated. Researchers and analysts use variables of this kind in studying the effects of accounting reports on security prices. (Chapter 8 discusses the literature on security price effects of accounting reports.)

Another use of an index model is to show the analyst where to devote resources in the forecasting effort. For firms highly dependent on macroeconomic or industry factors, accurate forecasts of those factors would seem crucial. For firms not highly sensitive to such factors, greater attention might be given to the financial statements and other firm-specific variables such as managerial ability, marketing talent, or rights to technological processes.

Research Findings

Relationships among firms' annual earnings changes were initially studied by Brown and Ball (1967) and Brealey (1968). Based on work that explored the extent of correlation among firms' security returns (King [1966]), Brown and Ball applied the same research techniques to accounting return measures. Their results conclusively reveal the presence of similarities in the patterns describing firms' annual earnings numbers. For the 1947-1965 period, 316 large industrial firms were analyzed. Industry groups were based on two-digit standard industrial classification (SIC) codes. The results

---

[8]Relative risk is defined as the covariance of a firm's security return with the return on the market portfolio divided by the variance of the return on the market portfolio. (See Chapter 8 for further details.)

are twofold: First, 35-40 percent of earnings variability on average was explained by a market-wide index of earnings; second, 10-15 percent of the remaining variability was explained by an index of earnings for the industry. "Clearly," according to Brown and Ball, "accounting measurements of net income reflect both events which affect all firms and, at least to some degree, events which affect only those firms that are members of a given industry" (page 65). A similar analysis is reported by Brealey (1968) except that earnings changes, not earnings levels, were examined. Industry- and economy-wide indexes of earnings changes were able to explain roughly 40 percent of the average firm's change in earnings.

Subsequent research by Gonedes (1973) and Magee (1974) strengthened these initial results. Index models based on the change in earnings were shown to be more descriptively valid than those based on earnings themselves. Moreover, index models based on change in annual earnings were better in predictive tests relative to other index models, though they were not a significant improvement over a strict random-walk model, that is, one that does not utilize information about changes in other firms' earnings. Magee added an industry index to the model (using earnings changes) examined in Gonedes. The industry index was constructed to be uncorrelated with the market index of earnings. Using four-digit SIC codes, Magee "found that the industry effects on earnings are [of] approximately the same magnitude as the economy-wide effects" (page 273). Forecasting ability of the model using two indexes (economy and industry), however, was not examined.[9]

Following the general trend of research on the time-series properties of earnings, Hopwood (1980) studied the impact of market and industry indexes on the behavior of quarterly earnings. A time-series technique called *transfer function analysis* was used. Transfer function analysis attempts to establish an "optimal" description of the relationship between the time-series behavior of a particular firm's earnings and the time-series behavior of a set of variables that might explain the firm's patterns of earnings (e.g., industry- and economy-wide indexes of earnings). Hopwood, however, runs into methodological difficulties. While some transfer function models proved to be adequate descriptors of the underlying relationships,

---

[9]Magee tested the index models in terms of their strength of association with security prices. Industry factors were found to be reflected in security prices.

the transfer functions did not predict at all well. The theoretical benefits of this multivariate approach seem almost entirely blurred by issues of implementation.

Analysis of Accounting Ratios

As the research documented in the remaining chapters indicates, accounting ratios are used extensively by investors, creditors, analysts, and others.[10] Horrigan (1965) notes: "It is inconceivable that accounting data can be analyzed without transforming it into ratios, in one way or another; and thus, a justification of financial ratios would also be an important justification of financial accounting" (page 568). The purpose of this section is (1) to discuss ways of using ratios more effectively and (2) to bring together various empirical studies on the properties of accounting ratios.

Making Ratios More Informative

Numerous factors determine the informational value of accounting ratios. First, most ratios are concerned with the issue of specifying a relevant economic or financial relationship. For example, a primary determinant of net income or earnings is the financial capital invested (e.g., owners' equity). Consequently, it is usually more "meaningful" to examine the ratio of income to capital in comparing interfirm performance than to examine absolute income. The implicit hypothesis is that one variable—in this case financial capital—is a dominant reason for differences in income.

The most common form of ratio adjusts for differences in scale or size (measured as assets, sales, equity, value of the same variable in the preceding period, etc.). Supposedly, this allows the user to concentrate on other reasons why the accounting numbers might differ. However, ratios are not always an appropriate means to adjust for the effects of size. Lev and Sunder (1979) discuss conditions under which size can be adequately adjusted by using ratios. The principal condition is that size and the underlying variable of interest (e.g., market power) be strictly proportional, that is, the

---

[10]Ratios are also used in investor, creditor, and management contracts and hence may have direct financial consequences for those involved. For an interesting case on the use of financial ratios in management compensation contracts, see Loomis (1980).

ratio of the variable of interest to size be a constant. If proportionality does not hold, Lev and Sunder recommend other kinds of adjustment techniques, such as including size as an additional variable in a regression analysis.

Negative numbers can create problems in the construction of ratios, especially if they enter as denominator variables. For example, percentage change in earnings (a ratio) can reflect the opposite of what is intended. If earnings are reported in 3 consecutive years as, say, $4, -$1, and $6, the percentage change in the third period is a negative 700 percent. Earnings, though, have improved substantially.

Assuming the ratio is properly adjusted for size effects and negative-number problems have been dealt with, the next step is to compare the ratio with some benchmark or ideal standard. Those include predetermined (budgetary) goals, historical ratios of the same firm, and ratios of other firms usually as industry- or economy-wide averages. Complex issues arise in the determination of industry- or economy-wide benchmarks. These include: the choice of weights in computing the index, how to deal with firms that are outliers (which arises, for instance, if a denominator variable is close to zero), and how to define the population that the index purports to represent (e.g., an "industry" definition could be based on products, markets, growth rates, etc.). In brief, the construction and appropriate use of ratios is not always a simple operation. One must consider the economic relationship that underlies the ratio in addition to various measurement issues. Careful attention to both aspects will make accounting ratios more informative.

Empirical Research

The work done on the properties of ratios thus far is limited. First, the research suggests industries differ in the distribution of financial ratios. Statistical analysis by Gupta and Huefner (1972), for instance, "found that cluster analysis groupings of the ratio data correspond highly with both the judgmental classifications of economists and with numerous qualitatively expressed economic characteristics of the industries involved" (page 90). In other words, groupings of firms determined by similarity of accounting ratios matched groupings based on conventional industry classifications. Second, within an industry, firms' ratios tend to become more alike over time. (See Lev [1969] and Foster [1978] for details.) The idea that ratios converge to an industry norm is consistent with several explanations; for example, the presence of competition among firms in the industry, the idea that firms in an industry eventually tend to follow similar accounting methods, and the fact that random factors in one firm's ratios, if unrelated with other firms', tend to cancel out over time.

Since accounting ratios are increasingly being used in modeling economic relationships and predicting significant events, two further issues are addressed. Many economic modeling techniques require that the explanatory or predictor variables be distributed as a normal curve, yet the evidence suggests that most accounting ratios are not normally distributed (Deakin [1976]). Also, according to Horrigan (1965) and Foster (1978), there is evidence of positive skewness. (The tail of the frequency distribution is stretched to the right.) Such skewness appears to be sufficient to reject the assumption that most ratios are distributed as the bell-shaped, normal curve.[11]

A related concern in using advanced econometric techniques is that ratios may be affected by common industry- and economy-wide factors. The ratios of one firm are thus not independent of another firm. Since most statistical modeling techniques require independent observations, the analysis may have to be modified if the independence assumption is violated. One straightforward approach is to express the data as a deviation from a benchmark (e.g., the firm's ratio less an industry norm).

Further problems arise if several ratios for the same firm are analyzed concurrently. Different financial ratios for the same firm are usually significantly related. (For results based on 1948-1957 data, see Horrigan [1965].) This means that in statistical analysis such as multiple regression, the significance level of any one explanatory variable will tend to be unreliable. Consequently, relationships that the analyst is looking for may be disguised. However, there are techniques available (e.g., principal components analysis) that enable large sets of ratios to be reduced to smaller numbers of uncorrelated

---

[11]A logarithmic transformation of the empirical data is appropriate in most cases. Positive skewness is reduced by such a transformation since the right tail of the distribution is pulled in toward the mean and the left tail is stretched out away from the mean. The researcher can also adopt nonparametric statistical procedures which make fewer assumptions about the characteristics or parameters of the distribution.

explanatory factors. Pinches, Mingo, and Caruthers (1973), for example, summarized (explained) 40 ratios by only 7 uncorrelated factors. Those 7 factors summarized 90 percent of the information inherent in all 40 ratios. The cross-sectional stability of those dimensions was evaluated by Johnson (1979), who essentially confirmed the Pinches et al. findings. A few carefully selected ratios (e.g., return on investment, leverage, liquidity, turnover, etc.) can thus be chosen to represent most aspects of firm behavior.

Summary

Improving the use of accounting ratios for estimation and prediction requires not only that the impact that different accounting methods have on ratios be understood, but also that statistical assumptions of the prediction model be evaluated by empirical analysis. Unless the data is appropriate, incorrect forecasts or other unwarranted inferences might be drawn. Unfortunately, except for knowing that a few well-chosen ratios are better for analysis than are numerous conventional ratios and that cross-sectional arrays of ratios are noticeably unlike a normal, bell-shaped curve, relatively little empirical evidence on the statistical properties of ratios is available. (This is in contrast to research on the distributional properties of stock prices.) The implications of the preceding discussion for accounting and reporting policy are indirect. Accounting standard setters do not usually make choices about the ratios that users will compute. However, those who may select or evaluate accounting alternatives should not remain unaware of the issues involved, in part because the selected accounting alternative could alter the characteristics of the data. Indeed, a prediction rule valid under one accounting method may not be valid under another.

Concluding Comments

This chapter has discussed certain statistical properties of accounting numbers and ratios, an understanding of which should enable investors, creditors, and their advisors to use more effectively the various modeling or forecasting techniques available. Most of the research effort concentrates on the properties of historical series of annual and interim earnings, and comparisons of those forecasts with published forecasts by analysts and management. However, since most accounting information is analyzed in ratio form, certain properties of accounting ratios are described with a view to enhancing statistically derived predictions. A primary objective in almost all the research examined is the prediction of future reported earnings, which should aid in assessing the future returns on firms' securities.

For those who must often select or evaluate accounting alternatives (e.g., the FASB), the potential benefit of the research discussed is that it may eventually provide clues about (1) how earnings and other information might change as a consequence of changes in the measurement methods used and other attributes of the firm and (2) the extent to which one firm's earnings patterns might differ from another firm's as a function of the choice of accounting techniques. To date, however, the studies provide little concrete guidance regarding the expected effects on the behavior of earnings due to changes in particular standards or measurement rules.

REFERENCES

Abdel-khalik, A. Rashad, and Espejo, Jose. "Expectations Data and the Predictive Value of Interim Reporting." *Journal of Accounting Research,* Spring 1978, pp. 1-13.

Albrecht, W. Steve; Lookabill, Larry L.; and McKeown, James C. "The Time-Series Properties of Annual Earnings." *Journal of Accounting Research,* Autumn 1977, pp. 226-44.

Ball, Ray, and Watts, Ross. "Some Time Series Properties of Accounting Income." *The Journal of Finance,* June 1972, pp. 663-81.

_____. "Reply to Salamon and Smith." *The Journal of Finance,* December 1977, pp. 1802-8.

Basi, Bart A.; Carey, Kenneth J.; and Twark, Richard D. "A Comparison of the Accuracy of Corporate and Security Analysts' Forecasts of Earnings." *The Accounting Review,* April 1976, pp. 244-54.

Basu, S. "Investment Performance of Common Stocks in Relation to Their Price-Earnings Ratios: A Test of the Efficient Market Hypothesis." *The Journal of Finance,* June 1977, pp. 663-82.

_____. "The Effect of Earnings Yield on Assessments of the Association between Annual Accounting Income Numbers and Security Prices." *The Accounting Review,* July 1978, pp. 599-625.

Beaver, William H. "The Time Series Behavior of Earnings." *Journal of Accounting Research.* Supplement, *Empirical Research in Accounting: Selected Studies, 1970,* pp. 62-99.

Beaver, William H.; Lambert, R.; and Morse, D. "The Information Content of Security Prices." *Journal of Accounting and Economics,* March 1980.

Beaver, William H., and Morse, Dale. "What Determines Price-Earnings Ratios?" *Financial Analysts Journal,* July/August 1978, pp. 65-76.

Box, George E. P., and Jenkins, Gwilyn M. *Time Series Analysis: Forecasting and Control.* San Francisco: Holden-Day, Inc., 1970.

Brealey, Richard. "Some Implications of the Comovement of Company Earnings." Paper presented at the Seminar on the Analysis of Security Prices, November 15, 1968, at the University of Chicago.

_____. *An Introduction to Risk and Return from Common Stocks.* Cambridge: The Massachusetts Institute of Technology, 1969.

Brooks, LeRoy D., and Buckmaster, Dale A. "Further Evidence of the Time Series Properties of Accounting Income." *The Journal of Finance,* December 1976, pp. 1359-73.

Brown, Lawrence D. "Accounting Changes and Analyst Earnings Forecast Accuracy." Research paper. Buffalo: State University of New York, May 1981.

Brown, Lawrence D.; Hughes, John S.; Rozeff, Michael S.; and Vanderweide, James H. "Expectations Data and the Predictive Value of Interim Reporting: A Comment." *Journal of Accounting Research,* Spring 1980, pp. 278-88.

Brown, Lawrence D., and Rozeff, Michael S. "Univariate Time-Series Models of Quarterly Accounting Earnings per Share: A Proposed Model." *Journal of Accounting Research,* Spring 1979, pp. 179-89.

Brown, Philip, and Ball, Ray. "Some Preliminary Findings on the Association between the Earnings of a Firm, Its Industry, and the Economy." *Journal of Accounting Research.* Supplement, *Empirical Research in Accounting: Selected Studies, 1967,* pp. 55-77.

Brown, Philip, and Niederhoffer, Victor. "The Predictive Content of Quarterly Earnings." *The Journal of Business,* October 1968, pp. 488-97.

Coates, Robert. "The Predictive Content of Interim Reports—A Time Series Analysis." *Journal of Accounting Research.* Supplement, *Empirical Research in Accounting: Selected Studies, 1972,* pp. 132-44.

Collins, Daniel W. "Predicting Earnings with Sub-Entity Data: Some Further Evidence." *Journal of Accounting Research,* Spring 1976, pp. 163-77.

Collins, William A., and Hopwood, William S. "A Multivariate Analysis of Annual Earnings Forecasts Generated from Quarterly Forecasts of Financial Analysts and Univariate Time-Series Models." *Journal of Accounting Research,* Autumn 1980, pp. 390-406.

Copeland, Ronald M., and Marioni, Robert J. "Executives' Forecasts of Earnings per Share versus Forecasts of Naive Models." *The Journal of Business,* October 1972, pp. 497-512.

Cragg, J. G., and Malkiel, Burton G. "The Consensus and Accuracy of Some Predictions of the Growth of Corporate Earnings." *The Journal of Finance,* March 1968, pp. 67-84.

Crichfield, Timothy; Dyckman, Thomas; and Lakonishok, Josef. "An Evaluation of Security Analysts' Forecasts." *The Accounting Review,* July 1978, pp. 651-68.

Deakin, Edward B. "Distributions of Financial Accounting Ratios: Some Empirical Evidence." *The Accounting Review,* January 1976, pp. 90-96.

Dopuch, Nicholas, and Watts, Ross. "Using Time-Series Models to Assess the Significance of Accounting Changes." *Journal of Accounting Research,* Spring 1972, pp. 180-94.

Elton, Edwin J., and Gruber, Martin J. "Earnings Estimates and the Accuracy of Expectational Data." *Management Science,* April 1972, pp. B409-24.

Foster, George. "Quarterly Accounting Data: Time-Series Properties and Predictive-Ability Results." *The Accounting Review,* January 1977, pp. 1-21.

_____. *Financial Statement Analysis.* Englewood Cliffs, N.J.: Prentice-Hall, Inc., 1978.

Gonedes, Nicholas J. "Properties of Accounting Numbers: Models and Tests." *Journal of Accounting Research,* Autumn 1973, pp. 212-37.

Gray, William S. "The Role of Forecast Information in Investment Decisions." In *Public Reporting of Corporate Financial Forecasts,* edited by Prem Prakash and Alfred Rappaport, pp. 47-79. Chicago: Commerce Clearing House, 1974.

Green, David, Jr., and Segall, Joel. "The Predictive Power of First-Quarter Earnings Reports: A Replication." *Journal of Accounting Research.* Supplement, *Empirical Research in Accounting: Selected Studies, 1966,* pp. 21-36.

_____. "The Predictive Power of First-Quarter Earnings Reports." *The Journal of Business,* January 1967, pp. 44-55.

Griffin, Paul A. "The Time-Series Behavior of Quarterly Earnings: Preliminary Evidence." *Journal of Accounting Research,* Spring 1977, pp. 71-83.

Gupta, Manak C., and Huefner, Ronald J. "A Cluster Analysis Study of Financial Ratios and Industry Characteristics." *Journal of Accounting Research,* Spring 1972, pp. 77-95.

Hopwood, William S. "The Transfer Function Relationship between Earnings and Market-Industry Indices: An Empirical Study." *Journal of Accounting Research,* Spring 1980, pp. 77-90.

Horrigan, James O. "Some Empirical Bases of Financial Ratio Analysis." *The Accounting Review,* July 1965, pp. 558-68.

Imhoff, Eugene A., Jr. "The Representativeness of Management Earnings Forecasts." *The Accounting Review,* October 1978, pp. 836-50.

Imhoff, Eugene A., Jr., and Paré, Paul V. "Analysis and Comparison of Earnings Forecast Agents." Research paper. Ann Arbor: The University of Michigan, October 1980.

Jaggi, Bikki. "Further Evidence on the Accuracy of Management Forecasts vis-à-vis Analysts' Forecasts." *The Accounting Review,* January 1980, pp. 96-101.

Johnson, W. Bruce. "The Cross-Sectional Stability of Financial Ratio Patterns." *Journal of Financial and Quantitative Analysis,* December 1979, pp. 1035-48.

King, Benjamin F. "Market and Industry Factors in Stock Price Behavior." *The Journal of Business,* January 1966, pp. 139-90.

Kinney, William R., Jr. "Predicting Earnings: Entity versus Subentity Data." *Journal of Accounting Research,* Spring 1971, pp. 127-36.

Lev, Baruch. "Industry Averages as Targets for Financial Ratios." *Journal of Accounting Research,* Autumn 1969, pp. 290-99.

Lev, Baruch, and Sunder, Shyam. "Methodological Issues in the Use of Financial Ratios." *Journal of Accounting and Economics,* December 1979, pp. 187-210.

Little, I. M. D. "Higgledy Piggledy Growth." *Bulletin of the Oxford Institute of Economics and Statistics,* November 1962, pp. 389-412.

Lookabill, Larry L. "Some Additional Evidence on the Time Series Properties of Accounting Earnings." *The Accounting Review,* October 1976, pp. 724-38.

Loomis, Carol J. "Archie McCardell's Absolution." *Fortune,* December 15, 1980, p. 89.

Lorek, Kenneth S. "Predicting Annual Net Earnings with Quarterly Earnings Time-Series Models." *Journal of Accounting Research,* Spring 1979, pp. 190-204.

Lorek, Kenneth S.; McDonald, Charles L.; and Patz, Dennis H. "A Comparative Examination of Management Forecasts and Box-Jenkins Forecasts of Earnings." *The Accounting Review,* April 1976, pp. 321-30.

Magee, Robert P. "Industry-Wide Commonalities in Earnings." *Journal of Accounting Research,* Autumn 1974, pp. 270-87.

Manegold, James G. "Time-Series Properties of Earnings: A Comparison of Extrapolative and Component Models." *Journal of Accounting Research,* Autumn 1981, pp. 360-73.

Pinches, George E.; Mingo, Kent A.; and Caruthers, J. Kent. "The Stability of Financial Patterns in Industrial Organizations." *The Journal of Finance,* May 1973, pp. 389-96.

Rayner, A. C., and Little, I. M. D. *Higgledy Piggledy Growth Again.* Oxford, England: Basil Blackwell, 1966.

Reilly, Frank K.; Morgenson, David L.; and West, Marilyn. "The Predictive Ability of Alternative Parts of Interim Financial Statements." *Journal of Accounting Research.* Supplement, *Empirical Research in Accounting: Selected Studies, 1972,* pp. 105-24.

Ronen, Joshua; Sadan, Simcha; and Snow, Charles. "Income Smoothing: A Review." *The Accounting Journal,* Spring 1977, pp. 11-26.

Ruland, William. "The Accuracy of Forecasts by Management and by Financial Analysts." *The Accounting Review,* April 1978, pp. 439-47.

Salamon, Gerald L., and Smith, E. Dan. "Additional Evidence on the Time Series Properties of Reported Earnings per Share: Comment." *The Journal of Finance,* December 1977, pp. 1795-1801.

Van Breda, Michael F. "Modelling Earnings Behavior." Research paper. Cambridge: Sloan School of Management, Massachusetts Institute of Technology, 1980.

Watts, Ross L. "The Time Series of Accounting Earnings." In "The Information Content of Dividends." Ph.D. dissertation, University of Chicago, 1970, Appendix A.

_____. "The Time Series Behavior of Quarterly Earnings." Draft working paper. New South Wales: Department of Commerce, University of Newcastle, April 1975.

Watts, Ross L., and Leftwich, Richard W. "The Time Series of Annual Accounting Earnings." *Journal of Accounting Research,* Autumn 1977, pp. 253-71.

CHAPTER 6—BEHAVIORAL RESEARCH AND FINANCIAL ACCOUNTING STANDARDS

by Michael Gibbins and Patricia Brennan*
Faculty of Commerce and Business Administration
The University of British Columbia

Vast amounts of research effort are being given to the study of the ways in which people use information and make decisions. Behavioral research, as it applies to financial accounting, uses empirical methods (such as field studies, protocol analyses, interviews, and questionnaires) arising from psychology and similar disciplines to seek general explanations of how accounting information is used. This area of research is at present young, unfocused, and conceptually underdeveloped. However, a review of the research to date uncovers interesting possibilities for future study as well as potential shortcomings of such study in general.

Because conceptions of behavioral research and the Financial Accounting Standards Board's interest in it vary, it is best to begin by clarifying the scope of our review. The analysis concentrates on the issues of efficiency and effectiveness of standard setting in accounting rather than on normative (and political) questions about the existence of the FASB or its own preferences for outcomes. We focus on the behavior of investors, creditors, and similar decision makers—the principal users of general purpose financial reports (see Concepts Statement 2, paragraphs 22-26). The behavior of managers, auditors, and others will be referred to where relevant, but we make no systematic review of the extensive behavioral literature in areas such as management accounting, auditing, and personnel management (in public accounting). Moreover, the bulk of the work reviewed deals with the behavior of *individuals* rather than organizations or markets, which are dealt with in other chapters. (See Chapter 8, for example.)

This chapter has two major parts. The first reviews the behavioral research relevant to the evaluation of financial information by investors and creditors. The second attempts to draw conclusions that we hope are of interest to the FASB and its constituency. These

*The authors thank participants in research workshops at the University of Alberta, the University of British Columbia, and the University of Washington for their very helpful comments on earlier drafts of this chapter.

conclusions are based on the research itself, and on certain characteristics of the research that should be considered when evaluating the contribution it makes to a discussion of issues raised in this and other chapters.

Before we go further, we must emphasize that, so far, strong conclusions of direct applicability to standard setters have eluded us. Behavioral research in financial accounting emphasizes descriptive explanations of the world as it is and, as such, is not particularly well suited to examining the *desirability* of alternative accounting standards. In our review and conclusions, therefore, we try to clarify not only what is known but also the limits of that knowledge. We wish to inform the reader about the kinds of topics studied in behavioral accounting and allied research and to explain how the orientation of that research tempers the conclusions that can be drawn.

A. Review of Behavioral Research in Financial Accounting

Large amounts of behavioral research could be considered relevant to this review, so we have tried to avoid sins of omission by taking a broad view in this section. One difficulty with this approach is that no conceptual framework for relating behavioral research to investment and lending decisions and standard setting exists. Notwithstanding periodic commentary about this situation (e.g., Gonedes and Dopuch [1974]; American Accounting Association [1977a]; Dyckman, Gibbins, and Swieringa [1978, pages 79-81]), researchers have failed to rally to any generally agreed solution. As a result, we have adopted a simple and somewhat arbitrary scheme for classifying the behavioral research we review:[1]

1. People's response to information in general
2. Additional issues related to financial accounting
3. Specific users of accounting information
4. Influences of the accounting environment on action

---

[1]For behavioral accounting research earlier than 1975, the reader is referred to Dyckman et al. (1978) for financial accounting studies; American Accounting Association (1976) for managerial accounting studies; and Gibbins (1977) for auditing studies. In addition, reviews specifically related to "human information processing" research, which emphasizes individuals' thought processes rather than their behavior, are available. (See, for example, American Accounting Association [1977b] and Libby and Lewis [1977].)

100

Most of the research cited or reviewed deals with the behavior of *individuals* rather than that of groups, markets, or other aggregates. We believe that the aggregate effects of individual behavior are important in evaluating the contribution of behavioral financial accounting research. Unfortunately, there is a paucity of behavioral research on either aggregate behavior or the link between the individual and the aggregate. Questions of aggregation are discussed in the second part of this chapter.

People's Response to Information in General

As stated earlier, a great amount of research attention is being given to the ways in which people use information and make decisions. A recent bibliography of empirical research, for example, includes more than 850 articles and books on the subject (Naylor [1979]). Relevant to this study are four interrelated results drawn from the literature reviewed:

1. In studying how people make choices, empirical results do not compare well with results predicted by models of how one ought to behave in a given situation (normative models).
2. People are not really conscious of their own decision-making styles or, in most cases, what information is important to their decisions.
3. Some statistical models are fairly robust approximations of the way judgments are made. Such models often outperform the decisions or judgments made by people.
4. People's responses in making decisions reflect a variety of simplifications, fixations, and perceptual distortions of their environment.

We examine each of these results below, citing key studies where appropriate.

Predictions from Decision Models

Many attempts have been made to test empirically the predictive ability of normative (rational) models of judgment and decision making. Overall, the findings indicate little predictive success for such models, suggesting that they are poor representations of actual behavior. The normative theory of decision making based on "subjective expected utilities" has been extensively studied in this regard (e.g., Slovic, Fischhoff, and Lichtenstein [1977]). The evidence is reasonably clear: People make choices that are inconsistent, contaminated by supposedly irrelevant considerations, or otherwise improper in terms of the prescriptions of the theory. Nobel laureate Herbert Simon (1979) summarized the state of affairs:

> . . . The refutation of the theory has to do with the *substance* of the decisions, and not just the process by which they are reached. It is not that people do not go through the calculations that would be required to reach the [subjective expected utility] decision—neoclassical thought has never claimed that they did. What has been shown is that they do not even behave as if they had carried out those calculations, and that result is a direct refutation of the neoclassical assumptions. [page 507]

Other decision-making models have encountered similar difficulties. An example is the well-known "Bayesian probability revision model" that considers the activity of revising an event's estimated probability on the basis of new information. People's revisions of probability assessments do not follow the Bayes model well in that they are often "conservative," that is, they give less weight to arriving information than the model prescribes. An example of conservative behavior would be changing one's estimate of the probability of loan default from one percent to two percent upon the arrival of new information, whereas the Bayes formula would revise the probability to greater than two percent. There is much debate about the phenomenon of "conservatism," but the principal findings have led many researchers to claim that the Bayesian model is fundamentally invalid as an explanation of the way people evaluate probabilities (Kahneman and Tversky [1972, page 450]; Hogarth [1975, page 273]; Shafer [1978]).

These theories of decision making, of course, involve only one image of humans as processors of information (Libby [1976]; Watts and Zimmerman [1979]). Among the more empirically oriented alternative models of choice behavior are some that are rational in spirit yet adjusted to meet empirical realities. Simon (1979) has argued that rationality is bounded by several human limitations in processing information. Such limitations include failure to adequately consider new evidence (anchoring), inability to make proper probability judgments, and preoccupation with personal experience. Additionally, Kahneman and Tversky (1979) suggest that people edit information and hence change its meaning before using it in decision making (Newman [1980]). Some of the newer approaches reflect entirely different conceptions of the choice process. March (1978), for example, suggests that people may reasonably prefer ambiguity and lack of coherence concerning their tastes, preferences, and inclinations to act. Finally, Nisbett and Wilson (1977) and Weick (1979) have questioned the conventional interpretation of rational behavior (i.e., consistent with prescribed "rational" axioms), suggesting that rationality might be viewed as rationalization—as an attempt to explain behavior to ourselves after the fact, rather than as a determinant of behavior.

An important assumption in the normative theory of investment choice, referred to in other chapters, is that investors use information (e.g., financial statements) to assess the probabilities of future returns to various investment alternatives. In such a context, information is useful only if it allows an "improved" assessment of uncertain returns. Unfortunately, this concept of information, and the kinds of probability assessments it implies, have received little behavioral investigation in accounting as yet, though some work on developing ways of getting managers to verbalize the probability of occurrence of events has begun (Chesley [1978]). Recent findings pertaining to judgment processes (see reviews by Hammond, McCelland, and Mumpower [1980]; Hogarth [1980]; Einhorn and Hogarth [1981]) are undoubtedly consistent with the concept of information in terms of its role to change or confirm beliefs, but direct connections between the concept and the evidence are still only speculative. As explained elsewhere in this chapter, behavioral research is still struggling with the identification of major components of people's decision making, both in accounting and in general.

The relationship between normative decision models and behavioral research findings has been a matter of much debate (Mock and Vasarhelyi [1978]; Hilton [1980]; Butterworth, Gibbins, and King [1981]; Einhorn and Hogarth [1981]). Once considered divergent schools of thought, the normative and behavioral frameworks now appear to have a lot in common—mostly as a result of more precise analytical expressions of the observed behavior. The debate has doubtless had positive effects. For example, taking normative models as first approximations of purposeful decision making has drawn attention to decision aids and other methods of improving decisions (Slovic et al. [1977, pages 17-28]). Accountants have long recognized the value of such aids. Much of standard presentation in financial statements, such as the notes, calculations of earnings per share, and so on, are directed at helping people use the information more effectively. Behavioral evaluation of the design of decision aids in financial accounting has not yet begun, though there is some progress in the auditing area (e.g., Chesley [1978]) and in research on computer aids (e.g., Benbasat and Dexter [1979]).

Lack of Self-Knowledge about Decision Making

People, including those with apparent expertise in the decision or judgment to be made, are not consciously aware of their own decision-making thought processes. For example, Gray (1979) claims that people's ability to *make* judgments exceeds their ability to understand how they *reached* those judgments. The evidence is mixed, however. Some studies have found that auditors exhibit sub-stantial understanding of the factors that affect their judgments (Ashton [1974]; Schultz and Gustavson [1978]). Savich (1977) and Wright (1977a and 1979) also found good understanding among business students. However, all but Savich's study used a statistical research technique known as the "Brunswik lens model," a tech-nique that requires a large number of repetitive decisions in a tightly controlled setting. This may encourage the research participant to develop a simple decision strategy just to cope with the repetition · (Ashton [1974]). Similarly, Nisbett and Wilson (1977) suggest that people's reports on their own thought processes are based on their own theories about what seems plausible in the situation, rather than on any true introspection. Consequently, what appears to be "self-knowledge" may be a function more of the situation than of the person.

People also tend to be overconfident in their judgments, com-pared with the confidence implied by reasonable statistical models (e.g., Slovic et al. [1977]). This is a fairly persistent phenomenon and seems to involve a failure to understand the limitations of the information being used in the judgment, though Gibbins (in press) demonstrates that statistical models may support higher confidence than had been thought.

For years psychologists have recognized that simple statistical models tend to perform well in representing decision makers, or in competing with them (Meehl [1954]). One class of models, called *linear models* assumes that the various pieces of information "add together" in terms of their combined effect on the decision or judgment.[2] Certain simple models may even predict a person's own judgments better than that person could predict alone. For example, if error in the information leads to noise or uncertainty, the simple statistical model, which ignores the noise, may cope better than an ostensibly sophisticated human who might be confused or sidetracked by it (Slovic et al. [1977, page 12]; Ogilvie and Schmitt [1979]). Moreover, composites of people's judgments often outperform all but the most successful individuals (Libby [1975a]; Wright [1979]). Such findings are frequent (Libby [1975b]; Wright [1977b]; Abdel-khalik and El-Sheshai [1980]) though not universal (Libby [1976]; Libby and Lewis [1977]; Libby and Blashfield [1978]) and may be a function partly of the research instruments.

Yet little is really known about how people actually combine information in reaching a decision. While the above simple models appear to be approximating *some* fundamental underlying processes, it is not obvious what those are. However, researchers such as Eggleton (1976) and Biggs (1979) are attempting to generate deeper understanding by developing ways of "tracing" people's use of information through a decision, and by trying to model the brain's storage and retrieval processes.

In sum, the conclusions drawn in most of the literature suggest that while the simple statistical models are not necessarily valid representations of a decision maker's actual thought processes, they can be useful aids in predicting or replacing the human's decision tasks (Dawes [1979]).

---

[2]A simple linear model could appear as follows: $Y = aX_1 + bX_2 + cX_3$. Each variable is measured numerically. Y represents the decision or judgment that is explained by pieces of information X_1, X_2, and X_3. Since each piece of information is of differing importance, they are each weighted differently (by a, b, and c, respectively). Y is referred to as the dependent variable, the Xs are independent variables, and a, b, and c are coefficients.

A tendency observed in many studies is that people seem to simplify the situation when making decisions, particularly if the task is complex or repetitive. These simplifications take many forms, including a disregard for information and a failure to recognize changes in the situation since the previous decision.

One class of simplifications, dubbed *heuristics,* applies rules of thumb to the information used. Heuristics, for example, may give too much importance to immediately available information or to the imagined results of an alternative action. A previous result may be given too much importance as well or be remembered as having been better than it actually was. The concept of "materiality" in accounting and auditing is a generally accepted heuristic based on the size of the discrepancy relative to expectations. (For studies of materiality and other simplifying techniques, see Pattillo [1976], Hofstedt and Hughes [1977], Dyckman et al. [1978], Firth [1979], and Moriarity and Barron [1979].)

Another simplification that has received considerable attention from accounting researchers is the so-called functional-fixation hypothesis: People stick doggedly to previously used ways of evaluating information because they fail to recognize the changing aspects of the situation. The hypothesis has been supported in experimental settings and as such appears to be valid (Ashton [1976]; Chang and Birnberg [1977]; Abdel-khalik and Keller [1979]; Swieringa, Dyckman, and Hoskin [1979]). For example, Abdel-khalik and Keller reported that the investment officers and securities analysts who participated in their study

> indicated an understanding of the impact of switching to LIFO on reported earnings and on cash flows. In spite of this apparent understanding, respondents generally preferred a firm using FIFO over an identical firm that had decided to switch to LIFO in an inflationary economy. . . . Our explanation is consistent with the posited hypothesis of functional fixation—subjects do not readily change the weights assigned to reported earnings in forming expectations about the prospects of the firm. [page 50]

It is not yet known how people choose heuristics (or similar decision rules) or to what range of phenomena they might apply. In a recent experiment, Abdel-khalik and El-Sheshai (1980) found that default predictions by lending officers were more affected by the officers' choice of information than by the officers' use of the chosen information. In other words, it is what a person selects as information and not how that is combined with other data that is important. Neither is it known whether biases in individuals' decisions affect stock market or other aggregate behavior; they may "cancel out" or otherwise be mitigated in the aggregation process.

To summarize, behavioral research on the whole has shown generally inconclusive results about people's decision making. There are, however, a few valuable results. Normative decision models, despite their broad conceptual appeal, appear to be poor representations of what people actually do. People's judgments can be represented better by simple statistical models based on empirical analysis. Also, people are not very aware of their own thought processes, which seem subject to a variety of biases and distortions.

Additional Issues Related to Financial Accounting

Though there has been much nonbehavioral research and other writing on accounting measurement (including the FASB's Statements of Financial Accounting Concepts), behavioral investigation of accounting measurement concepts has been sparse. Dyckman et al. (1978, pages 53-55) reported several studies in the early 1970s on aggregation and entropy (i.e., loss of information through aggregation), communication effectiveness, reliability, and semantic meaning, but there have been few recent studies. Adelberg (1979) and Moriarity (1979) demonstrated intriguing techniques for assessing communication effectiveness. Adelberg asked respondents to try to fill in randomly deleted words from financial statement narratives. Moriarity translated financial reports into schematic human faces and asked respondents to use them in bankruptcy predictions. Ashton (1977) proposed a consensus approach to the evaluation of objectivity, and Belkaoui (1978) suggested that the accounting "language" be examined using linguistic techniques. Interest continues in how (as distinct from what) accounting information is communicated, but no general conclusions have yet emerged.

There has been some research on financial statements containing numbers expressed as confidence intervals or ranges (Birnberg and Slevin [1976]; Keys [1978]; Collins and Yeakel [1979]), but the evidence is that such statements are not helpful to users. Keys, for example, found that bank officers' decisions on loans were not affected by the presence of confidence interval information. Apparently, users feel comfortable with single-figure estimates, and some believe that the presence of ranges implies inaccuracy in the accounting information.

There is a large amount of literature questioning the adequacy of historical cost financial statements in the present inflationary environment and suggesting alternative ways of producing inflation-adjusted reports. In spite of this, Dyckman et al. (1978, pages 63-66) reported that behavioral studies had generally discovered that decision makers had little interest in inflation-adjusted numbers or in other alternatives to the traditional historical cost model. Benston and Krasney (1978) also found little enthusiasm for alternatives to historical cost among investment officers in life insurance companies, particularly among the more experienced officers. Additionally, Eyes and Tabb (1978) found that bank managers did not strongly desire inflation-adjusted statements. More recently, a study conducted by Louis Harris and Associates (1980) for the Financial Accounting Foundation indicates that the current cost data is viewed more positively now than in the past by a variety of influential persons. A survey by Arthur Young & Company (1981) shows that preparers favor current cost over constant dollar information, although many respondents oppose both. And two additional surveys (Casey and Sandretto [1981]; Schwarzbach and Swanson [1981]) indicate that managers are beginning to use the changing prices data for decision making. An FASB Research Report by Frishkoff (1982) reviews those and other studies in more detail.

The results of a business game task (Benbasat and Dexter [1979]) support the contention that users prefer to draw their own conclusions from information about economic events, rather than being given summarized information that might obscure the events and doubtless contains assumptions about users' particular needs. However, not all of the users studied by Benbasat and Dexter preferred the nonaggregated information; those who did prefer it did not perform any better in the task.

Proposals to supplement financial statements with information on a firm's management of human resources and attention to various "social responsibilities" have received reasonable research effort, some of it behavioral. Most behavioral research, though, has found little enthusiasm for information regarding the use of social or human resources (Hendricks [1976]; Flamholtz and Cook [1978]; Buzby and Falk [1979]; Snowball [1979]). However, Williams (1980) reports some evidence of interest in such data by managers for their own performance evaluations, and Schwan (1976) observed some effects on decisions of bankers, as did Acland (1976), who studied analysts.

To conclude, behavioral research has uncovered little support for alternatives to the historical cost financial accounting model and has as yet given only scattered attention to the underlying measurement characteristics of that model. Behavioral financial accounting research has produced rather less conclusive results than has the more general decision-making research reviewed in the previous section.

Specific Users of Accounting Information

We now turn to the large amount of behavioral research concerned with the needs of particular users of financial statements. Dyckman et al. (1978) commented:

> . . . More sophisticated users, in terms of their understanding and appreciation of accounting data, tend to rely more heavily on the accounting data supplied to them in financial reports, rather than on the nonaccounting portions of such reports. Unsophisticated users, on the other hand, rely more on the nonaccounting data. . . . Sophisticated users are more likely to be able to perceive economic realities underlying alternative reporting methods. These user characteristics are job-related and are probably related to the user's experience as well. Therefore, the effect of alternative reporting practices is likely to be influenced by the same factors. [page 76]

These conclusions were based largely on survey research published in the late 1960s and early 1970s.

Since then, additional experimental research (conducted in laboratories and other controlled settings) has examined individual differences among information users (Driver and Mock [1975]; Savich [1977]; McGhee, Shields, and Birnberg [1978]; Benbasat and

Dexter [1979]; Lusk [1979]; Pratt [1980]). These recent studies normally have used student subjects and have focused principally on differences in personality and "style" of information use (e.g., preference for complex versus simplified information). Such studies involve sorting student users into groups and examining differences among groups, and so do not provide much detail about the use of accounting information by individuals.

Surveys of preferences for information by various user groups, which were plentiful in the early 1970s, have almost disappeared from the academic accounting literature. They are also rare in professional accounting journals. Recent studies include only a sprinkling of user groups: Epstein (1975), Lewellen, Lease, and Schlarbaum (1977), and Reckers and Stagliano (1980) studied individual investors; Ferris (1976) and Chandra and Greenball (1977) studied managers; Fuller and Metcalf (1978) and Carper, Barton, and Wunder (1979) studied financial analysts; and Benjamin and Stanga (1977) and Most and Chang (1979) studied a variety of users.

The findings from these studies and the earlier ones examined by Dyckman et al. (1978) are often contradictory. For example, Epstein (1975) reported that financial statements are of little value (or at least are little used) in making investment decisions, whereas Most and Chang (1979) reported the opposite, that is, respondents felt financial statements were very useful in such decisions. Such contradictory findings may be a function of differences in the questions asked (most are surveys), response rates, alternatives provided, and other differences in research approach. The methodological difficulties and contradictory results of surveys, together with people's earlier-noted lack of conscious awareness of their own use of information, make survey results hard to interpret, although some conclusions may tentatively be drawn.

Investors have difficulty understanding financial statements and show little interest in using them. Financial analysts are more able and inclined to use financial statements but do not appear to depend very much on them and do not see much value in the inclusion of information (e.g., forecasts) that they already develop for themselves. As remarked in Chapter 4, the SEC's Advisory Committee on Corporate Disclosure (1977) found that analysts relied on more informal sources of information. Nevertheless, Patton (1976) surveyed users of municipal financial statements and found some interest in improving the statements' format. In a subsequent study, however, Patton (1978) did not succeed in establishing experimen-

110

tally that varying the degree of funds consolidation in such statements made a difference to municipal officers' estimates of interest rates for the debt of other municipalities.

A large subset of behavioral research in this area has focused on bankers and loan officers (Kennedy [1975]; Libby [1975a, 1975b, 1979a, and 1979b]; Estes and Reimer [1977]; Eyes and Tabb [1978]; Stanga and Benjamin [1978]; Abdel-khalik and El-Sheshai [1980]; Casey [1980b]; Zimmer [1980]). Much of this has involved carefully controlled experimental settings, with considerable emphasis on providing the bankers and loan officers with realistic tasks. Because the phenomena of interest vary from study to study, the specific tasks and surrounding information vary also. For example, in one study, Libby (1979a) used only audit reports, with no accompanying financial statements; in a second study, Libby (1979b) used full financial statements, including an audit report and a "management evaluation" and an "uncertainty" report; Casey (1980b) used ratios only; and Abdel-khalik and El-Sheshai (1980) used a set of 18 ratio and trend numbers computed from the statements. No particular picture of bankers' and loan officers' decision processes has therefore emerged, but it is clear that these people do use financial statements in their credit decisions, that they are sensitive to information related to credit risk, and that they seem to pay attention to only a few dimensions of each set of information (as we might expect from the earlier discussion on decision makers' simplifications of their environment).

The conclusion drawn from behavioral research on particular users of financial statements is that users' needs are specific and relate to each job, decision-making task, or environment. No general summary of needs or informational priorities has emerged; indeed, the research suggests that none will emerge. Researcher interest is thus shifting away from the earlier (optimistic) attempts to summarize users' general-purpose needs or preferences and toward the study of the actual thought processes inherent in making investment decisions. Several of the above-noted studies of bankers and loan officers are typical of this newer, "human information processing" approach. There is also increased interest in the environmental factors affecting users' decisions, to which we turn next.

Influences of the Accounting Environment on Action

This section considers the response of individuals to financial information in relation to the informational, organizational, and economic *environment* of accounting and reporting. We hope that by examining some behavioral concepts relevant to that environment, a richer understanding of individual response and action may develop. This section presents some environmental influences offered by behavioral research as relevant to understanding a person's response to accounting information. Some of the points made are tentative, for much of the research is recent and little has been conducted yet in the financial accounting area. However, the discussion provides necessary background to the conclusions we draw later. The environmental picture we outline is a highly interactive one; the points discussed, therefore, are highly interrelated.

(1) Most people who come in contact with accounting information do not act in isolation but, instead, interact as members of organizations, professions, or other groups. (See Hayes [1977] for a demonstration of this in a management accounting setting.) In so interacting, people respond and contribute to an array of processes that cause organizations to act and, hence, change. Those processes can be subtle, are often political, and are frequently not explicitly directed to the organization's goals (Cohen and March [1974]; March [1978]; Weick [1979]).

The conception of an organization's actions as not necessarily deliberate, even though individuals within the organization may act deliberately, is causing many researchers on organizational behavior to rethink their discipline. This is contributing to an increased interest in studying the ways organizations actually decide things (similar to the earlier-noted increased interest in "human information processing" at the individual level). Interest in this conception also reflects the increasing awareness that study of individual behavior does not necessarily provide insights about the aggregate behavior of organizations or markets. We touch on the issue of organizational choice later in this section.

(2) People, to a degree, cause or create their own environment. Their actions, a part of the ongoing events, in effect physically shape or determine their world. Under this view, prophecies can indeed be self-fulfilling. Further, because the effects of their own (and others') acts are often not easily observable, people construct explanations based on what they perceive to be happening, which

may not always coincide with what actually is happening (Nisbett and Wilson [1977]). Their learning is in relation to an environment that may at first be hypothetical but that through their actions may gain some physical reality. For example, if an investor has some belief about the market's behavior (e.g., prospects will improve) and acts accordingly, that investor's acts will contribute, even if in only a small way, to the events that determine whether or not the belief is founded.

(3) It has been theorized (e.g., Weick [1979]) that organizational behavior is a product of dual tendencies to stability and change. Such tendencies are generally thought to operate in a kind of balance. Information, for example, is needed both about ongoing environmental change and about the organization's accumulated experience and wisdom. An imbalance toward the former would tend to produce erratic or stop-and-go policies through attempts to respond to every change, while an imbalance in the other direction would produce a tendency to stagnation through lack of response to change. Information such as financial statement data no doubt contributes both to the assessment of future returns to the investor and to the assessment of past behavior by the investor's agents (management). How such dual roles work, which role is predominant in a particular setting, and how they affect each other is largely unknown (Butterworth et al. [1981]). But, as noted in Chapter 4, research effort (none of it as yet behavioral) is now being directed to the role that (accounting) information plays in organizations' contractual arrangements and other mechanisms.

(4) Organizations' reward and management systems constitute massive constraints on a person's response to accounting information. An analyst who fails to respond to an accounting change may recognize the information but respond instead to the firm's guidelines concerning investment in particular industries. This response may be similarly influenced if there is to be an evaluation by a method believed to be insensitive to the accounting change. Similarly, an auditor facing a conflict with a client about an accounting policy will consider the business risk involved, the probability of losing the client, and so on. Behavioral research has not yet contributed to a substantial understanding of the organizational settings within which people respond to financial accounting information, though recent "human information processing" research offers promise in this regard.

(5) The role of financial accounting information as a control sys-

tem on individual behavior is important, perhaps more important than its role as a basis for predictions (Butterworth et al. [1981]). Recent work on the economic theory of principal and agent relationships and its implications for financial accounting (Watts and Zimmerman [1978 and 1981]; Atkinson and Feltham [1981]), information evaluation (Uecker [1978 and 1980]), and behavior that anticipates information (Prakash and Rappaport [1977]) is giving new attention to the traditional but heretofore neglected concepts of stewardship and control. Accounting information *influences* behavior. It not only provides neutral information for decision making, but it also motivates, influences, and otherwise induces behavior by way of feeding back the results of decisions in a variety of ways and by acting as a "scoring system" for measuring results. For example, if a bond indenture imposes restrictions on management's actions on the basis of particular accounting results, there must be a way of calculating those results. Future behavioral accounting research is likely to give more emphasis to control and feedback effects and less to a decision maker's ability to make predictions using accounting numbers.

(6) Even if the individual decision maker is responding entirely without the assistance of others and is using accounting information to decide on how to respond, the role of that information can be understood only if it is related to the individual's available information sources. If shareholders do not use financial statements in making decisions, then what do they use? Epstein (1975, page 71) conjectures that they ask their stockbroker for advice. But how does the broker formulate this advice? We have noted that analysts, for example, rely extensively on information from informal sources. What informal information systems are used?

The existence of other information sources means that financial accounting information must be evaluated on the basis of marginal benefits and costs. Regarding marginal benefits, an investor who believes profits are a function of uncontrollable market effects would have little incentive to seek better information for investment decisions. As Watts (1977) commented with respect to individuals' willingness to vote in elections, the incremental benefits are negligible. Even if there were a perceived marginal benefit, it may not outweigh the marginal costs. Lack of interest in changing the content of financial reports, therefore, does not necessarily imply no desire for information; it may simply indicate a perceived excess of marginal costs over marginal benefits. Marginal analysis, moreover, must take into account any other existing sources of similar information. Lev (1976) observes that financial statements do not and should not monopolize the provision of information to the capital markets. In the inflation-accounting area, for example, if a decision maker requires information on the effects of inflation but can and does estimate most of the effects from other sources, an improved financial accounting standard, even if perfect, can provide only a limited benefit. That benefit might not be worth the incremental cost to implement the new standard. Evaluations of this sort may well influence potential respondents to the FASB, who are aware of their information alternatives, to express little enthusiasm for accounting changes.

(7) The set of individuals whose actions are relevant to standard setting is very broad: included are analysts, auditors, creditors, managers, regulators, shareholders, union members, and so on (Watts and Zimmerman [1978 and 1979]; Dopuch and Sunder [1980]). This breadth, combined with our earlier remarks about the role of financial accounting as a behavioral control system, suggests that major effects of financial accounting information will be observed not only in stock prices after the new information is released, but also in altered behavior of managers, auditors, and others during the periods before and after first public disclosure. If an accounting standard is changed to assist investors in adapting to changing external circumstances, its result may be to alter managerial behavior or investor expectations so as to head off stock price fluctuations that would otherwise have occurred. In other words, lack of effect on stock prices can be evidence that the accounting change is working, not that it is ineffective.

(8) External forces such as increased regulation, endemic inflation, and increasing business internationalization (Brennan [1979]; Gray [1980]; Scott and Troberg [1980]) are likely to affect various user groups differently and to affect the role financial accounting plays in influencing each group's behavior. The role of financial accounting information may be quite subtle. Stock market behavior, for example, will not necessarily reflect that role if external events affect the market differently than they do other components of the economy. Shank, Dillard, and Murdock (1980) interviewed financial managers about their responses to the FASB's Statement 8 on foreign currency translation and found that, in spite of an apparent lack of reaction by stock markets to the standard, the managers undertook action in the foreign currency area that would

increase expected costs and risk levels, in order to preserve "desired" relationships in accounting numbers.

In summary, a consideration of the statement user's decision environment and the factors that influence it as studied by other researchers provides behavioral financial accounting researchers with examples of potential contributions. Yet to be explored are accounting's role as a behavioral control system and its role in organizational decision making. The environmental review also raises issues that may help to explain the earlier-noted lack of conclusiveness of behavioral financial accounting research, for example, the problems of making deductions about market behavior from individual behavior and the need for marginal cost and benefit alternatives as part of the research in the use of accounting information.

B. Conclusions and Implications for Standard Setting

This section draws conclusions of interest to the FASB and its constituency from the preceding review and makes connections to points raised in other chapters. Because behavioral financial accounting research has not been particularly oriented to standard-setting issues, because individual research results have seldom been conclusive, and because we wish to avoid potentially misleading speculation, our conclusions must be general ones.

Financial accounting is a difficult subject to study using behavioral methods, because such methods emphasize empirical fact finding and do not deal well with questions of desirability (of alternative standards, of the FASB's political effects, etc.). Setting financial accounting standards involves not only an assessment of what likely effects will occur, but also an evaluation of whether those effects are desirable for all affected parties. Empirical research's focus on assessing the effects therefore produces results that, from a standard setter's viewpoint, are incomplete. While research on questions of social desirability may be conducted by appealing to integrated theories in economics, decision theory, and statistics, empirical behavioral accounting research has no integrated theory. It is not in the nature of the underlying behavioral disciplines to provide such theory. Real progress in behavioral research on financial accounting issues may therefore have to await the development of a hybrid approach, such as the empirical study of people's responses to information prepared in accordance with rules deemed desirable by others.

Behavioral Accounting Research Relates to Individuals, Not Aggregates

Virtually all the research reviewed has been directed at the behaviors and perceptions of individual decision makers who use accounting information. Of course, the information is usually aggregated to develop descriptions of average perceptions, to distinguish the responses of different types of decision makers, and so on, but the behavior of such aggregates as firms, markets, or professions has seldom been studied. As has been noted already, aggregate behavior is unlikely to have properties deducible from separately observed individual actions (Milgram and Toch [1968]; Beaver [1972]; Schelling [1978]). Further, the processes by which individual actions or values are aggregated into market or social behavior have been subjected to only rudimentary analytical or behavioral analysis as yet (e.g., Schelling [1978]; Demski [1980]; Plott and Sunder [1981]). Schelling, for example, developed simple models to explain what happens when the collective good of the aggregate (such as a nation wanting reduced energy consumption) is not matched by the wishes of each individual (a person who will suffer if heat is absent and who knows that the use of fuel makes no real difference to total consumption). Plott and Sunder studied the formation of "security markets" in a controlled laboratory setting.

The FASB appears to have an interest in both aggregate and individual behavior. On the one hand, the Board's mandate—to set generally accepted accounting standards—implies an interest in general effects that might be observed in such aggregates as stock markets, professions, organizations, or governments. The FASB's publications (e.g., Concepts Statements 1 and 2) make references to efficient resource allocation—an aggregate concept. On the other hand, those same FASB publications refer to individual investors, creditors, and people without access to sophisticated analysis. Regardless of how aggregation works, it is composed somehow of individual actions—and certain ones may significantly impact the whole (e.g., powerful individuals or those involved in precedent-setting court cases). Our discussions with academic researchers indicate agreement that the FASB should be concerned with aggregate behavior but no agreement that the Board should be concerned with individual behavior.

If the factors explaining individual behavior cannot be assumed to translate readily into aggregate behavior, specific conclusions about market or organizational effects from behavioral research at the individual level cannot be drawn without conjecture. If the FASB is concerned with both levels of behavior, it should encourage research that would build connections between the two. For instance, a useful connection would relate the limitations of individuals' decision making (e.g., heuristics, biases, functional fixation, conservatism) to market behavior. Are such limitations also evident in market behavior? And if not, why not? Attempts to improve financial accounting will be frustrated if they are ignored or distorted by the presumed beneficiaries.

On the other hand, research reviewed in other chapters (e.g., Chapters 4 and 8) indicates that the market is neither unresponsive nor naive with respect to understanding the impacts of changes in accounting methods. This suggests, from an aggregate perspective, that the expenditure of resources by a body such as the FASB to alter financial reporting so as to, for example, reduce functional fixation, make probability revisions less conservative, or otherwise "improve" individuals' decision making may not be needed.

If our economic and societal institutions have some sophistication with respect to the problems of relating financial accounting information to individual behavior, these institutions are likely to bring about changes to mitigate such problems. For example, if people have difficulty with complex accounting information, a profession (e.g., analysts) arises to cope with the problem and, in the process, becomes part of the mechanism of informational use itself. If an efficient and effective method of adjustment exists for a given difficulty, changing financial accounting to deal with that difficulty may be not only unnecessary but inefficient. The relative efficiencies of the present methods of adjustment and the proposed financial accounting change must be known in order to evaluate whether the change is worthwhile.

Settings in Which Accounting Is Used Are Not Well Specified

The uses of financial accounting information are varied and complex. Certainly, uses extend beyond making investment decisions. Moreover, the role that such information plays, even in investment settings, is unclear. Accounting information is used together with other information, so that the contribution of such information (or of accounting standards) must be argued on marginal grounds. Behavioral research can assist in untangling settings in which information is used and possibly can permit such marginal analysis. However, it has not yet done so except in one or two isolated cases, such as in experimental studies of bankers and financial analysts.

Decision Making Is Not Well Understood

Behavioral research on the use of financial accounting information has produced generally inconclusive findings. The processes of people's decision making, revision of probabilities, and formation of perceptions are not well known. Moreover, there has been little success in applying such concepts as rationality or consistency to empirical research on information use. In short, it has been difficult to demonstrate clearly that accounting information matters to individual investors, creditors, analysts, etc., notwithstanding the studies reviewed in other chapters (e.g., Chapter 8) that find evidence of market effects—produced unquestionably by many individuals acting in response to information.

To be sure, the behavioral findings suggest caution when making assumptions about how people use accounting information, in particular about assuming that the user carefully weighs all the facts before making a decision. An interesting corollary to this discussion concerns the concept of rationality (e.g., paragraph 34 of Concepts Statement 1). We believe that concept is empirically elusive. Reference to it in accounting standards would not seem to help in predicting the effects of such standards, especially since, given the behavioral findings, the concept implies inappropriate expectations about users' decision-making behavior.

If the FASB is interested in the behavior of individuals, it should encourage research into decision makers' actual thought processes. Assumptions in economics and decision theory appear to be descriptively invalid and, since alternative theories of decision making are not well developed, there is somewhat of a vacuum in this important area of research.

Accounting Information Is Not Neutral

Because accounting information has many uses and seems to have behavioral effects, it gains characteristics of a control system in addition to its role as a "dispassionate" information system. At least three such aspects appear relevant to financial accounting. First, people are influenced to act in accordance with the way their actions are reported. There are, therefore, issues regarding education and persuasion to consider in the development of financial accounting standards. If the FASB's directives contain declarations about cause and effect that users can be persuaded to believe (e.g., current cost information improves forecasts of enterprise cash flows), those users' actions, by reflecting (for better or worse) such declarations, can partly determine whether the declarations are true (for example, that current cost data do indeed predict cash flows better). Second, the FASB, by designing features of the accounting information structure, prescribes or promotes certain decision-making approaches or biases, or triggers decision makers' "heuristics" or other rules of thumb. Third, if an accounting standard does have effects on individual behavior, those effects are unlikely to be the same from person to person or from group to group. In the research reviewed, little support for widespread change in financial accounting has been detected. Rather, the research suggests that various personal, institutional, and informational variables interact so substantially that one would not predict similar evaluations of a standard's effects or neutrality by different individuals or groups. The behavioral research here is consistent with arguments advanced elsewhere against the general desirability of particular standards (Demski [1973]; American Accounting Association [1977a]; Dopuch and Sunder [1980]).

Surveys Should Be Used with Care

One means of obtaining broadly based opinions about accounting alternatives is to conduct questionnaire surveys of various groups of presumed users. Lack of consistency in survey results and people's lack of awareness of their own thought patterns imply, however, that surveys of users' preferences for or confidence in accounting alternatives are unlikely to be reliable indicators of the real impact of accounting alternatives.

Surveys have a variety of uses, nonetheless, including adding credibility to the Board's conclusions (as part of the FASB's due process system) and developing political commitment or consensus. Hence, we are not advocating discontinuance of surveys as part of the FASB's research function. However, we caution that surveys should be supplemented with detailed empirical analyses, such as in-depth case studies, experimental investigations, and other procedures, to verify the survey findings. Also, we suggest that the use of survey results to rank accounting alternatives should not be encouraged. Direct evidence of decision behavior should be sought in preference to self-reports on informational preferences.

C. A Final Comment

In this chapter, we have considered behavioral research published primarily within the accounting literature. Conclusions about the implications of that research for standard setting have been drawn. Several of those conclusions, however, point to a lack of reliable findings, due in part to the fact that behavioral research in accounting is a young and relatively unfocused discipline. We hope that this chapter has informed the reader about the present state of the research and has made a good case for additional research to improve our understanding of the complex relationships between financial accounting information and individual behavior. However, we have not been able to identify key implications of *immediate* relevance to accounting policymakers. The body of "solid" research findings as yet is small, especially compared with the number of unresolved questions and unexplored issues. Only as our knowledge expands will more direct implications be evident.

REFERENCES

Abdel-khalik, A. Rashad, and El-Sheshai, Kamal M. "Information Choice and Utilization in an Experiment on Default Prediction." *Journal of Accounting Research,* Autumn 1980, pp. 325-42.

Abdel-khalik, A. Rashad, and Keller, Thomas F. *Earnings or Cash Flows: An Experiment on Functional Fixation and the Valuation of the Firm.* Studies in Accounting Research, no. 16. Sarasota, Fla.: American Accounting Association, 1979.

Acland, Derek. "The Effects of Behavioural Indicators on Investor Decisions: An Exploratory Study." *Accounting, Organizations and Society,* nos. 2/3 (1976), pp. 133-42.

Adelberg, Arthur Harris. "A Methodology for Measuring the Understandability of Financial Report Messages." *Journal of Accounting Research,* Autumn 1979, pp. 565-92.

Advisory Committee on Corporate Disclosure. *Report of the Advisory Committee on Corporate Disclosure to the Securities and Exchange Commission.* Washington, D.C.: U.S. Government Printing Office, November 3, 1977.

American Accounting Association, Committee on Concepts and Standards—Management Planning and Control. "Managerial Accounting Literature Abstracts." Mimeographed. Sarasota, Fla.: American Accounting Association, October 1976.

American Accounting Association, Committee on Concepts and Standards for External Financial Reports. *Statement on Accounting Theory and Theory Acceptance.* Sarasota, Fla.: American Accounting Association, 1977. (1977a)

American Accounting Association, Committee on Human Information Processing. "Report of the Committee on Human Information Processing." Mimeographed. Sarasota, Fla.: American Accounting Association, 1977. (1977b)

Arthur Young & Company. *Financial Reporting and Changing Prices: A Survey of Preparer's Views and Practices.* New York: Arthur Young & Company, 1981.

Ashton, Robert H. "The Predictive-Ability Criterion and User Prediction Models." *The Accounting Review,* October 1974, pp. 719-32.

_____. "Cognitive Changes Induced by Accounting Changes: Experimental Evidence on the Functional Fixation Hypothesis." *Journal of Accounting Research.* Supplement 1976, *Studies on Human Information Processing in Accounting,* pp. 1-17.

_____. "Objectivity of Accounting Measures: A Multivariant-Multidimensional Approach." *The Accounting Review,* July 1977, pp. 567-75.

Atkinson, A. A., and Feltham, G. A. "Information in Capital Markets: An Agency Theory Perspective." Working paper. Vancouver: Faculty of Commerce, University of British Columbia, January 1981.

Beaver, William H. "The Behavior of Security Prices and Its Implications for Accounting Research (Methods)." In "Report of the Committee on Research Methodology in Accounting." *The Accounting Review,* Supplement 1972, pp. 407-37.

Belkaoui, Ahmed. "Linguistic Relativity in Accounting." *Accounting, Organizations and Society,* no. 2 (1978), pp. 97-104.

Benbasat, Izak, and Dexter, Albert S. "Value and Events Approaches to Accounting: An Experimental Evaluation." *The Accounting Review,* October 1979, pp. 735-49.

Benjamin, James J., and Stanga, Keith G. "Differences in Disclosure Needs of Major Users of Financial Statements." *Accounting and Business Research,* Summer 1977, pp. 187-92.

Benston, George J., and Krasney, Melvin A. "DAAM: The Demand for Alternative Accounting Measurements." *Journal of Accounting Research.* Supplement 1978, *Studies on Accounting for Changes in General and Specific Prices: Empirical Research and Public Policy Issues,* pp. 1-30.

Biggs, Stanley F. "An Empirical Investigation of the Information Processes Underlying Four Models of Choice Behavior." In *Behavioral Experiments in Accounting II,* edited by Thomas J. Burns, pp. 35-81. Columbus: The Ohio State University, 1979.

Birnberg, Jacob G., and Slevin, Dennis P. "A Note on the Use of Confidence Interval Statements in Financial Reporting." *Journal of Accounting Research,* Spring 1976, pp. 153-57.

Brennan, W. John, ed. *The Internationalization of the Accounting Profession.* Toronto: The Canadian Institute of Chartered Accountants, 1979.

Butterworth, John E.; Gibbins, Michael; and King, Raymond. "The Structure of Accounting Theory: Some Basic Conceptual and Methodological Issues." Prepared for the Clarkson, Gordon Foundation research symposium, "The Nature and Role of Research to Support Standard-Setting in Financial Accounting in Canada." Mimeographed. Toronto: Clarkson, Gordon Foundation, May 1981.

Buzby, Stephen L., and Falk, Haim. "Demand for Social Responsibility Information by University Investors." *The Accounting Review,* January 1979, pp. 23-37.

Carper, Wm. Brent; Barton, M. Frank, Jr.; and Wunder, Haroldene F. "The Future of Forecasting." *Management Accounting,* August 1979, pp. 27-31.

Casey, Cornelius J., Jr. "The Usefulness of Accounting Ratios for Subjects' Predictions of Corporate Failure: Replication and Extensions." *Journal of Accounting Research,* Autumn 1980, pp. 603-13. (1980b)

Casey, Cornelius J., and Sandretto, Michael J. "Internal Uses of Accounting for Inflation." *Harvard Business Review,* November/December 1981, pp. 149-56.

Chandra, Gyan, and Greenball, Melvin N. "Management Reluctance to Disclose: An Empirical Study." *Abacus,* December 1977, pp. 141-54.

Chang, Davis L., and Birnberg, Jacob B. "Functional Fixity in Accounting Research: Perspective and New Data." *Journal of Accounting Research,* Autumn 1977, pp. 300-312.

Chesley, G. R. "Subjective Probability Elicitation Techniques: A Performance Comparison." *Journal of Accounting Research,* Autumn 1978, pp. 225-41.

Cohen, Michael D., and March, James G. *Leadership and Ambiguity: The American College President.* Report prepared for the Carnegie Commission on Higher Education. New York: McGraw-Hill, Inc., 1974.

Collins, Frank, and Yeakel, John A. "Range Estimates in Financial Statements: Help or Hindrance?" *Journal of Accountancy,* July 1979, pp. 73-78.

Dawes, Robyn M. "The Robust Beauty of Improper Linear Models in Decision Making." *American Psychologist,* July 1979, pp. 571-82.

Demski, Joel S. "The General Impossibility of Normative Accounting Standards." *The Accounting Review,* October 1973, pp. 718-23.

_____. "The Value of Financial Accounting." Research paper. Stanford, Calif.: Graduate School of Business, Stanford University, January 1980.

Dopuch, Nicholas, and Sunder, Shyam. "FASB's Statements on Objectives and Elements of Financial Accounting: A Review." *The Accounting Review,* January 1980, pp. 1-21.

Driver, Michael J., and Mock, Theodore J. "Human Information Processing, Decision Style Theory, and Accounting Information Systems." *The Accounting Review,* July 1975, pp. 490-508.

Dyckman, Thomas R.; Gibbins, Michael; and Swieringa, Robert J. "Experimental and Survey Research in Financial Accounting: A Review and Evaluation." In *The Impact of Accounting Research on Practice and Disclosure,* edited by A. Rashad Abdel-khalik and Thomas F. Keller, pp. 48-105. Durham, N.C.: Duke University Press, 1978.

Eggleton, Ian R. C. "Patterns, Prototypes, and Predictions: An Exploratory Study." *Journal of Accounting Research.* Supplement 1976, *Studies on Human Information Processing in Accounting,* pp. 68-131.

Einhorn, Hillel J., and Hogarth, Robin M. "Behavioral Decision Theory: Processes of Judgment and Choice." *Journal of Accounting Research,* Spring 1981, pp. 1-41.

Epstein, M. J. *The Usefulness of Annual Reports to Corporate Shareholders.* Los Angeles: Bureau of Business and Economic Research, California State University, 1975.

Estes, Ralph, and Reimer, Marvin. "A Study of the Effect of Qualified Auditors' Opinions on Bankers' Lending Decisions." *Accounting and Business Research,* Autumn 1977, pp. 250-59.

Eyes, Alan D., and Tabb, J. Bruce. "Bank Managers' Use of Financial Statements." *The Accountants' Journal,* April 1978, pp. 81-85.

Ferris, Kenneth R. "The Apparent Effects of Profit Forecast Disclosure on Managerial Behaviour: An Empirical Examination." *Journal of Business Finance & Accounting,* Autumn 1976, pp. 53-66.

Firth, Michael. "Consensus Views and Judgment Models in Materiality Decisions." *Accounting, Organizations and Society,* no. 4 (1979), pp. 283-95.

Flamholtz, Eric, and Cook, Ellen. "Connotative Meaning and Its Role in Accounting Change: A Field Study." *Accounting, Organizations and Society,* no. 2 (1978), pp. 115-39.

Frishkoff, Paul. FASB Research Report, *Financial Reporting and Changing Prices: A Review of Empirical Research.* Stamford, Conn.: FASB, 1982.

Fuller, Russell J., and Metcalf, Richard W. "Management Disclosures: Analysts Prefer Facts to Management's Predictions." *Financial Analysts Journal,* March/April 1978, pp. 55-57.

Gibbins, Michael. "A Behavioral Approach to Auditing Research." In Audit Group at the University of Illinois at Urbana-Champaign, *Symposium on Auditing Research II,* pp. 141-86. Urbana-Champaign: The Board of Trustees of the University of Illinois, 1977.

_____. "Regression and Other Statistical Implications for Research on Judgment Using Intercorrelated Data Sources." *Journal of Accounting Research,* in press.

Gonedes, Nicholas, and Dopuch, Nicholas. "Capital Market Equilibrium, Information Production, and Selecting Accounting Techniques: Theoretical Framework and Review of Empirical Work." *Journal of Accounting Research.* Supplement, *Studies on Financial Accounting Objectives 1974,* pp. 48-129.

Gray, Clifton W. "Ingredients of Intuitive Regression." *Organizational Behavior and Human Performance,* February 1979, pp. 30-48.

Gray, S. J. "The Impact of International Accounting Differences from a Security-Analysis Perspective: Some European Evidence." *Journal of Accounting Research,* Spring 1980, pp. 64-76.

Hammond, Kenneth R.; McCelland, Gary H.; and Mumpower, Jeryl. *Human Judgment and Decision Making: Theories, Methods, and Procedures.* New York: Praeger Publishers, 1980.

Hayes, David C. "The Contingency Theory of Managerial Accounting." *The Accounting Review,* January 1977, pp. 22-39.

127

Hendricks, James A. "The Impact of Human Resource Accounting Information on Stock Investment Decisions: An Empirical Study." *The Accounting Review,* April 1976, pp. 292-305.

Hilton, Ronald W. "Integrating Normative and Descriptive Theories of Information Processing." *Journal of Accounting Research,* Autumn 1980, pp. 477-505.

Hofstedt, Thomas R., and Hughes, G. David. "An Experimental Study of the Judgment Element in Disclosure Decisions." *The Accounting Review,* April 1977, pp. 379-95.

Hogarth, Robin M. "Cognitive Processes and the Assessment of Subjective Probability Distributions." *Journal of the American Statistical Association,* June 1975, pp. 271-91.

_____. *Judgement and Choice: The Psychology of Decision.* Chichester, England: John Wiley, 1980.

Kahneman, Daniel, and Tversky, Amos. "Subjective Probability: A Judgment of Representativeness." *Cognitive Psychology,* July 1972, pp. 430-54.

_____. "Prospect Theory: An Analysis of Decision under Risk." *Econometrica,* March 1979, pp. 263-91.

Kennedy, Henry A. "A Behavioral Study of the Usefulness of Four Financial Ratios." *Journal of Accounting Research,* Spring 1975, pp. 97-116.

Keys, David E. "Confidence Interval Financial Statements: An Empirical Investigation." *Journal of Accounting Research,* Autumn 1978, pp. 389-99.

Lev, Baruch. "On the Adequacy of Publicly Available Financial Information for Security Analysis." In *Financial Information Requirements for Security Analysis,* edited by A. Rashad Abdel-khalik and Thomas F. Keller, pp. 123-43. Duke Second Accounting Symposium, December 2-3, 1976. Durham, N.C.: Graduate School of Business Administration, Duke University, December 1976.

Lewellen, Wilbur G.; Lease, Ronald C.; and Schlarbaum, Gary G. "Patterns of Investment Strategy and Behavior among Individual Investors." *The Journal of Business,* July 1977, pp. 296-333.

Libby, Robert. "Accounting Ratios and the Prediction of Failure: Some Behavioral Evidence." *Journal of Accounting Research,* Spring 1975, pp. 150-61. (1975a)

_____. "The Use of Simulated Decision Makers in Information Evaluation." *The Accounting Review,* July 1975, pp. 475-89. (1975b)

_____. "Man versus Model of Man: Some Conflicting Evidence." *Organizational Behavior and Human Performance,* June 1976, pp. 1-12.

_____. "Bankers' and Auditors' Perceptions of the Message Communicated by the Audit Report." *Journal of Accounting Research,* Spring 1979, pp. 99-122. (1979a)

_____. "The Impact of Uncertainty Reporting on the Loan Decision." *Journal of Accounting Research.* Supplement 1979, *Studies on Auditing—Selections from the "Research Opportunities in Auditing" Program,* pp. 35-57. (1979b)

Libby, Robert, and Blashfield, Roger K. "Performance of a Composite as a Function of the Number of Judges." *Organizational Behavior and Human Performance,* April 1978, pp. 121-29.

Libby, Robert, and Lewis, Barry L. "Human Information Processing Research in Accounting: The State of the Art." *Accounting, Organizations and Society,* no. 3 (1977), pp. 245-68.

Louis Harris and Associates, Inc. *A Study of the Attitudes toward and an Assessment of the Financial Accounting Standards Board.* Stamford, Conn.: Financial Accounting Foundation, 1980.

Lusk, Edward J. "A Test of Differential Performance Peaking for a Disembedding Task." *Journal of Accounting Research,* Spring 1979, pp. 286-94.

129

March, James G. "Bounded Rationality, Ambiguity, and the Engineering of Choice." *The Bell Journal of Economics,* Autumn 1978, pp. 587-608.

McGhee, Walter; Shields, Michael D.; and Birnberg, Jacob G. "The Effects of Personality on a Subject's Information Processing." *The Accounting Review,* July 1978, pp. 681-97.

Meehl, Paul E. *Clinical versus Statistical Prediction: A Theoretical Analysis and a Review of the Evidence.* Minneapolis: University of Minnesota Press, 1954.

Milgram, S., and Toch, H. "Collective Behavior: Crowds and Social Movements." In *Handbook of Social Psychology,* edited by Gardner Lindzey and E. Aronson. 2d ed. Reading, Mass.: Addison-Wesley Publishing Company, Inc., 1968. Vol. 4, *Group Psychology and Phenomena of Interaction,* pp. 507-10.

Mock, Theodore J., and Vasarhelyi, Miklos Antal. "A Synthesis of the Information Economics and Lens Models." *Journal of Accounting Research,* Autumn 1978, pp. 414-23.

Moriarity, Shane. "Communicating Financial Information through Multidimensional Graphics." *Journal of Accounting Research,* Spring 1979, pp. 205-24.

Moriarity, Shane, and Barron, F. Hutton. "A Judgment-Based Definition of Materiality." *Journal of Accounting Research,* Supplement 1979, *Studies on Auditing—Selections from the "Research Opportunities in Auditing" Program,* pp. 114-35.

Most, Kenneth S., and Chang, Lucia S. "How Useful Are Annual Reports to Investors?" *Journal of Accountancy,* September 1979, pp. 111-13.

Naylor, J. C. "A Bibliography of Research Related to Human Judgment and Choice Behavior." Research paper. Lafayette, Ind.: Purdue University, August 1979.

Newman, D. Paul. "Prospect Theory: Implications for Information Evaluation." *Accounting, Organizations and Society,* no. 2 (1980), pp. 217-30.

Nisbett, Richard E., and Wilson, Timothy DeCamp. "Telling More Than We Can Know: Verbal Reports on Mental Processes." *Psychological Review,* May 1977, pp. 231-59.

Ogilvie, John R., and Schmitt, Neal. "Situational Influences on Linear and Nonlinear Use of Information." *Organizational Behavior and Human Performance,* April 1979, pp. 292-306.

Pattillo, James W. *The Concept of Materiality in Financial Reporting,* vol. 1. Research study. New York: Financial Executives Research Foundation, 1976.

Patton, James M. "Standardization and Utility of Municipal Accounting and Financial Reporting Practices: A Survey." *Governmental Finance,* May 1976, pp. 15-20.

_____. "An Experimental Investigation of Some Effects of Consolidating Municipal Financial Reports." *The Accounting Review,* April 1978, pp. 402-14.

Plott, Charles R., and Sunder, Shyam. "Efficiency of Experimental Security Markets with Insider Information: An Application of Rational Expectations Models." Social Science working paper, 331, revised. Pasadena: Division of the Humanities and Social Sciences, California Institute of Technology, January 1981.

Prakash, Prem, and Rappaport, Alfred. "Information Inductance and Its Significance for Accounting." *Accounting, Organizations and Society,* no. 1 (1977), pp. 29-38.

Pratt, Jamie. "The Effects of Personality on a Subject's Information Processing: A Comment." *The Accounting Review,* July 1980, pp. 501-6.

Reckers, Phillip M. R., and Stagliano, A. J. "How Good Are Investor's Data Sources?" *Financial Executive,* April 1980, p. 26.

Savich, Richard S. "The Use of Accounting Information in Decision Making." *The Accounting Review,* July 1977, pp. 642-52.

Schelling, Thomas C. *Micromotives and Macrobehavior.* New York: Norton & Company, Inc., 1978.

Schultz, Joseph J., Jr., and Gustavson, Sandra G. "Actuaries' Perceptions of Variables Affecting the Independent Auditor's Legal Liability." *The Accounting Review,* July 1978, pp. 626-41.

Schwan, Edward S. "The Effects of Human Resource Accounting Data on Financial Decisions: An Empirical Test." *Accounting, Organizations and Society,* nos. 2/3 (1976), pp. 219-37.

Schwarzbach, Henry R., and Swanson, Edward P. "The Use of Replacement Cost Accounting Information for Decision Making during Inflationary Times." *Journal of Contemporary Business,* August 1981, pp. 65-76.

Scott, George M., and Troberg, Pontus. *Eighty-eight International Accounting Problems in Rank Order of Importance: A DELPHI Evaluation.* Sarasota, Fla.: American Accounting Association, 1980.

Shafer, Glenn. "Two Theories of Probability." Technical Report no. 1. National Science Foundation Grant MCS78-01887. Lawrence: Department of Mathematics, The University of Kansas, October 1978.

Shank, John K.; Dillard, Jesse F.; and Murdock, Richard J. "FASB No. 8 and the Decision-Makers." *Financial Executive,* February 1980, pp. 18-23.

Simon, Herbert A. "Rational Decision Making in Business Organizations." *The American Economic Review,* September 1979, pp. 493-513.

Slovic, Paul; Fischhoff, Baruch; and Lichtenstein, Sarah. "Behavioral Decision Theory." *Annual Review of Psychology,* 1977, pp. 1-39.

Snowball, Doug. "Human Resource Accounting Information: A Comment concerning Demand Characteristics." *The Accounting Review,* January 1979, pp. 199-204.

Sorter, George H. "An 'Events' Approach to Basic Accounting Theory." *The Accounting Review,* January 1969, pp. 12-19.

Stanga, Keith G., and Benjamin, James J. "Information Needs of Bankers." *Management Accounting,* June 1978, pp. 17-21.

Swieringa, Robert; Dyckman, Thomas R.; and Hoskin, Robert E. "Empirical Evidence about the Effects of an Accounting Change on Information Processing." In *Behavioral Experiments in Accounting II,* edited by Thomas Burns, pp. 225-59. Columbus: The Ohio State University, 1979.

Uecker, Wilfred C. "A Behavioral Study of Information System Choice." *Journal of Accounting Research,* Spring 1978, pp. 169-89.

_____. "The Effects of Knowledge of the User's Decision Model in Simplified Information Evaluation." *Journal of Accounting Research,* Spring 1980, pp. 191-213.

Watts, Ross L. "Corporate Financial Statements: A Product of the Market and Political Processes." *Australian Journal of Management,* April 1977, pp. 53-75.

Watts, Ross L., and Zimmerman, Jerold L. "Towards a Positive Theory of the Determination of Accounting Standards." *The Accounting Review,* January 1978, pp. 112-34.

_____. "The Demand for and Supply of Accounting Theories: The Market for Excuses." *The Accounting Review,* April 1979, pp. 273-305.

_____. "Auditors and the Determination of Accounting Standards." Working paper, no. GPB 78-06, revised. Rochester, N.Y.: Graduate School of Management, The University of Rochester, November 1981.

Weick, Karl E. *The Social Psychology of Organizing.* Reading, Mass.: Addison-Wesley Publishing Company, Inc., 1979.

Williams, Paul F. "The Evaluative Relevance of Social Data." *The Accounting Review,* January 1980, pp. 62-77.

Wright, William F. "Self-Insight into the Cognitive Processing of Financial Information." *Accounting, Organizations and Society,* no. 4 (1977), pp. 323-31. (1977a)

_____. "Financial Information Processing Models: An Empirical Study." *The Accounting Review,* July 1977, pp. 676-89. (1977b)

_____. "Properties of Judgment Models in a Financial Setting." *Organizational Behavior and Human Performance,* February 1979, pp. 73-85.

Zimmer, Ian. "A Lens Study of the Prediction of Corporate Failure by Bank Loan Officers." *Journal of Accounting Research,* Autumn 1980, pp. 629-36.

CHAPTER 7—PREDICTIVE VALUE OF
ACCOUNTING INFORMATION

The idea that accounting issues could be "evaluated in terms of their ability to predict events of interest to decision makers" was perhaps first formalized by Beaver, Kennelly, and Voss (1968). In fact, before 1960, predictive value was not widely recognized as a criterion for the evaluation of accounting information. However, during the 1960s, researchers shifted their emphasis from largely prescriptive or normative topics to those involving empirical analysis and hypothesis testing. This shift brought predictive value into the spotlight as an important characteristic of accounting information.

Initially, the criterion of predictive value (or predictive ability) in accounting met with some controversy. The discussions usually centered on whether accounting numbers are useful for predictive purposes as well as nonpredictive purposes.[1] Today, however, its conceptual merit seems firmly established—as an integral aspect of, though not a sole arbiter in, the accounting choice problem. Policymakers and others who must evaluate informational alternatives often invoke predictive value to suggest that a proposed disclosure or alternative accounting procedure is more informative than those presently in use.

For example, Statement 33, on financial reporting and changing prices, states that investors' and creditors' abilities to assess future cash flows "will be severely limited" (paragraph 10) unless certain supplementary information about the effects of inflation and changing prices is included in financial reports. The primary object of prediction in this case is prospective cash flows to the firm. Concepts Statement 2, on the qualitative characteristics of accounting information, directly links predictive value to "relevance." Predictive value is a primary ingredient of relevance together with "feedback value" and "timeliness." "To be relevant . . . ," Concepts Statement 2 notes, "accounting information must be capable of making a difference in a decision by helping users to form predictions about the outcomes of past, present, and future events or to

---

[1]The term *nonpredictive purposes* refers to the use of such data for performance evaluation and in legal and fiduciary contracts or arrangements. For a criticism of the predictive-value approach, see Greenball (1971). See Carsberg, Arnold, and Hope (1977) for support for that approach.

confirm or correct expectations" (paragraph 47). The emphasis here is on predictions about "outcomes" of events.

This chapter documents those studies that have explored the utility of the information in financial reports in particular predictive contexts. Following a brief conceptual discussion of factors that constitute relevant predictions for information evaluation, studies that deal with enterprise failure and financial distress, judgments by rating agencies, lending and credit decisions, mergers and acquisitions, assessment of prospective cash flows, and the behavior of those who participate in the accounting regulatory process are addressed. (The reader not wishing to pursue the conceptual discussion should skip the next section and proceed directly to the sections on the evidence.)

One area not reviewed in this chapter is research on the extrapolation of accounting numbers. The relationship between past patterns in time series and future values of those series has already been discussed in Chapter 5. Another area, research on the relationship between security prices and financial report information, is discussed in Chapter 8. The objects of assessment (or prediction) in that chapter are not events or actions but the prospective returns to the holder of a portfolio of securities and covariability relationships among returns within the portfolio. Nonetheless, securities market variables—current price, for instance—have been used as predictors in some studies (e.g., research on the prediction of failure and on financial distress) rather than as objects of prediction, and are included in the discussion.

Relevant Predictions for Information Evaluation

There are two ways of expressing the connection between uncertain events and predictor (accounting) variables. The first is to ascribe probabilities to the possible events that the decision maker is interested in (e.g., the firm fails), such probabilities depending on (1) the particular signal that might be transmitted (e.g., the firm's reported earnings), (2) the system that generates all possible signals for that decision maker (e.g., the firm's financial reporting system), and (3) a model that relates such signals to more basic financial numbers and provides a means of assembling the data (e.g., a statistical regression equation).[2] For example, a prediction of bankruptcy (*event*) might depend on whether earnings were good or bad (*signal*), were based on a historical or current cost accounting *system,* and how such earnings were assembled with other relevant accounting data (e.g., risk, liquidity, etc.).

A second means of expressing the relationship between events and predictor (accounting) variables is to assess a probability distribution on the predictor variable for every possible event. This approach assesses the likelihood of observing the various values of the relevant predictor variable or accounting signal (e.g., cash flow to total debt, etc.) given that an event will occur (e.g., loan default). Likelihoods are usually developed by observing historical data. In the immediately preceding case, one might specify, for those firms that failed in the past, an array of accounting ratios reported one, two, and three years prior to failure. Similarly, the values of the accounting ratios could be arrayed for those firms that did not fail in the past. Such arrays—in fact, probability distributions—are called *likelihood functions.*

The likelihood-function approach has a distinct advantage over the first approach, especially if the analyst and the decision maker are different people. The likelihood function does not require that the analyst specify the "prior" probabilities, namely, the probabilities associated with each possible event (e.g., failure or nonfailure) in the absence of the relevant predictor variable (e.g., cash flow to total debt, etc.). It merely provides the likelihoods (chances or odds) of the various values of the accounting variable, given that a particular event will occur. For example, for firms likely to fail, the odds that cash flow to debt will exceed 0.4 one year before failure are, perhaps, 1 chance in 10. The probability of occurrence of each event need not be stated.

---

[2]The probabilities associated with the events of interest might also depend upon a fourth factor, namely, the behavior of the decision maker. For example, prior knowledge of a prediction that the firm may be given a poor credit rating by some outside agency (an event in this case) may well prompt action on the part of management to change the firm's financial standing prior to that event (thus altering the likelihood that a poor rating will be given). Similarly, an audit report qualified as to the going-concern assumption may precipitate an action by a bank that otherwise might not have been taken. The audit qualification might well generate a self-fulfilling chain of events.

Someone other than the decision maker is often responsible for analyzing the informativeness of financial reporting alternatives. The accounting staff chooses accounting and reporting systems on behalf of management; analysts and other financial intermediaries process information on behalf of investors and creditors; and standard setters define aspects of the information system to be used by investors, creditors, and others. Predictions, therefore, must be made regarding a decision maker's actions or behavior. Sometimes that behavior may be thought to be completely rational—as if the decision maker was unconstrained—in ability to process information, in understanding the problem at hand, and in gathering more information if necessary. At other times, the decision maker may simplify the task. Rules of thumb (heuristics) may be used in making decisions. Moreover, the decision maker may be unable to visualize the problem clearly due to personal idiosyncrasies. Chapter 6 discusses the relevant research on the rationality (or irrationality) of human information processing, and such issues will not be elaborated. It should be mentioned, however, that almost all the predictive studies identified here involve behavioral issues of the kinds discussed in Chapter 6.

Predictions of a decision maker's beliefs and attitudes toward risk may also be required for a complete evaluation of the information. Differences in willingness to accept risk mean that the results or consequences of actions and events connote different payoffs to different people. An improved expected cash payoff to someone who enjoys taking risks might well be viewed very differently by a highly risk-averse person. (The latter would be willing to accept a more certain cash payoff of lower expected value.) If the analyst's prediction of the decision maker's preferences diverges significantly from actual preferences, the chances that the analyst will feed the decision maker the most "useful" information diminish commensurately. The FASB, for instance, might consider giving more emphasis to the production of information about risk (rather than return) to better satisfy the needs of risk-averse users of financial statements. On the other hand, such information would be of no value to an investor whose decisions were made solely on the basis of expected (average) cash payoff. Similarly, "best" decisions may not be made if the evaluator provides information based on probabilities of events diverging significantly from the decision maker's assessment of such probabilities. Indeed, at the extreme, the analyst or standard setter may be providing worthless information, that is, information that has absolutely no potential to change decision makers' beliefs about future events.

Often the analysis of predictive value is extended to the prediction of results, outcomes, or consequences—in other words, to the combination of events and actions. The present FASB focus—on the ability of accounting and other financial information to help investors, creditors, and others assess (or predict) the amounts, timing, and uncertainty of prospective cash flows to the enterprise—exemplifies this approach.[3]

In a securities market setting, the focus is altered slightly. The interaction of the plans of many investors and creditors is manifested in price and portfolio reallocations that, subsequently, determine returns. Assessments of security returns, of course, represent assessments of future cash flows in the form of dividends, interest, redemptions, maturities, etc. Predictions of results, outcomes, or consequences, however, indirectly reflect predictions of uncertain events. The assessment of prospective returns (and relationships among firms' securities), for example, always implicitly considers the different possible events that may occur (e.g., the state of the economy, war or peace, etc.).

Summary

This section has presented a brief discussion of factors pertaining to the "predictive value" criterion. In its most elementary form, the criterion is a probability relationship between events of interest to the decision maker and relevant predictor variables derived in part from accounting information. However, since decisions to produce or invest are not always made by people who evaluate information systems, additional issues become relevant. In order to distinguish "better" from "inferior" information systems, evaluators such as analysts, accountants, and standard setters may need to assess decision makers' likely actions, their beliefs, and their attitudes toward risk. All such considerations are relevant predictions for information evaluation.

---

[3]See, for example, Concepts Statements 1 and 2 and comments earlier in this chapter.

Evidence on the Predictive Value of Financial Information

The remainder of this chapter reviews the available evidence on the predictive value of accounting numbers, ratios, and other financial signals contained in corporate reports. The studies reviewed are organized under six topic headings: (1) enterprise failure and financial distress, (2) judgments by rating agencies, (3) trade credit and bank lending decisions, (4) mergers and acquisitions, (5) prospective cash flow assessments, and (6) concerns expressed in submissions to standard-setting bodies. The first and fourth areas involve the prediction of events of decision-maker interest, and the second and third areas concern the prediction of decision-maker behavior; the fifth area deals with the prediction of consequences; and the sixth area involves the prediction of preferences of those who participate in the process that determines accounting standards. Accounting information can be useful in all such predictive contexts.

Enterprise Failure and Financial Distress

The possibility that a firm will fail is a prime consideration in investment and lending decisions. On occasion, the decision maker will want to separate firms into those that are expected to fail and those that are not. But that is a very crude partition of the set of possibilities. The more relevant information is the probability of failure or some means of distinguishing among firms based on the chances that the uncertain event will occur. Financial theorists commonly denote the scale of possible contingencies as degrees of "financial distress."

There are numerous examples of the use of models to predict financial distress. Auditors sometimes need to assess whether the going-concern assumption is satisfied. Regulatory agencies (e.g., the Federal Deposit Insurance Corporation) often assess whether a regulated company is in danger of failing. Lawmakers must occasionally pass judgment on whether a company satisfies the "failing company doctrine."[4] Portfolio managers must periodically

---

[4]The failing-company doctrine is an argument available to companies to support mergers that are likely to reduce competition. The defense (e.g., the bidding firm) must establish that the firm subject to acquisition is "in imminent danger" of failing.

screen their investments and loans for signs of possible weakness. All lending decisions are, of course, concerned with expected loss due to financial distress.

Methodological Issues

Before summarizing the different results, some methodological issues warrant discussion. First, the research process is one of inference. The studies examine observable events, such as legal bankruptcy, loan default, and omission of preferred dividend, in order to infer something that cannot be observed, namely, financial distress. Hence, financial distress—not actual bankruptcy or some similar uncertain event—is the object of analysis for predictive purposes. This is not always directly stated.[5]

Second, the usefulness of financial-distress models for investors and creditors hinges implicitly on an assessment of the costs associated with impending failure (i.e., the expected losses associated with each possible action available to the decision maker). The issues are subtle and may involve not only questions of loss to the security holder given legal bankruptcy but also the opportunity costs of mergers and other forms of feasible reorganization such as divestment and loan restructuring. In the context of a commercial loan decision, the expected losses are a function of the chances that a wrong decision will be made: Either (1) a firm whose loan is accepted will default or (2) a firm whose loan is rejected continues to be successful.[6]

---

[5]It should be noted that Zeta Services, Inc., which markets the Zeta model (Altman, Haldeman, and Narayanan [1977]), has expressly indicated that its model does not forecast failure or nonfailure and is not designed to do so. Rather, the objective is more modest. "It [the model] compares a company's operating and financial characteristics to those of over 50 firms **which have already failed**" (Zeta Services, Inc. [1979]). No doubt, possible claims by affected companies are minimized by such an approach. At the same time, there are usually many options open to management that would obviate the occurrence of legal bankruptcy or some similar unambiguous event. Indeed, large numbers of financially distressed firms may never be observed to enter bankruptcy proceedings.

[6]For a conceptual discussion of the costs involved, see Beaver (1966) and Neter (1966). Based on 1975 data, Altman (1977b) estimates the average loan loss for a commercial bank to be in the vicinity of 70 percent of the loan. (This is the cost of making a type-one error.) The costs associated with the rejection of a successful loan application (type-two error), however, are very small by comparison, because the funds can usually be lent elsewhere.

Third, financial distress has different shades of meaning to researchers and analysts. The particular context in which the predictions are being made is therefore important. This requires a careful definition of the events of interest. Beaver (1966), for example, defines failed firms broadly to include bankruptcies, bond defaults, overdrawn bank accounts, and firms that omitted preferred dividend payments. Subsequent authors have tended to restrict failure to legal bankruptcy. The Altman, Haldeman, and Narayanan (1977) formula is based on only those firms that filed bankruptcy petitions.[7] But some researchers argue that this also is misleading since the theory actually deals with a firm's failure to meet its financial obligations, and such failure would not ordinarily lead to bankruptcy. Problems of definition of financial distress can be severe in the noncorporate sector, such as in universities (Schipper [1977]).

Descriptive Modeling

The empirical literature on the prediction of financial distress falls into one of two main schools of thought. The first is primarily descriptive. The studies initially compare the financial characteristics of a sample of failed firms with those of a sample of nonfailed firms. They then combine those characteristics in a formula or model that best discriminates not only between the original samples but also between failed and nonfailed firms in a sample of firms not used to develop the model (hereafter, a validation or holdout sample). The groundwork was laid by Beaver (1966, 1968a, and 1968b). Beaver's 1966 study was most effective in showing that accounting ratios of firms that eventually fail diverge increasingly from those of nonfailed firms as the date of failure is approached. Using 1954-1964 data, Beaver compared 79 failed firms with 79 matched firms that had not failed in each of the 5 years prior to the failed firms' bankruptcy. Having the highest discriminatory power of the selected ratios was "cash flow to total debt." Five years before failure, an optimal prediction criterion based on this single accounting ratio misclassified only 22 percent of a sample not used in the criterion's development; 1 year prior to failure, the criterion misclassified only 13 percent of the validation sample. This is

---

[7]Five nonbankruptcy petition firms, however, were included. The firms involved either received substantial government support, were forced to merge, or had their business taken over by banks.

142

impressive, given that a random classification would produce a 50-percent error. Beaver (1968a) examined these results further. The study reports that nonliquid-asset measures (e.g., cash flow to total debt, net income to total assets, and total debt to total assets) seem to perform better than liquid asset measures, apparently because they represent more "permanent aspects" of the firm (page 117).[8]

Security prices also convey information about financial distress. Beaver (1968b) reports that, on the average, common stock return data have a lead time of about two and one-half years in discerning failure versus nonfailure status. This lead time runs slightly ahead of the lead times of the accounting ratios examined. However, Beaver does not examine the joint predictive power of accounting ratios and market price data. Still, his results are consistent with the idea that investors use accounting ratios in the assessment of financial distress as part of an overall evaluation of prospective security returns. More recently, Aharony, Jones, and Swary (1980) evaluated a rule that predicts the bankruptcy probability using quarterly security return data. Their results are consistent with Beaver's, indicating "that a solvency deterioration signal using capital market data is available some two years before the bankruptcy event" (page 1014).

Most of the post-Beaver studies adopted a multiple-variable approach to the prediction of financial distress, combining accounting and nonaccounting data in a variety of statistical formulas. Altman's (1968) model is perhaps the best known. Comparing 33 firms that failed in the 1946-1965 period with 33 similar successful firms, Altman develops an equation that optimally combines 5 ratios reflecting accounting and market data—namely, liquidity, profitability, leverage, solvency, and activity (i.e., sales to total assets). The discriminant-function criterion (commonly known as a "Z" score) predicted 24 out of 25 failed firms not used in developing the model—1 year ahead of the event. A second sample of 66 nonfailed firms with temporary earnings difficulties was examined. The Altman "Z" score criterion was in error in only 14 out of the 66 cases.

Studies using multiple variable statistical techniques subsequent to Altman include Deakin (1972), Edmister (1972, concentrating on small business failure), and Blum (1974). Deakin and Blum repli-

---

[8]For replications of the Beaver results, see Deakin (1972) and Blum (1974). The findings in these more recent studies are generally consistent with the earlier studies.

cated the Altman model. Subsequent research also includes investigations of the characteristics of failing firms in the nonindustrial sector: Altman (1973) on railroads, Sinkey (1975) on commercial banks,[9] Altman and Loris (1976) on broker-dealers, and Altman (1977a) on savings and loan institutions. In all the models developed—whether based on samples of industrials or of nonindustrials—the misclassification rates are low. Hence, the explanatory variables have significant predictive power. Ratios based on accounting earnings, reported cash flow, and book debt figure prominently in the various statistical formulas, especially those that apply to firms in the industrial sector.

Two of the most recent studies in this area are Altman et al. (1977) and Ohlson (1980). The Altman et al. research is important in that it is used by several major banks and spans well over 2,000 public companies (*Business Week,* March 24, 1980, page 106). The variables in the discriminant model (or Zeta model, as it is commercially known) are: retained earnings to total assets, leverage, earnings variability, return on assets, fixed charge coverage, current ratio, and asset size. The model is based on 53 firms filing for bankruptcy since 1970 and an equivalent number of industry-matched firms. It improves upon the Altman "Z" score, classifying 91 percent of a validation sample 1 year before the filing. Five years earlier, 77 percent of the validation sample is correctly analyzed. Having greatest weight in the equation are the variables "retained earnings to assets" (explains 25 percent of the difference between failed and nonfailed firms) and "stability of earnings" (explains 20 percent of the difference).

Ohlson (1980) uses an alternative statistical procedure called "logit" analysis. The logit approach avoids certain statistical problems inherent in discriminant analysis. No assumptions need be made regarding the prior probability that a firm belongs to the failed or nonfailed group. Less critical than in discriminant analysis are the assumptions that the data should be distributed as a normal curve and that there should be equality of the variances and covariances among variables across groups. Moreover, the model provides a score between zero and one as its output—directly interpretable as the probability of financial distress. Ohlson claims that significant predictive factors are size, liquidity, performance, and financial structure. However, the predictive ability of the model

---

[9]See also the section on trade credit and bank lending decisions in this chapter.

144

based on 1970-1976 data is lower than in previous studies. One possible reason, according to the author, is the relatively long lead time between failure and the most recent annual report, which was not always adequately recognized, and may have been understated, in prior studies. (The average lead time in the Ohlson study was 13 months.) The absence of market data in the model might also be a factor.

Accounting Alternatives

While the preceding discussion demonstrates that accounting information is useful in assessing the chances that a firm will fail, it is far from obvious that the ability to predict failure is a feasible criterion for the selection or evaluation of accounting alternatives. Standard setters would seem more interested in the latter issue, especially if an objective benchmark for judging the predictive success of accounting alternatives could be derived. Studies by Elam (1975), Ketz (1978), and Norton and Smith (1979) are relevant in this regard. Elam explored the proposition that predictive ability would improve when off-balance-sheet lease data were incorporated into the ratio calculations. Predictive power was not improved. Altman (1976), however, raises several issues of research design that cloud the validity of this finding. Similarly, Ketz tested the hypothesis that discriminatory power would increase when bankruptcy prediction was based on price-level-adjusted data rather than on historical cost data. While weak support is offered in favor of the price-level alternative, Patell's (1978) review of Ketz's paper also renders the results largely inconclusive. Testing the same hypothesis, Norton and Smith (1979) find little difference in price-level-based predictions of failure versus predictions based on historical cost numbers.[10]

In short, it appears that the test methodologies used in the research thus far have not been sufficiently exacting to detect an improvement due to an accounting change if in fact one was present. Additional research is obviously required. Still, attention to accounting rules and the extensive use of footnote data can only enhance the cross-sectional comparability of the primary ingre-

---

[10]For correspondence debating whether Norton and Smith failed to find support for the price-level alternative due to design problems, see the comment by Solomon and Beck (1980) and the response by Norton and Smith (1980).

dients of analysis. Altman et al. (1977) identified the incorporation of such reporting adjustments as one factor that led to an improvement in predictive ability relative to the original "Z" score model.

First Passage Time Models

The second main strand in the empirical literature emphasizes the use of a "theory" of bankruptcy based on special stochastic models (e.g., the Markov process). Initially, researchers used a "first passage time" or "gambler's ruin" approach. Such an approach is best visualized as a game played by the firm against the environment. Starting with an arbitrary sum, the firm (i.e., the gambler) wins one dollar from the opponent (the economic environment) with a given probability (p) of success and loses a dollar with the probability of one minus p. The game continues until either the firm loses all of its money (i.e., goes bankrupt) or the opponent loses. There are statistical expressions for the probability of ruin, the expected time lapse until ruin, and the expected gain or loss during the game. Wilcox (1971 and 1973) presents estimates of the probability of ruin based on measures of the firm's adjusted cash position (liquidation value) and adjusted cash flow.[11]

While Wilcox's (1973) results "yielded an improvement in risk-ranking power over the various financial ratios tested by Beaver" (page 167), Kinney (1973), in his review comments, notes that the formula is not meaningful for roughly one-half of the sample. Kinney also notes that on an adjusted basis the Wilcox criterion is no more accurate than one based on a single cash-flow-to-total-debt ratio. Even extended tests by Wilcox (1976) rendered no significant improvement in the accuracy of the first-passage time model.

More recent models have been offered by Santomero and Vinso (1977) and Vinso (1979). These models are probably more realistic in recognizing that most firms never reach the "ruin" state. (Ultimate ruin is certain to occur under the "gambler's ruin" model.) Vinso tests his theory on electric utilities with medium- to high-grade outstanding bonds. He reports that his "safety index" is predictably correlated with bond rating, security beta, and various

---

[11]Wilcox (1973) defines *adjusted cash position* as: cash + (0.7)(noncash current assets) + (0.5)(long-term assets) - (1.0)(liabilities). *Adjusted cash flow* is defined as: net income + stock issued in merger - dividends - (0.3)(increase in noncash current assets) - (0.5)(increase in long-term assets).

scores from well-known bankruptcy prediction models. However, his model is not evaluated on a validation sample, although further tests are expected. The ability of such stochastic modeling approaches that attempt to integrate economic theory and statistical analysis is encouraging.

Judgments by Rating Agencies

The predictive aspects associated with bond ratings are twofold. At one level, researchers have developed models that would predict ratings and rating changes. The object is to describe how raters make their judgments. Usually a mathematical expression is developed with "judgment" in the form of a rating on one side of the equation and the accounting and other data that would explain or predict such judgments on the other. A second level of predictive analysis is suggested by asking: For what purpose might one want to represent a complex judgment process by a mathematical expression? For bondholders and bond analysts, presumably, their ultimate concern is the prediction or assessment of bond price changes or yields. Empirical analysis should enable them to understand better the nature and impact of bond ratings and rating changes as signals that change assessments of returns and yields.

This section addresses two issues: (1) It discusses whether bond ratings (and rating changes) have an impact on security prices. (2) It highlights the work done to evaluate how well a rater's judgments can be predicted or replicated by various statistical models. Some brief comments on the function of rating agencies are made at the outset.

The Bond-Rating Function

A bond rating is a signal about bond investment quality. Consistent with the previous section, a rating is viewed as an indicator of a firm's financial distress, namely, the probability of default or loss of market value due to deterioration of a firm's future prospects. Rating agencies themselves emphasize that the rating is the minimum sustainable level of overall bond quality that the company can expect to maintain under presently known circumstances.[12]

---

[12]For example, *Moody's Bond Record* (July 1976) notes: "Since ratings involve a judgment about the future, on the one hand, and since they are used by investors as a means of protection, on the other, the effort is made when assigning ratings, to look at 'worst' potentialities in the 'visible' future rather than solely at the past record and the status of the present" (p.1).

The importance of a particular rating stems directly from its impact on bond yield—either at the date of issuance or at any point before redemption or maturity. Low-grade bonds with, say, B or lower ratings require higher yields than quality bonds with AA or AAA ratings. Ratings and yields are thus negatively correlated. So too are rating changes and yield changes. A downgrade is normally associated with a commensurate increase in required yield. Bond price changes and reclassifications, up or down, should thus be positively correlated.

However, in an age of rapid information processing, with adequate numbers of skilled analysts evaluating bond quality, it is not obvious whether the rating announcement, or the rating process in its entirety, exerts a substantial effect on yield. Rating and yield might be correlated due to a third factor, namely, publicly available information. One means of assessing whether bond ratings per se (as opposed to more basic information, such as accounting data) affect buyers and sellers of securities is to study the impact of rating announcements on common stock and bond prices. The next several paragraphs consider the research to date.

Is There a Market Impact?

The evidence suggests that ratings are anticipated substantially due to accounting or other financial data that flow continuously to the market in earlier periods. Weinstein (1977) suggests that the rate-changing lag (i.e., the difference between the market's recognition of new information and the agency's response to that information as a reclassification) is at least six months for bonds. The rating lag may be even longer for common stocks. Pinches and Singleton (1978), for instance, report that the estimated rating lag is 15-18 months, except when a company-specific event (e.g., issuance of new securities) may have precipitated a review of existing debt, in which case the rating lag is less than 6 months. In brief, ratings per se provide little in the way of new information to investors and creditors.

In light of the discrete nature of ratings (AAA, AA, etc.), it is of course reasonable that there should be a lag, although that lag may well have diminished due to the recent introduction of the "plus" and "minus" designations within rating classes. Still, the rating process may reveal a limited amount of nonpublic information to investors and creditors by way of the agency-management interactions that frequently precede a bond upgrading or downgrading.[13] Hence, the possibility of market reaction to the rating per se cannot be ruled out. In this regard, there is conflicting evidence regarding the abnormal price movements six months or less prior to reclassification. Weinstein indicates that there is little bond market response to the announcement of a reclassification. However, Griffin and Sanvicente (in press) report that firms with reclassifications exhibited significantly different common stock price behavior less than 12 months prior to the rating change compared with that of a control sample. Moreover, the abnormal price changes for downgrades were significantly negative in the month of rating change announcement. These results are consistent with the proposition that the rating process obtains the release of what otherwise might remain private information. Limited evidence of security price movement after the announcement has been reported, though upward or downward drifts in security prices following announcement can only be considered anomalies in light of the evidence on market efficiency.[14]

Overall, then, investors and creditors probably do pay attention to ratings, and thus to the accounting data on which they are based. But while there may be specific announcement effects, most of the financial information inherent in the rating (or rating change) has already been impounded into bond and stock prices due to the efficient nature of the U.S. securities markets. This suggests that investors and creditors are able to anticipate ratings with reasonable accuracy.

Predicting Agency Judgments

A variety of models that would forecast bond raters' judgments has been developed using accounting and other financial information as inputs. Such models explain as much as 80 percent of the judgments made by the raters themselves and thus underscore the usefulness of accounting data. However, the ability of these models to explain either newly rated bonds or rating changes is somewhat

---

[13]Ross (1976) and Backer and Gosman (1978) report examples of such discussions.
[14]See Katz (1974), Grier and Katz (1976), and Hettenhouse and Sartoris (1976). Regarding these studies, Weinstein (1977) comments: ". . . None of them examines the statistical properties of the data they use in sufficient detail. Further, each study imposes biases on the sample of ratings that they examine . . ." (p. 330).

lower. For example, one of the more successful models proposed in Kaplan and Urwitz (1979) correctly classifies about two-thirds of a sample of new bond issues.[15]

The more popular modeling techniques used in this research are multiple regression and discriminant analysis, although so-called probit or logit techniques may offer advantages in the estimation process. (See the discussion earlier in this chapter.) The models provide formulas that tell in what category the bond should be classified. The statistical formulas are generally designed to minimize error in misclassification, but care is required in defining exactly what is an error. When the agency and the researcher's model disagree, it is far from obvious who, at the time, is right and who is wrong.

Moreover, it is difficult to compare the various models because the models employed as benchmarks are often overly naive. Also, the predictive success depends on the number of rating categories examined; and the use of validation samples varies. Some of the better known studies are Horrigan (1966), Pogue and Soldofsky (1969), West (1970 and 1973), and Pinches and Mingo (1973). These are comprehensively discussed in Kaplan and Urwitz (1979), who comment also on the many unresolved methodological issues.

While many technical aspects of the models have been well documented, the uses of such models have not. The models should be helpful in the development of in-house services by investment firms and, to a lesser extent, should assist enterprise managers and their advisors in the evaluation of new or existing debt obligations. Further, the agencies themselves may use models to predict or replicate ratings in order to identify biases among raters, minimize judgmental factors at early stages of the rating process, and monitor large samples of firms for potential in-depth analysis.

Finally, it is worthwhile to comment on the role of the rating agency in accounting and reporting policy. While historically the raters appear to have shown little interest in the improvement of accounting and reporting standards, a new trend may be emerging. Policy at Standard & Poor's with respect to municipalities, for example, now regards failure to adopt acceptable accounting and timely reporting standards as a negative factor in the rating process.[16] This suggests that accounting policymakers may have a new

---

[15]This model is based on four variables: long-term debt to total assets, total assets, subordination status, and security (market) beta.

[16]See Standard & Poor's policy statement, *Fixed Income Investor,* May 3, 1980, p. 781.

ally in their quest for improved accounting and financial reporting. Presently, much less public disclosure is required of municipalities and public agencies than of corporations. Standard & Poor's action is also consistent with their desire to preserve their reputation for accurate ratings.

Other Debt Securities

The discussion so far has focused on the nature and impact of industrial bond ratings because most of the research is in that area. However, the rating agencies work with debt securities other than bonds (e.g., convertibles, leases, commercial paper) and also rate nonindustrials (e.g., regulated enterprises, financial institutions, and nonprofit state and local governmental organizations). Among the empirical studies in the nonindustrial sector are Altman and Katz (1976) on electric utility ratings, Carleton and Lerner (1969) and Horton (1970) on municipalities, and Harmelink (1973) on the bond ratings of insurance companies. Again, the statistical models are good approximations of the agency's judgment process. Horton's study of general obligation bonds, for example, found that a model developed using discriminant analysis was able to classify correctly as much as 80 percent of a validation sample of 25 investment-quality and 25 noninvestment-quality municipal bonds. The model of Altman and Katz successfully predicted just over 75 percent of a validation sample.

Little research appears to have been performed on commercial paper ratings. However, Backer and Gosman (1978) suggest that analytical procedures used by commercial paper raters are virtually identical to those used by bond analysts and the bond-rating agencies. The ratings ascribed to senior long-term debt and commercial paper are seldom inconsistent.

To summarize, research on the nature of ratings and their effects on bonds and other debt securities suggests that accounting and other financial data make an important contribution in at least two respects: First, such data appear to be relevant to predicting what a firm's ratings ought to be. Second, the finding that no widespread price reaction occurs at the time a rating change is announced is consistent with the contention that investors' and creditors' assessments of bond quality—based on timely accounting and other financial data—are not systematically wrong.

Trade Credit and Bank Lending Decisions

Trade Credit

Most firms devote significant resources to the evaluation of the credit risks associated with existing and prospective customers. The principal supplier of information in this process is Dun & Bradstreet, Inc., though other organizations such as National Credit Office, National Association of Credit Management, The Robert Morris Associates, and various industry trade associations also engage in credit analysis. Unquestionably, a basic ingredient in the credit-rating process is accounting information.

But the use of accounting and other financial information to evaluate trade credit has received only sparing attention by researchers. The research issue, as in the bond-rating case, is to replicate or predict the credit evaluation or change therein. Ewert (1980) evaluated the extent to which financial ratios could be used to distinguish good from bad accounts, bad accounts being those either placed for collection or written off as uncollectible. Data were collected from the 1970-1974 period. Slightly more than 80 percent of a sample of firms not used in developing the model were correctly analyzed. Backer and Gosman (1978) studied differences in financial ratios among a group of firms that had been downgraded in 1974-1976 by Dun & Bradstreet and a matched sample that had not experienced a change in credit rating. The Backer and Gosman discriminant formula demonstrated a somewhat lower ability to classify the groups correctly. Using the most recent annual data, 66 to 74 percent of the original sample were correctly classified as belonging to the Dun & Bradstreet group.[17] But despite modest success, the models are still rather mechanical and suffer from design problems (common to most analysis of this general kind). They are thus unlikely to be implemented without modification in practical settings, except perhaps as broad screening devices. It should be recognized that the extension of credit is not one but a sequence of decisions involving interest rates, timing of payments, collateral, and other factors.

---

[17]But their statistical findings "failed to confirm D&B's own description of its decision model" (p. 178). While profitability variables were significant in the research, Dun & Bradstreet apparently emphasize short-term liquidity ratios, which were not significant.

In contrast to research on the provision of commercial credit, the bank lending process has been the focus of considerable empirical research. This section identifies and discusses four principal strands in the literature. The first deals with models that attempt to describe aspects of a bank's investment and lending processes using simulation techniques; the second area concerns statistical models of components of the bank lending process such as loan classification; the third studies sensitivity of a loan officer's behavior to accounting changes; and the fourth involves estimation and prediction of commercial bank financial distress.

Studies in the first area include Clarkson (1962) and Cohen, Gilmore, and Singer (1966). Clarkson developed a computer model that simulates a trust investment officer's decisions in a medium-sized national bank. Specifically, he investigated the investment of customers' funds in common stock portfolios. The trust officer was modeled as a sequential decision maker using a relatively small number of heuristics or "rules of thumb." Such heuristics were able to specify a greater proportion of correct securities than were the alternative models. Clarkson's main contribution, however, is that he describes the interactions among a bank officer's information, expectations, and decisions, thus showing that it is possible to remove the aura of mystery and to identify assumptions that are implicit in the traditional approach to investment analysis and portfolio selection. Financial information plays a prominent part in the simulation analysis, though always in a comparative sense (i.e., relative to bankers' expectations). Dutton and Starbuck (1971) provide a criticism of the Clarkson study.

Others have devoted their energies to a second area—the development of statistical models of components of the bank lending process. The exploration of numerical loan-rating systems is one such component. The objective is to develop a model that facilitates the monitoring of existing loans and the evaluation of possible new accounts. Some commercial banks apparently have implemented such scoring systems with relative success, although there is a tendency to use the models mostly in the loan-monitoring phase. According to Backer and Gosman, ". . . competition often plays a greater role than inherent loan risk in the determination of the interest rate to be charged" (page 189).

Orgler (1970), for example, presents a multiple-regression model that is able to replicate the Federal Deposit Insurance Corporation's classification of bank loans into their "criticized" and "uncriticized" categories. Some 300 loans were analyzed and tested on a second sample of 40 criticized and 80 uncriticized loans. A 6-variable regression equation correctly classified 75 percent of the criticized loans and 35 percent of the latter group. The relatively high percentage of errors made in attempting to classify loans as uncriticized detracts from any practical use. Given a sample of loans, it appears that the model would incorrectly predict loans in good standing as "criticized" loans much too often.

A more recent investigation of the commercial loan classification decision is by Dietrich and Kaplan (1982). Based on 327 loan classifications made in 1975-1976 at a large money center bank, a statistical "logit" model was constructed to explain and predict four classes of loans—from those that are "current/in good standing" to those that are "doubtful." The statistical prediction formula gave the greatest weights to (1) debt to total assets and (2) funds flow to fixed commitments. A sales-trend variable was also significant. One version of the model, developed from 1975 classifications and 1974 accounting data, predicted 117 out of 140 classifications made in 1976. However, the predictive accuracy (117/140) should be assessed relative to a benchmark. A naive model that predicted all loans as current would have predictive accuracy of 109/140. Thus, the model suggested by Dietrich and Kaplan is an improvement. The model was also superior to previous bankruptcy models in predicting the four classes of loans. However, its accuracy might well be increased by the use of more timely (e.g., quarterly) data. The model could respond more quickly to changing economic circumstances.

The third strand in the literature addresses laboratory studies that test the sensitivity of a loan officer's behavior (e.g., ability to predict bankruptcy, decision to lend, etc.) to changes in accounting methods and, more generally, to changes in information available to the decision maker. Studies in this category include Oliver (1972), who reports that bankers did not alter hypothetical loan decisions when given financial statements containing confidence interval data; Abdel-khalik (1973), whose results suggest that the high degree of aggregation in accounting data is a negative factor in the loan evaluation process only when the firm being evaluated is close to default; Casey (1978), who finds that loan officers who were overloaded with accounting data in bankruptcy prediction experienced an *"overall* poorer [forecasting] performance" (page 57)

154

relative to those who were given lesser amounts of accounting data; and Abdel-khalik and El-Sheshai (1980), who conclude that a decision maker's choice, not processing, of information is a major contributory factor in predicting whether and when a firm will default on its debt.[18]

Finally, the fourth area of research involves the estimation and prediction of commercial bank financial distress, primarily for purposes of constructing early warning systems for federal and state bank regulators. The objective is to develop classification rules based on comparisons of banks with criticized loans and banks with uncriticized loans, problem banks and nonproblem banks, and failed banks and nonfailed banks.

Consistent with the general research on financial distress, studies involving banks focus on the ability of accounting data to predict to which population a given firm is likely to belong. Sinkey's model (1979), based on the variables (1) operating expenses to operating income and (2) investments to assets, is such an example. The model was able to predict 15 out of 16 bank failures in a validation sample one year before their failure, and 14 out of 16 two years before. The model also worked well in classifying nonproblem banks as such. Equally noteworthy is Sinkey's finding that the 2-variable (accounting) model appears to signal a "red flag" (on average) approximately 66 weeks ahead of the date of the examiner's on-site review that led to the bank's being placed on the FDIC problem-bank list. Pettway and Sinkey (1980) follow up this research with an analysis of market- and accounting-based screening models. According to the authors, ". . . the accounting screen provides valuable lead time that regulators could have used to carry out more effectively their statutory responsibilities" (page 145). A dual market and accounting screen produced similar results.[19]

In sum, the findings on the use of accounting and other information in lending and credit decisions, while limited in scope, are encouraging. There is firm evidence that models based on account-

---

[18]Dawes and Corrigan (1974) assert that the trick is to decide which variables to examine and then to know how to add.

[19]The screen was based on whether the bank experienced successive negative weekly price changes. The market screen, of course, attempts to capitalize on the notion that the market for bank securities is efficient. Recent research by Fraser and McCormack (1978) on bond price reactions and by Pettway (1980) on common stock price adjustments appears to be consistent with the efficiency hypothesis. Earlier studies on early-warning systems for banks are by Sinkey (1975) and Hanweck (1977).

ing data capture key aspects of lending behavior, although attempts to capture the entire process have been less successful and certainly have not attracted researcher attention in recent years. Also, statistical formulas are available to predict a bank's status as a "problem" bank with reasonable accuracy. Such findings should prove useful to bank regulators. For regulators of accounting information (e.g., the FASB), however, the research offers few surprises. Still, it is reassuring to know that accounting data are primary inputs in numerous decision aids, screening devices, and other evaluative devices that bankers and other lenders appear to use.

Mergers and Acquisitions

Two areas of research regarding mergers and acquisitions provide evidence that may help investors gain from these transactions. The first concerns the stock price behavior of acquired and acquiring firms in the period preceding the merger or tender offer announcement. Obviously, a knowledge of those anticipatory movements provides a rationale for the second area of research—the development of models that use accounting and other information to assess the probability of merger or acquisition. The empirical studies agree that the analyst who picks firms subject to merger or tender offer obtains dramatic abnormal returns—the longer the lead time the better. And, even in those cases for which the offer is turned down, the shares seldom revert to their former levels. This section summarizes those two research areas. The relevant studies include Halpern (1973), Mandelker (1974), Langetieg (1978), and Dodd (1980), who studied the impact of mergers; and Dodd and Ruback (1977) and Kummer and Hoffmeister (1978), who estimated the price response to tender offers.

The methodologies of the studies reviewed are similar in that firms subject to tender offer or merger are grouped into a single portfolio. Their periodic returns (daily, weekly, etc.) are aligned so that the announcement date of tender offer or merger is time "zero." Then the returns are averaged cross-sectionally and are usually adjusted for risk and market-wide movements using the market model technique. (See Chapter 4 for an expanded discussion.)

Halpern studied 155 mergers from the 1950-1965 period. Both the smaller and the larger firms combined in the merger transaction experienced gains in stock price. The larger firms increased by about 6 percent; the smaller firms by roughly 30 percent. Mandelker divided his sample of mergers occurring in 1941-1962 into 252 acquired firms and 241 acquiring firms. Date "zero" was the month of consummation of the merger. The stockholders of acquired firms earned abnormal returns of approximately 14 percent over months -6 to 0. The acquiring firms experienced positive but insignificant excess returns over the same period. Langetieg amended Mandelker's procedures employing a more detailed methodology involving multi-index models and a nonmerging control group. The average excess return for 149 acquired firms is reported as 13 percent over the months -6 to -1. There is little evidence of anticipatory movement prior to six months before the merger. The acquiring firms gained to the extent of 6 percent in the months -18 to -7. However, the average price for those firms dropped in months -6 to 1.

Finally, Dodd used daily price change data to measure the magnitude of response to the first public announcement of the proposed merger. During trading days -10 to 10, target companies' prices improved by 34 percent on the average. Even target companies with tender offers subsequently vetoed by the incumbent management earned 11 percent abnormal returns in the -10 to 10 trading period. For these companies, a permanent revaluation of the target's stock occurred. On the other hand, the prices of the bidding firms' common stock dipped slightly (7 percent) during the same 21-trading-day period.

Two studies deal with the price effects of tender offers. The Dodd and Ruback (1977) sample covers successful and unsuccessful offers in the period 1958-1975. During the month of announcement, successful target companies rose 21 percent in price (after adjustment for market-wide effects). Also, for the unsuccessful target and "clean up" offers, the abnormal return was 19 percent and 17 percent, respectively. Note that the price rise for unsuccessful mergers and clean-up offers was not reversed in the months immediately thereafter. Kummer and Hoffmeister (1978) analyzed three groups with tender offers: (1) takeover was resisted and unsuccessful, (2) takeover was resisted and turned out successful, and (3) takeover

157

was not resisted and turned out successful. The price response in month zero is similar to that reported in Dodd and Ruback. However, prior to six months before the tender offer, the excess returns were negative. All firms performed poorly relative to the market portfolio. Group 1 firms fared worst, suffering a 22-percent negative return in months -40 to -4.

In short, the target-company or acquired-firm stockholders gain handsomely from mergers or tender offers. The evidence on whether the stockholders of merger-active, acquiring firms win or lose in terms of short-term price movements is less clear-cut. None of the studies implies, however, that mergers impose significant costs on the stockholders of acquiring firms, despite allegations to that effect.

Predicting the Candidates

A logical next step is to pursue the possibility of an early identification of merger and acquisition candidates using accounting information. Studies have been made of the financial characteristics of acquired versus nonacquired firms and whether such characteristics can optimally be combined to predict or classify correctly those firms likely to be acquired. Studies by Simkowitz and Monroe (1971) and Stevens (1973) are representative of the work in this area of research. Simkowitz and Monroe, for example, use discriminant analysis to evaluate differences between 23 "absorbed" firms and 25 "nonabsorbed" firms. Their conclusions: ". . . 1) The ability to discriminate and classify is upheld at better than the .01 level of significance; 2) Indications are that non-financial characteristics are important and should be included in any subsequent work; . . . and 3) The acquired firms appeared to have lower price: earnings ratios, to be smaller, and to have under-utilized their borrowing capabilities" (page 2).

Stevens raises questions about the Simkowitz-Monroe methodology. Using 40 acquired and 40 nonacquired firms, Stevens first applied factor analysis to highlight an appropriate group of uncorrelated explanatory variables before developing a discriminant model to predict possible takeover candidates. Four accounting-based ratios are shown to have a 68-percent accuracy on a validation sample (versus 50 percent with random prediction). The variables are, unfortunately, different from those identified in the Simkowitz-Monroe study. The author attributes such differences to design factors.

Thus, in conclusion, the limited research on merger prediction has shown only marginal success to date. Unresolved methodological issues are no doubt hampering further developments. None of the studies so far has dealt adequately with the usual shortcomings of work of this kind (e.g., failure to use random samples, violation of statistical assumptions, historical orientation, etc.). Nevertheless, even the crudest models based on published financial data have some practical merit, partly because there is usually very little to lose in picking a stock that is *not* taken over. One infrequent winner may well be enough to make a statistical stock selection strategy work most profitably. The strategy of certain mutual funds apparently functions in this manner (e.g., Over-the-Counter Securities Fund Inc., as reported in *Business Week,* January 14, 1980, page 101). Analysts, also, periodically release news sheets indicating the most likely takeover candidates. (See, for example, Maxwell [1977 and 1978].)

Prospective Cash Flow Assessments

The extent to which cash flows can be forecasted using alternative sets of accounting information poses an interesting empirical issue. As Chapter 4 indicates, the FASB holds one point of view: Financial reporting based on accrual accounting provides information about future cash flows that is better than other methods of reporting the underlying events and transactions (e.g., financial reporting based on cash receipts and payments). Today, however, many securities analysts stress an evaluation of past cash flows rather than past earnings. (See, for instance, Hawkins and Campbell [1978].)

Unfortunately, while the debate over cash flow versus accrual concepts is long-standing in accounting, there is almost no research that evaluates that issue empirically. One reason is that enterprise cash flows are generated in diverse ways over many periods and, hence, are not measurable in simple terms. Cash flows derive from the complex interactions of production, marketing, investment, and financing decisions made during the life of the enterprise. In a similar vein, studies of the predictability of cash flow from earnings are of only limited relevance. Cash flow from earnings (e.g., net earnings plus depreciation) is biased toward accounting procedures presently in use, which of course are accrual based. Historical cash flow, therefore, is not a good criterion for the evaluation of accounting alternatives. For example, Beaver, Griffin, and Landsman (1981) studied the ability of various measures of earnings growth to explain differences in security returns among 313 firms that filed replacement-cost data with the SEC. The correlations between security returns and percentage changes in historical cost earnings (0.37 for 1978 and 0.37 for 1977) were greater than those between security returns and percentage change in cash flow from earnings (0.31 for 1978 and 0.29 for 1977). Ball and Brown (1968) report similar results, although cash flow in their study was approximated by operating income.

Predicting Future Dividends

Only studies that specifically address the prediction of dividends are discussed here. The studies are of an extrapolative, time-series nature and more often than not rely on the methodologies and analytical techniques discussed in Chapter 5 (on the time-series properties of accounting numbers). Examples include Fama and Babiak (1968) and Fama (1974).[20]

Fama and Babiak test the "partial-adjustment model" suggested by Lintner (1956) which says that next period's change in dividends is a fraction of the difference between (1) management's target dividend payout (assumed proportional to next period's reported earnings) and (2) dividend payout this period. Based on data for 392 firms in years 1946-1964, Fama and Babiak conclude that the Lintner model with current earnings as an extra explanatory variable provides the best predictions of next period's dividend change relative to other versions of the partial-adjustment regression model. Certain naive models (e.g., next period's change in dividends equals this period's change in dividends), however, performed well relative to the various regression models.

Fama expands the number of explanatory variables to include past earnings and dividends as well as several investment- and output-related variables. According to Fama, the partial-adjustment model (with the constant term dropped) "does better than all other dividend regression models" (page 308). Further, its

---

[20]Studies that address the securities market reaction to changes in dividend policy are not addressed in this section. Brief reference is made to such studies in Chapter 8, in a discussion of the joint effects of earnings changes and dividend changes on security prices.

predictive ability was 20 percent or more greater than a naive model whose prediction was that changes in dividends in 1967 and 1968 were equal to the average annual change for the period 1946-1966. (Fama's tests were based on 298 firms; the models were developed from 1946-1966 data and the predictions were evaluated using 1967-1968 data.)

Thus, past earnings and past dividends would appear to be moderately successful in predicting future dividend payout, appropriately combined according to the Lintner formula. Unfortunately, the preceding results lack comparison with publicly available forecasts (e.g., by management) that in most cases are based on more extensive information. Penman (1981) provides an indirect test of ability to predict dividends using management's forecasts of earnings, rather than past earnings or dividends. This test evaluates the predictive ability of the following alternative earnings forecast models: (1) a forecast that assumes earnings is a random walk, (2) published management forecasts, and (3) a model based on forecasted dividend information derived from the Lintner model. The results show that the dividend-based forecasts of next year's reported earnings are "superior to both the martingale [random-walk] and the direct [management] forecast on all criteria except at the median where the direct forecast is slightly better" (page 12). Hence, while the partial-adjustment model is not the last word in dividend forecasting, dividend expectations are, apparently, useful in the assessment of next year's earnings.[21] Note, however, that the analysis is tied to earnings (as the object of prediction), not to prospective cash flow.

Concerns Expressed in Submissions to Standard-Setting Bodies

Research attempting to explain or predict a firm's or an individual's preferences with respect to an accounting standard is a relatively new branch of accounting research. The research finds encouragement in tentative new "theories" of regulatory behavior based on notions of self-interest. Watts and Zimmerman (1978), for

---

[21]That expectations of earnings based on dividend expectations (and past dividends) might in certain instances be more accurate than expectations of earnings based directly on management forecasts should not be too surprising. Management forecasts of earnings are subject to bias (e.g., optimism). Dividend policy, on the other hand, can reveal much about the future prospects of the firm.

instance, argue that management lobbies for or against accounting standards based on its private interests. Factors affecting a manager's welfare are purported to be taxes, regulation, political costs, and management compensation. The empirical analysis seeks to evaluate whether such factors are important determinants in a manager's decision to oppose or support an accounting proposal. The specific accounting issue studied by Watts and Zimmerman was the 1974 FASB proposal to require general price level accounting, later withdrawn and superseded by Statement 33. Watts and Zimmerman report that the strongest factor in discerning those for versus those against the general price level requirement is firm size—which they contend is a surrogate for the political costs faced by the firm. Small firms, being less visible, are apparently less sensitive to losses of wealth due to political costs than are large firms.

The observed size effect, however, was not uniformly supported by Hagerman and Zmijewski (1979), who studied whether choices regarding accounting methods for inventory, investment tax credits, depreciation, and past service pension costs were related to more basic economic factors. They were led to conclude, ". . . the important explanatory variables tend to be different for each accounting principle tested. This fact suggests that management may act as if they use different variables to make each decision" (page 157). In a later study, however, Zmijewski and Hagerman (1981) analyzed four accounting policies jointly. They concluded that firm size, existence of a profit-sharing plan, industry concentration, and leverage all influence the choice of a firm's accounting policy.

Two further preliminary investigations should be mentioned. Griffin's study (in press) of managements' responses to changes in foreign currency accounting rules identifies size as a statistically significant discriminatory variable. The larger and more highly leveraged firms were more likely to oppose the requirement of Statement 8 that foreign exchange gains and losses,whether realized or unrealized, be shown immediately in income.[22] Bowen, Lacey, and Noreen (1981) also suggest the importance of a size variable in explaining the preferences of firms with respect to the FASB's proposal to capitalize interest costs. Due to the potential impact of political costs, the largest firms in the oil industry did not encourage the interest capitalization alternative, which tends to increase both assets and earnings.

---

[22]See also Dhaliwal (1980).

Despite the advancement of tentative theories, the present research is mostly exploratory. An ultimate objective, however, is to understand better the regulatory process and, hence, predict the responses of those who participate in the standard-setting process. Such descriptive analysis could be useful in assessing the attitudes of investors, managers, and others toward proposed accounting changes, perhaps even before exposure to the public for comment. Also, nonrespondent views might be assessed by such descriptive analysis (i.e., inferred from an economic and statistical model). Knowledge of the likely comments of persons who do not participate in the standard-setting process could be potentially useful for policy, especially if the views of those who respond are biased.

In brief, these studies suggest that financial accounting and other economic data might be useful for understanding regulatory activity.[23] But research of this kind can only indirectly increase the usefulness of information in financial reports for investors and creditors. Its aim is to make the regulatory process more efficient, thus eventually benefiting all groups within the standard setter's purview (including investors and creditors).

Summary

The purpose of this chapter has been, first, to identify and discuss conceptual aspects relating to the "predictive value" of accounting information and, second, to examine and summarize the empirical research in six contexts for which accounting information has been examined for predictive ability. In some areas the research is comprehensive (e.g., on the prediction of financial distress); yet investigations in the other areas have barely scratched the surface (e.g., on the prediction of enterprise cash flows). While this body of knowledge should ultimately lead to better decision making by investors and creditors and their advisors—as in certain instances it has already done—it is doubtful that the empirical research has produced tangible results of direct applicability to those who must evaluate or select accounting alternatives. Attempts to adopt "ability to predict failure" as a criterion for ranking accounting alternatives have been unsuccessful so far.

---

[23]The idea is not unlike the notion that a firm displays a "corporate personality" in its financial statements. Sorter and Becker (1964) are generally attributed with introducing this idea into the accounting literature. The notion of corporate personality also pervades the popular view that firms have liberal versus conservative attitudes in their selection of accounting practices.

REFERENCES

Abdel-khalik, A. Rashad. "The Effect of Aggregating Accounting Reports on the Quality of the Lending Decision: An Empirical Investigation." *Journal of Accounting Research.* Supplement, *Empirical Research in Accounting: Selected Studies, 1973,* pp. 104-38.

Abdel-Khalik, A. Rashad, and El-Sheshai, Kamal M. "Information Choice and Utilization in an Experiment on Default Prediction." *Journal of Accounting Research,* Autumn 1980, pp. 325-42.

Aharony, Joseph; Jones, Charles P.; and Swary, Itzhak. "An Analysis of Risk and Return Characteristics of Corporate Bankruptcy Using Capital Market Data." *The Journal of Finance,* September 1980, pp. 1001-16.

Altman, Edward I. "Financial Ratios, Discriminant Analysis and the Prediction of Corporate Bankruptcy." *The Journal of Finance,* September 1968, pp. 589-609.

_____. "Predicting Railroad Bankruptcies in America." *The Bell Journal of Economics and Management Science,* Spring 1973, pp. 184-211.

_____. "Capitalization of Leases and the Predictability of Financial Results: A Comment." *The Accounting Review,* April 1976, pp. 408-12.

_____. "Predicting Performance in the Savings and Loan Association Industry." *Journal of Monetary Economics,* 1977. (1977a)

_____. "Some Estimates of the Cost of Lending Errors for Commercial Banks." *The Journal of Commercial Bank Lending,* October 1977, pp. 51-58. (1977b)

Altman, Edward I.; Haldeman, Robert G.; and Narayanan, P. "ZETA Analysis: A New Model to Identify Bankruptcy Risk of Corporations." *Journal of Banking and Finance,* June 1977, pp. 29-54.

Altman, Edward I., and Katz, Steven. "Statistical Bond Rating Classification Using Financial and Accounting Data." In *Proceedings of the Conference on Topical Research in Accounting,* edited by Michael Schiff and George Sorter, pp. 205-39. New York: Ross Institute of Accounting Research, New York University, 1976.

Altman, Edward I., and Loris, Bettina. "A Financial Early Warning System for Over-the-Counter Broker-Dealers." *The Journal of Finance,* September 1976, pp. 1201-17.

Backer, Morton, and Gosman, Martin L. *Financial Reporting and Business Liquidity.* New York: National Association of Accountants, 1978.

Ball, Ray, and Brown, Philip. "An Empirical Evaluation of Accounting Income Numbers." *Journal of Accounting Research,* Autumn 1968, pp. 159-78.

Beaver, William H. "Financial Ratios as Predictors of Failure." *Journal of Accounting Research.* Supplement, *Empirical Research in Accounting: Selected Studies, 1966,* pp. 71-111.

_____. "Alternative Accounting Measures as Predictors of Failure." *The Accounting Review,* January 1968, pp. 113-22. (1968a)

_____. "Market Prices, Financial Ratios, and the Prediction of Failure." *Journal of Accounting Research,* Autumn 1968, pp. 179-92. (1968b)

Beaver, William H.; Griffin, Paul A.; and Landsman, Wayne R. "The Correlation of Replacement Cost Earnings with Security Returns." Research paper, revised. Stanford, Calif.: Graduate School of Business, Stanford University, July 1981.

Beaver, William H.; Kennelly, John W.; and Voss, William M. "Predictive Ability as a Criterion for the Evaluation of Accounting Data." *The Accounting Review,* October 1968, pp. 675-83.

Blum, Marc. "Failing Company Discriminant Analysis." *Journal of Accounting Research,* Spring 1974, pp. 1-25.

Bowen, Robert; Lacey, John; and Noreen, Eric. "Determinants of the Corporate Decision to Capitalize Interest." *Journal of Accounting and Economics,* August 1981, pp. 150-70.

Carleton, Willard T., and Lerner, Eugene M. "Statistical Credit Scoring of Municipal Bonds." *Journal of Money, Credit and Banking,* November 1969, pp. 750-64.

Carsberg, Bryan; Arnold, John; and Hope, Anthony. "Predictive Value: A Criterion for Choice of Accounting Method." In *Studies in Accounting,* edited by W. T. Baxter and Sidney Davidson, pp. 403-23. 3d ed. London: The Institute of Chartered Accountants in England and Wales, 1977.

Casey, Cornelius J., Jr. "The Effect of Accounting Information Load on Bank Loan Officers' Predictions of Bankruptcy." *The Journal of Commercial Bank Lending,* August 1978, pp. 46-60.

Clarkson, Geoffrey P. E. *Portfolio Selection: A Simulation of Trust Investment.* Englewood Cliffs, N.J.: Prentice-Hall, Inc., 1962.

Cohen, Kalman J.; Gilmore, T. C.; and Singer, F. A. "Bank Procedures for Analyzing Business Loan Applications." In *Analytical Methods in Banking,* edited by Kalman J. Cohen and Frederick S. Hammer. The Irwin Series in Finance. Homewood, Ill.: Richard D. Irwin, Inc., 1966.

Dawes, Robyn M., and Corrigan, Bernard. "Linear Models in Decision Making." *Psychological Bulletin,* February 1974, pp. 95-106.

Deakin, Edward B. "A Discriminant Analysis of Predictors of Business Failure." *Journal of Accounting Research,* Spring 1972, pp. 167-79.

Dhaliwal, Dan S. "The Effect of the Firm's Capital Structure on the Choice of Accounting Methods." *The Accounting Review,* January 1980, pp. 78-84.

Dietrich, J. Richard, and Kaplan, Robert S. "Empirical Analysis of the Commercial Loan Classification Decision." *The Accounting Review,* January 1982, pp. 18-38.

166

Dodd, Peter. "Merger Proposals, Management Discretion and Stockholder Wealth." *Journal of Financial Economics,* June 1980, pp. 105-37.

Dodd, Peter, and Ruback, Richard. "Tender Offers and Stockholder Returns: An Empirical Analysis." *Journal of Financial Economics,* December 1977, pp. 351-73.

Dutton, John M., and Starbuck, William H. *Computer Simulation of Human Behavior.* New York: John Wiley & Sons, Inc., 1971.

Edmister, Robert O. "An Empirical Test of Financial Ratio Analysis for Small Business Failure Prediction." *Journal of Financial and Quantitative Analysis,* March 1972, pp. 1477-93.

Elam, Rick. "The Effect of Lease Data on the Predictive Ability of Financial Ratios." *The Accounting Review,* January 1975, pp. 25-43.

Ewert, David C. *Trade Credit Management: Selection of Accounts Receivable Using a Statistical Model.* Research monograph, no. 79. Atlanta: College of Business Administration, Georgia State University, 1980.

Fama, Eugene F. "The Empirical Relationships between the Dividend and Investment Decisions of Firms." *The American Economic Review,* June 1974, pp. 304-18.

Fama, Eugene F., and Babiak, Harvey. "Dividend Policy: An Empirical Analysis." *Journal of the American Statistical Association,* December 1968, pp. 1132-61.

Fraser, Donald R., and McCormack, J. Patrick. "Large Bank Failures and Investor Risk Perceptions: Evidence from the Debt Market." *Journal of Financial and Quantitative Analysis,* September 1978, pp. 527-32.

Greenball, M. N. "The Predictive-Ability Criterion: Its Relevance in Evaluating Accounting Data." *Abacus,* July 1971, pp. 1-7.

Grier, Paul, and Katz, Steven. "The Differential Effects of Bond Rating Changes among Industrial and Public Utility Bonds by

Maturity." *The Journal of Business,* April 1976, pp. 226-39.

Griffin, Paul A. "Foreign Exchange Gains and Losses: Impact on Reported Earnings." *Abacus,* in press.

Griffin, Paul A., and Sanvicente, Antonio Z. "Common Stock Returns and Rating Changes: A Methodological Comparison." *The Journal of Finance,* in press.

Hagerman, Robert L., and Zmijewski, Mark E. "Some Economic Determinants of Accounting Policy Choice." *Journal of Accounting & Economics,* August 1979, pp. 141-61.

Halpern, Paul J. "Empirical Estimates of the Amount and Distribution of Gains to Companies in Mergers." *The Journal of Business,* October 1973, pp. 554-75.

Hanweck, Gerald A. "Predicting Bank Failure." Research Papers in Banking and Financial Economics. Washington, D.C.: Financial Studies Section, Division of Research and Statistics, Board of Governors of the Federal Reserve System, November 1977.

Harmelink, Philip J. "An Empirical Examination of the Predictive Ability of Alternate Sets of Insurance Company Accounting Data." *Journal of Accounting Research,* Spring 1973, pp. 146-58.

Hawkins, David F., and Campbell, Walter J. *Equity Valuation: Models, Analysis and Implications.* Research study and report. New York: Financial Executives Research Foundation, 1978.

Hettenhouse, George W., and Sartoris, William L. "An Analysis of the Informational Value of Bond-Rating Changes." *The Quarterly Review of Economics & Business,* Summer 1976, pp. 65-78.

Horrigan, James O. "The Determination of Long-Term Credit Standing with Financial Ratios." *Journal of Accounting Research.* Supplement, *Empirical Research in Accounting: Selected Studies, 1966,* pp. 44-62.

Horton, Joseph J., Jr. "Statistical Classification of Municipal Bonds." *Journal of Bank Research,* Autumn 1970, pp. 29-40.

Kaplan, Robert S., and Urwitz, Gabriel. "Statistical Models of Bond Ratings: A Methodological Inquiry." *The Journal of Business,* April 1979, pp. 231-61.

Katz, Steven. "The Price Adjustment Process of Bonds to Rating Reclassifications: A Test of Bond Market Efficiency." *The Journal of Finance,* May 1974, pp. 551-59.

Ketz, J. Edward. "The Effect of General Price-Level Adjustments on the Predictive Ability of Financial Ratios." *Journal of Accounting Research.* Supplement 1978, *Studies on Accounting for Changes in General and Specific Prices: Empirical Research and Public Policy Issues,* pp. 273-84.

Kinney, William R., Jr. "Discussion of a Prediction of Business Failure Using Accounting Data." *Journal of Accounting Research.* Supplement, *Empirical Research in Accounting: Selected Studies, 1973,* pp. 183-87.

Kummer, Donald R., and Hoffmeister, Ronald. "Valuation Consequences of Cash Tender Offers." *The Journal of Finance,* May 1978, pp. 505-16.

Langetieg, Terence C. "An Application of a Three-Factor Performance Index to Measure Stockholder Gains from Merger." *Journal of Financial Economics,* December 1978, pp. 365-83.

Lintner, John. "Distribution of Incomes of Corporations among Dividends, Retained Earnings, and Taxes." *The American Economic Review,* May 1956, pp. 97-113.

Mandelker, Gershon. "Risk and Return: The Case of Merging Firms." *Journal of Financial Economics,* December 1974, pp. 303-35.

Maxwell, F. Rollins. "Acquisition Candidates." Mimeographed. New York: E.F. Hutton Investment Research Department, December 28, 1977.

169

_____. "Acquisition Candidates II." Mimeographed. New York: E.F. Hutton Investment Research Department, May 15, 1978.

Moody's Investors Service, Inc. *Moody's Bond Record,* July 1976.

Neter, John. "Discussion of Financial Ratios as Predictors of Failure." *Journal of Accounting Research.* Supplement, *Empirical Research in Accounting: Selected Studies, 1966,* pp. 112-18.

Norton, Curtis L., and Smith, Ralph E. "A Comparison of General Price Level and Historical Cost Financial Statements in the Prediction of Bankruptcy." *The Accounting Review,* January 1979, pp. 72-87.

_____. "A Comparison of General Price Level and Historical Cost Financial Statements in the Prediction of Bankruptcy: A Reply." *The Accounting Review,* July 1980, pp. 516-21.

Ohlson, James A. "Financial Ratios and the Probabilistic Prediction of Bankruptcy." *Journal of Accounting Research,* Spring 1980, pp. 109-31.

Oliver, Bruce L. "A Study of Confidence Interval Financial Statements." *Journal of Accounting Research,* Spring 1972, pp. 154-66.

Orgler, Yair E. "A Credit Scoring Model for Commercial Loans." *Journal of Money, Credit and Banking,* vol. 2, November 1970, pp. 435-45.

Patell, James M. "Discussion of the Impact of Price-Level Adjustment in the Context of Risk Assessment and the Effect of General Price-Level Adjustments on the Predictive Ability of Financial Ratios." *Journal of Accounting Research.* Supplement 1978, *Studies on Accounting for Changes in General and Specific Prices: Empirical Research and Public Policy Issues,* pp. 293-300.

Penman, Stephen H. "Tests of Dividend-Signaling: A Comparative Analysis." Research paper. Berkeley: School of Business Administration, University of California, September 1981.

Pettway, Richard H. "Potential Insolvency, Market Efficiency, and Bank Regulation of Large Commercial Banks." *Journal of Financial and Quantitative Analysis,* March 1980, pp. 219-36.

Pettway, Richard H., and Sinkey, Joseph F., Jr. "Establishing On-Site Bank Examination Priorities: An Early-Warning System Using Accounting and Market Information." *The Journal of Finance,* March 1980, pp. 137-50.

Pinches, George E., and Mingo, Kent A. "A Multivariate Analysis of Industrial Bond Ratings." *The Journal of Finance,* March 1973, pp. 1-18.

Pinches, George E., and Singleton, J. Clay. "The Adjustment of Stock Prices to Bond Rating Changes." *The Journal of Finance,* March 1978, pp. 29-44.

Pogue, Thomas F., and Soldofsky, Robert M. "What's in a Bond Rating?" *Journal of Financial and Quantitative Analysis,* June 1969, pp. 201-28.

Ross, Irwin. "Higher Stakes in the Bond-Rating Game." *Fortune,* April 1976, p. 133.

Santomero, Anthony M., and Vinso, Joseph D. "Estimating the Probability of Failure for Commercial Banks and Banking System." *Journal of Banking and Finance,* October 1977, pp. 185-205.

Schipper, Katherine. "Financial Distress in Private Colleges." *Journal of Accounting Research.* Supplement 1977, *Studies on Measurement and Evaluation of the Economic Efficiency of Public and Private Nonprofit Institutions,* pp. 1-40.

Simkowitz, Michael, and Monroe, Robert J. "A Discriminant Analysis Function for Conglomerate Targets." Extracted from *The Southern Journal of Business,* November 1971, pp. 1-16.

Sinkey, Joseph F., Jr. "A Multivariate Statistical Analysis of the Characteristic of Problem Banks." *The Journal of Finance,* March 1975, pp. 21-36.

Solomon, Ira, and Beck, Paul J. "A Comparison of General Price Level and Historical Cost Financial Statements in the Prediction of Bankruptcy: A Comment." *The Accounting Review,* July 1980, pp. 511-15.

Sorter, George H., and Becker, Selwyn W.; assisted by Archibald, T. R., and Beaver, W. "Corporate Personality as Reflected in Accounting Decisions: Some Preliminary Findings." *Journal of Accounting Research,* Autumn 1964, pp. 183-96.

Stevens, Donald L. "Financial Characteristics of Merged Firms: A Multivariate Analysis." *Journal of Financial and Quantitative Analysis,* March 1973, pp. 149-58.

Vinso, Joseph D. "A Determination of the Risk of Ruin." *Journal of Financial and Quantitative Analysis,* March 1979, pp. 77-100.

Watts, Ross L., and Zimmerman, Jerold L. "Towards a Positive Theory of the Determination of Accounting Standards." *The Accounting Review,* January 1978, pp. 112-34.

Weinstein, Mark I. "The Effect of a Rating Change Announcement on Bond Price." *Journal of Financial Economics,* December 1977, pp. 329-50.

West, Richard R. "An Alternative Approach to Predicting Corporate Bond Ratings." *Journal of Accounting Research,* Spring 1970, pp. 118-25.

_____. "Bond Ratings, Bond Yields and Financial Regulation: Some Findings." *The Journal of Law and Economics,* April 1973, pp. 159-68.

Wilcox, Jarrod W. "A Simple Theory of Financial Ratios as Predictors of Failure." *Journal of Accounting Research,* Autumn 1971, pp. 389-95.

_____. "A Prediction of Business Failure Using Accounting Data." *Journal of Accounting Research.* Supplement, *Empirical Research in Accounting: Selected Studies, 1973,* pp. 163-79.

_____. "The Gambler's Ruin Approach to Business Risk." *Sloan Management Review,* Fall 1976, pp. 33-46.

Zeta Services, Inc. "Zeta." Mimeographed. Mountainside, N.J.: Zeta Services, Inc., 1979.

Zmijewski, Mark E., and Hagerman, Robert L. "An Income Strategy Approach to the Positive Theory of Accounting Standard Setting/Choice." *Journal of Accounting and Economics,* August 1981, pp. 129-49.

CHAPTER 8—RESEARCH ON THE USE OF INFORMATION IN CAPITAL MARKETS

The evaluation of accounting numbers and other financial disclosures will be greatly enhanced by an understanding of the relationship between the financial reporting process and the behavior of securities markets. Market behavior summarizes the activities of all traders competing under conditions of risk and uncertainty. As such, an analysis of market response to accounting information provides more objective indicators of investors' and creditors' activities than other means (e.g., questionnaires or interviews) of explaining or predicting those activities.

The growth in this area of research, since about 1968, has been extraordinary—probably greater than any other area of accounting research. Armed with a theoretical framework, an empirical methodology, and comprehensive stock price histories, accounting researchers have been able to analyze an extensive array of issues concerning the informational content of accounting numbers. Most observers would agree that their efforts have been fruitful.

However, much depends on how the phrase *the informational content of accounting numbers* is defined. As Gonedes and Dopuch (1974) cogently argue, knowledge of certain links between security prices and accounting alternatives does not by itself provide an ordering of the "*desirability* of alternative accounting techniques or regulations" (page 114). Nonetheless, as discussed throughout this chapter, that knowledge may be of considerable benefit to accounting policymakers and others who select or evaluate accounting and reporting alternatives.

It is important to examine not only the results of research, but also the methodology of that research. Some inquiries that purport to study informational content may be so deficient in their design that their results must be completely discounted. If that is the case, those studies are totally useless to accounting policymakers. Fortunately, issues of methodology are now receiving more attention. Accounting researchers—spurred by questions of the empirical validity of certain financial theories and aware of the limitations of their own previous analyses—are furthering their efforts with sharper statistical tests. Indeed, the whole province of security price research seems well poised to enter a new era—if it has not done so already.

Since several excellent surveys of the earlier studies are available (Beaver [1972]; Gonedes and Dopuch [1974]; Lev [1974]; Dyckman, Downes, and Magee [1975]; Foster [1978]; Kaplan [1978]), the emphasis in this chapter is on a review and synthesis of the more recent literature.[1] Overlap with the 1968-1978 literature, however, is unavoidable. The review begins with a discussion of the design of security price research studies. The material is then classified into five broad categories: (1) basic results: apparent use by investors; (2) earnings components, earnings versus dividends, and other disclosures; (3) accounting changes and alternative acceptable methods; (4) estimating and predicting relative risk; and (5) recent developments.

Research Design

The common thread that binds the various studies is their research design. Researchers must consider the following features of that design: (1) definition and measurement of statistical association, (2) what is "good" research? (3) specification of the dependent variable, (4) timing of the "event," and (5) selection of the independent variable. Each feature is looked at separately.

Statistical Association: Definition and Measurement

The most basic objective in every study is to estimate the association between changes in security prices (or a variant thereof) and some characteristic of the financial report, accounting system, etc., being examined. A significant association—measured as a degree of statistical dependency—is then viewed as consistent with the contention that the information, accounting system, etc., under consideration has an effect on security prices and hence possesses informational content.

A statistical association or dependency may be measured by one of three scales: nominal, ordinal, or interval. A "nominal" test of dependency simply examines whether prices (or returns) are different—with and without or before and after the new information (e.g., an earnings report). The second, an "ordinal" test, assesses whether returns are higher or lower when the new informa-

---

[1]Other recent surveys include Benston (1980) and Abdel-khalik and Ajinkya (1981).

tion is viewed positively or negatively, respectively. The test is dichotomous in that it assumes any two firms or portfolios can be ranked as exhibiting more or less of some dimension, or that they can be otherwise evaluated as good or bad, positive or negative, etc. Accounting signals may, for instance, be predicted to have positive or negative implications for purposes of assessing future cash flows. Alternative accounting systems may also be predicted to have adverse or salutary effects on the value of the firm. The third procedure, an "interval scale" test, evaluates an explicit functional relationship between prices and information. Linear or proportional relationships are the most common in the absence of evidence or theory that would suggest otherwise. A simple linear-regression equation involving price changes and earnings changes is frequently used in such tests.

In short, the objective in security price research is to observe whether a particular item of information, accounting system, or other accounting-related event has either (1) a security price effect (a nominal test), (2) a price effect in a predicted direction (an ordinal test), or (3) a price effect in a predicted direction and of a certain magnitude (an interval-scale test). Accounting researchers have utilized all three strategies.

What Is "Good" Research?

A good research methodology should satisfy two fundamental criteria. First, it should explain and specify the relationships to be tested, recognizing relevant theoretical and statistical considerations in constructing the test. Researchers call this *experimental design*. Second, it should control, hold constant, or otherwise extract all factors that might affect security prices at the same time as the information being examined. When an association is observed, an assurance that it is due to the variable(s) being tested, and not to some other (perhaps unknown) correlated factors, should be soundly established. The design should also minimize unwanted noise which might serve to obscure any relationships that exist between the variables in question. These latter aspects encompass the concept of *experimental control*.

Specification of the Dependent Variable

In security price research, the variable to be predicted or explained—the dependent variable—is change in security price (security return) or some variant such as yield, volatility, security beta, etc.[2] If security return is specified as the dependent variable, two broad design options are available to the researcher.

The first design option uses the market model, which splits return into two components—one component perfectly correlated with an index of return on the market portfolio, the other constructed to have no correlation with the market. It is this latter component, adjusted to have zero mean, that is a primary measure of the effects of information released by a firm. (Information that affects the returns of all firms, as reflected in a market index, is not reflected in this measure.) The measure goes by several names: unexpected return, unsystematic return, risk-adjusted return, abnormal return, excess return, or residual return, for example.

As the effects of the market are extracted before the statistical analysis, unexpected return based on a random sample of all firms in the economy should be only minimally influenced by factors beyond those that are company-specific. However, if the sample is small or restricted to a few industries, elements that are not company-specific may become factored into the overall results. Hence, unexpected return will not truly reflect company-specific phenomena. Should the information or event affect all firms similarly (e.g., the impact on earnings of a favorable tax ruling), unexpected return will not reflect such price effects since they are picked up in the market return (which by design is uncorrelated with unexpected return).

Rather than assume that returns conform to the market model, researchers often choose the second route: assuming a theoretical model of asset pricing and estimating expected return based on the predictions of that model. The difference between actual return and expected return (predicted just before the release of the information in question) is defined as the unexpected (abnormal, etc.) security return. Expected return could also be estimated by use of a control sample equivalent in all factors that influence return except the information in question. This approach, however, still assumes an implicit model of asset pricing.

In sum, researchers use two basic definitions of unexpected

---

[2]Recall that *yield* is a measure of average return for a period, *volatility* is generally measured as the variance or standard deviation of return, and *beta* is a risk measure reflecting the variation of a security's return with the return on the market index.

return—one based on the market model, the other based on an asset-pricing model.[3]

Timing of the "Event"

All tests of informational content must state *when* the information becomes available for use by investors and creditors. Only if the precise timing is known (e.g., to the hour or even the minute and second) can one make reasonably sure statements about whether, when, and possibly how much the market reacted to the release of information. Unfortunately, assumptions must often be made either because it is costly for the researcher to do otherwise or because the information may have reached the public in a roundabout manner. It is extremely difficult, for instance, to pinpoint when the market actually learns of changes in accounting and reporting pronouncements. Similarly, if information is costly, it may be available to one subset of investors and creditors but not to others. It is difficult to discern the exact time when information possessed by an analyst, for example, reaches an investment firm's preferred clients, as opposed to when that information finally reaches the public. Of course, all is not lost if assumptions as to timing are made. Cross-sectional and temporal averaging, a technique used in most studies, serves to reduce error as long as the error in timing for one firm is unrelated to the timing error of another firm.

Selection of Independent Variables

The explanatory or independent variables in security price research are derived from characteristics of the information in financial reports, the accounting system, or other accounting-related phenonema. Such variables are usually, though not always, accounting numbers. Two adjustments are typically made to those numbers before statistical analysis. The first is to estimate the

---

[3]In practical applications, of course, there exists a wide spectrum of unexpected return definitions, each dictated by the numerous decisions to be made in designing the actual "experiment." For example, one must specify the form of the return variable, the precise version of the market model or asset-pricing model, the appropriate market index, the expected timing of release of information (since such timing determines the selection of periods for the estimation of model parameters), methods of aggregation for the cross-sectional analysis, and so on.

"news" content of the number by comparing it with a forecast or expectation of the number known by investors and creditors before its release. In an informationally efficient market, that expectation would already be impounded in security prices. Second, a portion of that unexpected component is adjusted for any market-wide factors. For example, an unexpected change in a firm's earnings would normally be measured relative to past changes in that firm's earnings and relative to changes in earnings for the market as a whole. The idea is to focus on unanticipated changes in earnings not related to the unanticipated changes in the earnings of other firms (the average effect of which is captured by a market-earnings index). Unexpected earnings may be used to rank the firms or, more simply, to divide firms into groups. A useful grouping is to divide firms into those whose unexpected earnings are positive ("good news" is implied) and those whose unexpected earnings are negative ("bad news" is implied).[4]

Groupings not directly based on accounting numbers are also used. Examples of categories include: accounting system or method, form of disclosure, whether the accounting method has been changed, whether the new information is supplied voluntarily or involuntarily, and whether the firm opposes or supports the ruling. Further, numerical groupings may be combined with groupings based on categories. For instance, one might want to study the earnings impact (a numerical grouping) for firms that switched accounting methods versus those that did not (a categorical grouping). Most of the initial studies used just one independent variable to explain changes in market prices or returns.

Summary

To properly use the results from research, it is imperative to have some understanding of the concepts of research methodology. Research results are only as good as the methods by which they are

---

[4]The unexpected component of an accounting number (e.g., earnings), however, is not always adjusted for market-wide factors, especially if such factors are insignificant in explaining earnings changes. The decision to adjust often turns on the extent of correlation between the unexpected components of any two firms. If, for example, unexpected earnings were highly correlated because of a sharp, unanticipated downturn in the economy, the market adjustment would most likely be appropriate, since without it unexpected earnings for any two firms would be a mixture of firm-specific effects and common (market) factors.

produced. The studies summarized in this chapter focus on three measures of association between security prices (the dependent variable) and accounting information (the independent or explanatory variable): in terms of whether, at a point in time, there was (1) an effect on security prices, (2) an effect in the right direction, and (3) an effect in the right direction of a certain magnitude. Those effects are measured statistically using either a market-model or an asset-pricing model and then examined with respect to the release of information, change in accounting method, or other accounting phenomenon.

Basic Results: Apparent Use by Investors

Annual Reports

The initial question posed by researchers was the most basic of all: Is the information initially announced in *The Wall Street Journal* and subsequently published in annual reports used by investors? Benston (1967) and Ball and Brown (1968) performed the initial experiments on NYSE firms using unexpected security return as the dependent variable. Benston tested for a relationship between unexpected security returns and unexpected earnings and sales data. Based on a regression equation, Benston found that the responsiveness of price change to earnings change was small. The largest of the responsiveness coefficients was 0.18 (for sales), and the coefficients for earnings were in the vicinity of 0.02. In other words, if earnings were to double unexpectedly, Benston's research would predict a two-percent abnormal rise in stock prices. However, despite the low response of security prices to accounting data, both earnings and sales variables were statistically significant as explanatory factors in the regression equation.

Whereas Benston examined a regression relationship (an interval-scale test), the Ball and Brown study placed fewer demands on the data, focusing only on whether the sign of the change in unexpected earnings was positively correlated with the sign of the unexpected or abnormal price change (an ordinal test). Ball and Brown examined unexpected security returns measured over the 12 months before an annual earnings announcement. Unexpected annual earnings were measured dichotomously as either good news (positive unexpected earnings) or bad news (negative unexpected earnings). Ball and Brown found that good-news firms increased in price by roughly

181

7.3 percent in 12 months before the earnings announcement (months -11 to 0), while the firms with bad news declined by 9.5 percent in the same 12 months. They also observed that prices anticipated the annual earnings announcement by many months. Ball and Brown state, ". . . of the value of information contained in reported income, no more than about 10 to 15 per cent . . . has not been anticipated . . ." (page 175).

Such results are consistent with a market that uses a broad array of information, information that is correlated with the annual numbers, but preempts much of that information because of its timeliness (e.g., quarterly data). However, there is another explanation for the Ball and Brown result of little price effect in the month of annual earnings announcement.

Because the sign of unexpected earnings in Ball and Brown is based on previous annual data, the partitioning variable (i.e., good news versus bad news) becomes increasingly inaccurate as the date of announcement is approached. Whatever news is released in the intervening months, while obviously affecting market expectations during those months, is ignored in the research design. As Beaver (1981) states, ". . . it is hardly surprising that a residual earnings change, defined relative to a benchmark where the most recent firm-specific information is last year's earnings, has limited ability to predict the direction of the price change in the final month of the announcement" (pages 133 and 134).

The Ball and Brown approach has been evaluated in numerous contexts with similar results. Alternative research designs were examined in Beaver and Dukes (1972), who expanded the set of annual earnings variables and earnings expectations models, and Gonedes (1974), who expanded the set of accounting ratios to include variables other than earnings. The results have been replicated for exchanges other than the NYSE. (Foster [1975a] studied insurance companies on the over-the-counter market.) The results have also been replicated for exchanges in other countries. (Brown [1970] studied the Australian stock market; Deakin, Norwood, and Smith [1974] examined the Tokyo exchange; and Firth [1976] investigated firms in the United Kingdom.)

Interim Reports

The next logical step was to explore the association between price changes and quarterly earnings changes. Brown and Kennelly

(1972) and Foster (1977a) present the key findings based on NYSE firms. Brown and Kennelly demonstrated that monthly returns and unexpected quarterly earnings are correlated, even in the month that quarterly results are announced. Foster extends the analysis using daily unexpected return data and refined models of quarterly earnings expectations (Chapter 5). Foster reports that firms with positive unexpected changes in quarterly earnings experienced positive abnormal returns, and vice versa. Market reaction was observed in all four quarters to about the same degree. More important, perhaps, is that, unlike the Ball and Brown results, the strongest price response was felt on the day before and the day of *The Wall Street Journal*'s announcement of interim results. Earnings expectations based on past quarterly data, hence, appear to be relevant for the assessment of security return at the time of interim earnings announcement.

Overall, these studies present sound evidence to suggest that unexpected earnings changes—annual or quarterly—and unexpected price changes or returns move in the same direction. This basic result is but one means of ascribing informational content to accounting numbers.

Do Prices "Drift" after Earnings Announcement?

An interesting group of studies has examined so-called drifts in stock prices subsequent to the announcement of quarterly earnings. These investigations contend that the adjustment of prices to quarterly information is somehow delayed, thereby raising the possibility of a market inefficiency. Joy, Litzenberger, and McEnally (1977) on NYSE firms; Brown (1978) on NYSE and AMEX firms; Watts (1978) on NYSE firms; and other studies suggest that upward drift occurs for firms with large unexpected earnings increases in the two to three months following quarterly announcement. This led several authors to claim that the market is inefficient with respect to quarterly earnings. Watts, for example, in discussing other explanations, argues that the research "indicates that deficiencies in the capital asset pricing model cannot be accepted as an explanation of the observed abnormal returns" (page 146). However, preliminary analysis by Foster and Olsen (1980) on NYSE and AMEX firms, while confirming the drift in prices, suggests that differential firm size and dividend yield may account for a good portion of the drift, thus implying that the previous research may have been deficient in the estimation of unexpected return.

In sum, no single result appears to explain the drift phenomenon sufficiently well. Note that if the market is truly inefficient, investors are apparently not exploiting their knowledge of the drift that occurs (which ostensibly provides opportunity for excess returns). But why would rational individuals allow such a situation to persist for long periods? Surely, their investment strategies would eventually compete away such excess returns. The research thus far leaves that issue essentially unresolved.

Volatility Studies

Informational content may be ascribed to accounting numbers, accounting systems, etc., in a manner even more simple than the correlational analysis described in the preceding section. The idea is to estimate unexpected return before, during, and after the announcement of an "event" of interest (e.g., earnings disclosure, release of a financial report). The simpler approach, which researchers call a nominal test, makes no distinction between the positive and negative implications of the impact of the announcement. The only issue is whether the securities market's response at the time of the announcement is greater than the response of the market in a period during which no announcements are made. The inference is that the larger price responses observed are a result of the information conveyed in the announcement. One must obviously be careful in defining the no-announcement period. Such periods are generally considered as those during which the flow of information to the market is "normal."

Beaver (1968) provides the earliest application of this research procedure. Residual return variance (i.e., residual return squared) for noncalendar-year NYSE firms was shown to be 67 percent greater in the week of annual earnings announcement than residual return variance in the other weeks. Thus, unexpected price changes were noticeably larger when the market learned of reported annual earnings, relative to other times of the year.

The Beaver result has been replicated many times with essentially equivalent results. May (1971) examined the quarterly earnings announcements of AMEX firms using weekly data; Hagerman (1973) measured the effects of annual and quarterly announcements for over-the-counter bank stocks using weekly data; Jordan (1973), using NYSE daily data, measured responses to quarterly announcements of growth stocks; and Griffin (1977) and Foster and Vickrey (1978), using NYSE weekly prices, and Morse (1981), using daily prices from all exchanges, also report significant announcement effects. Morse, for example, shows that the strongest price reaction occurs on the day before and the day of the announcement in *The Wall Street Journal.*

The effects on return volatility of the filing of the SEC Form 10-K, reported in Foster and Vickrey, are only marginally significant. That is not surprising since the 10-K report is usually filed well after the preliminary earnings announcement and often after the release of the annual report. Finally, there is an application of the methodology to the New York bond market. In Davis, Boatsman, and Baskin (1978), percentage bond price changes adjusted for market-wide effects were tracked before, during, and after the announcement of earnings. Larger bond price changes were observed at the time of annual announcement for convertible issues. A diffused response was observed for nonconvertible bonds. The authors concluded that earnings data were informative to bondholders.

In brief, the volatility studies provide solid evidence concerning the effect the timing of an announcement has on security prices: Announcements of reported earnings are most definitely accompanied by larger than usual unexpected stock price changes. Further, the "spike" in return volatility happens with the timing of the announcement—to the day—even though the results of the preceding section suggest that much of the value of the information in accounting reports may have been preempted by more timely sources. Caution is advised, however, that such results can never "prove" that investors actually use the information in the announcements. But to the extent that the timing of the event and the price response are virtually synchronous, considerable doubt is cast over other possible explanations (e.g., that unknown variables trigger the response). The case for a "stimulus-response" relationship is thus well established. That conviction is corroborated by analysis of a third group of studies, discussed in the next section.

Magnitude and Responsiveness Effects

A third group of studies is concerned with not only the timing and direction of unexpected price changes, but also the relationship between unexpected price changes and the strength or magnitude of accounting variables. In the case of reported earnings, the researcher seeks to establish whether larger changes in unexpected earnings are positively correlated with larger abnormal price changes. Beaver, Clarke, and Wright (1979) conclude that such a relationship holds: The ranking of 25 NYSE-listed portfolios on the basis of *percentage change* in unexpected earnings per share was essentially the same as was achieved in ranking on the basis of unexpected price change. These rankings were not perfect, however; they showed a correlation coefficient of 0.74. Hence, there is strong indication of a positive relationship between the size of unexpected earnings and the amount of unexpected price change associated with their release.

However, such positive association in sign and magnitude does not imply that a change in one variable implies change of an equal amount in the other. As reported in one of the earliest security price studies (Benston [1967]), the responsiveness of price changes to earnings changes is rather small. Benston's responsiveness coefficient was "around two percent" for unexpected earnings. Beaver, Lambert, and Morse (1980) present more recent results. Using a somewhat different research design, Beaver et al. report that the responsiveness coefficient (for NYSE firms) averaged 0.12. An overall conclusion is thus established: Stock prices can be expected to change in the same direction as unexpected earnings, but only by a small fraction of the unexpected earnings change. The relationship is considerably less than one-to-one.

There are various interpretations of this result. Beaver et al., for example, suggest that investors perceive a portion of any unexpected earnings increase as short-lived, boosting only the current period's reported earnings, while the remainder is perceived to be permanent or sustainable and hence expected to affect future earnings and dividend-paying ability. Consequently, the larger this permanent component in earnings, the greater the price response is likely to be. The low responsiveness of prices to earnings may also be explained by the overall structure of the accounting and reporting process. For example, security prices may be responding to information more detailed than aggregate earnings (e.g., line-of-business data, nonaccounting information, or both). Also, earnings may change due to changes in measurement methods, which have few implications for the assessment of return.

Summary

The studies identified in this section present convincing evidence that accounting information—especially earnings—possesses informational content. The research shows three major results: (1) Securities prices respond contemporaneously with the announcement of earnings, despite the availability of other, more timely data such as dividend and forecast announcements. (2) At the time of announcement, unexpected earnings and unexpected price changes are positively correlated in both direction and magnitude. (3) The responsiveness of unexpected price changes to unexpected earnings is positive but small (though statistically significant). Hence, it is almost inconceivable that investors do not find information about earnings useful for investment decision making.

Annual Report and Other Disclosures

The findings presented thus far are mostly silent about whether and to what extent investors respond to the formal annual report and the numbers published therein. These issues are examined in this section. Evidence on three research questions is discussed: (1) Do the components of earnings possess informational content? (2) To what extent are earnings and dividend announcements providing similar information? (3) What has been the impact of various disclosure standards of the FASB and the SEC?

Earnings Components

First, attention is focused on the value of line-of-business information. Do such earnings components convey information to investors? Collins (1975) hypothesized that if investors can more accurately forecast earnings by using line-of-business information (rather than consolidated data alone) their investment strategies should benefit from this—provided the extra information was not publicly available. Using NYSE firms, Collins reported that in only two (1968 and 1969) of the three years examined could the non-public segment data (principally segment sales) have been used to increase returns. Yet, since excess returns were generated for two years, Collins implied that segmental results do have informational content in addition to aggregate sales or earnings.

Kochanek (1974), with extensions by Griffin and Nichols (1976), addressed a slightly different issue, concentrating on differences in the market's anticipation of reported annual earnings. The security prices of NYSE firms with extensive segmental data were found to adjust to future earnings announcements before the prices of those firms with minimal segmental data. The implication is that, other things equal, information regarding the former group of firms permits better forecasting of future earnings by users.[5]

Horwitz and Kolodny (1977) examined the impact of the 1970 SEC decision to require profit reporting by line of business. For NYSE or AMEX firms that voluntarily supplied segment sales data before 1970, the addition of segment earnings had no impact on security returns. Extended tests by Ajinkya (1980) confirmed this result. Security prices (NYSE) exhibited no change after implementation of the SEC's program. However, the returns for the experimental (affected by the SEC rule) and control (not affected by the SEC rule) samples were apparently more alike in the way they behaved after 1970. One possible interpretation is that there was a greater degree of consensus in assessments of return (between the experimental and control groups) after the SEC requirement took effect.

In sum, there is limited evidence that the data created by segmental reporting provides information of importance to market participants. Such informational content, however, seems to stem more from the disclosure of segmental sales data than from the disclosure rules mandated by the SEC.

Other Studies

Other studies that examine components of earnings include the following: Foster (1975b) showed that investors react in a way that recognizes the components of earnings of OTC-listed insurance companies (underwriting earnings, investment earnings, and capital gains and losses). For NYSE firms, Gonedes (1975 and 1978) and Eskew and Wright (1976) examined the association between security price changes and income before and after unusual (e.g., extraordinary) items.[6] The Gonedes and Eskew-Wright results provide

---

[5]See Chapter 5 for evidence of the superior relative accuracy of segment-based models in forecasting earnings.

[6] Gonedes (1975) uses the SEC's definition of an unusual item. The definition includes *extraordinary items* as defined by generally accepted accounting principles and *other disclosures* considered as "special" under various SEC rules (e.g., SEC ASR No. 159, *Notice of Adoption of Amendments to Guide 22* . . . [August 14, 1974]).

limited support for the proposition that investors make a distinction between operating and nonoperating income in assessing security returns.

Gonedes (1975) suggests that extraordinary accounting items "convey information pertinent to establishing firms' equilibrium values" (page 250). Firms with income-increasing extraordinary items exhibited higher returns than did firms with income-decreasing extraordinary items, after adjustment for differential risk. Eskew and Wright examined interrelationships among unexpected security returns, unexpected operating earnings, and the sign of the extraordinary item (positive if income-increasing). Their results are consistent with a market that responds to both the good and bad news conveyed by unexpected operating earnings and the extraordinary item. The response of the market to extraordinary items, however, was low relative to the response of the market to unexpected earnings. Also, the Eskew-Wright results appear to be sensitive to the type of extraordinary item reported.

Gonedes (1978), on NYSE firms, added a third variable—dividends—to examine the extent of relationships among unexpected earnings, unexpected dividends, and unexpected extraordinary items. Neither the dividend variable nor the extraordinary item variable was able to explain security returns beyond the information reflected in unexpected earnings. Gonedes attributed differences between his 1975 and 1978 results to methodology, mainly to differences in the definition of an "extraordinary" item.[7]

Finally, Manegold (1981), on NYSE firms, analyzed interrelationships among unexpected returns, operating income before depreciation and interest expense, depreciation, and interest expense. The unexpected-earnings variable, developed from a component-based forecast model, was slightly more positively correlated with unexpected return than were unexpected earnings derived from an extrapolation of aggregate earnings. Manegold's findings offer indirect support for the proposition that investors are cognizant of the components of earnings.

---

[7]Recognition of the ordinary and extraordinary components of earnings also supports the notion that investors perceive earnings as containing transitory and permanent components as discussed earlier in this chapter.

In assessing the information in earnings (as a correlation between unexpected earnings changes and unexpected price changes), researchers must contend with information that is correlated with earnings though not necessarily a perfect substitute for it. When accounting and nonaccounting data are released in the same period, one is not always sure of what is being responded to.

The separation of joint signals into "marginal" effects has a relatively long history with respect to dividend and earnings releases. Studies include Ashley (1962), Pettit (1972 and 1976), Watts (1973, 1976a, and 1976b), Brown and Hancock (1975), Griffin (1976a), Laub (1976), Gonedes (1978), Aharony and Swary (1980), and Penman (1981). Most of the investigations, with the primary exceptions of Watts and Gonedes, suggest that unexpected earnings and unexpected dividends do not provide identical information. It appears that earnings numbers are informative after consideration of the possible effects of dividend information. This is clearly demonstrated in the study by Aharony and Swary. Using NYSE daily return data, the authors report a strong price response to dividend changes when quarterly earnings are announced before a dividend change. Moreover, when both dividends and earnings increase, the price response at the date of earnings announcement is significant and positive, regardless of whether the dividend announcement preceded or followed the earnings announcement. Dividend and earnings decreases were not examined.

Interrelationships between earnings and corporate disclosures other than dividends have largely been ignored. Griffin and Ng (1978) present results involving unexpected earnings changes (for the current year) and unexpected analyst forecast data (for the ensuing year) released in the same month. The authors concluded that reported earnings information and new forecast information did not appear to provide the same information to users. Both the trading volume and price behavior of a sample of NYSE firms with similar signals (e.g., earnings increased, forecasts increased) differed from that of a sample of firms with conflicting signals (e.g., earnings increased, forecasts decreased). Foster (in press) studies the impact of earnings announcements by NYSE or AMEX firms in the same industry on a given company's stock price. Other firms' announcements were found to prompt significant changes in stock price, which says, in effect, that prices depend on information supplied by other firms. The effect was greatest for firms with one line of business as opposed to firms with many lines of business.

Other Disclosures

Another collection of studies concentrated on the security price effects of voluntary or required disclosures not necessarily having a *direct* impact on reported earnings. This section discusses disclosure effects in five areas: (1) effects of changing prices and inflation, (2) social responsibility and environmental impact, (3) sensitive foreign payments, (4) SEC Form 8-K filings, and (5) audit qualifications.

Effects of Changing Prices and Inflation

Based on numerous investigations, supplemental disclosures about asset-replacement costs and replacement or current cost expenses appear to have had no significant impact on security returns. This is despite the obvious and sometimes dramatic dip in accounting rate of return that results when historical cost earnings are converted to a current or replacement cost basis. Studies by Arbel and Jaggi (1978), Beaver, Christie, and Griffin (1980), Gheyara and Boatsman (1980), and Ro (1980) are virtually unanimous in this respect.[8] Beaver et al., for example, conclude "that ASR 190 replacement cost disclosures provided no information to the market during the fifteen trading days before and after the date that the requirement was first proposed, the date the requirement became effective, and the date that the data were first filed with the SEC" (page 155).

Nevertheless, any implication that such results mean investors did not find the replacement cost data useful remains unsubstantiated,[9] although there is evidence that similar measurements were available from analysts or could have been produced at low cost using a variety of indexes. The availability of substitutes means that the

---

[8]These studies, as well as other empirical studies dealing with the usefulness of changing prices data, are reviewed in more detail in an FASB Research Report by Frishkoff (1982).

[9]For a discussion of why such findings might say something about the costs and benefits of ASR No. 190, *Notice of Adoption of Amendments to Regulation S-X* . . ., and hence whether investors did or did not find the data useful, see Watts and Zimmerman (1980). There are many who would argue that such an inference is unwarranted, however.

marginal informational content of the new data was probably quite low. But the empirical results must be conditioned by the precision (or lack thereof) of the researchers' instruments. For example, the timing of the public availability of such data is difficult to pinpoint; in addition, investors may have been experiencing a "learning effect," thus responding gradually to the new data. The present methodologies may not be able to detect all such effects. Still, the results reported thus far are unchanged when examined under alternative research designs. Indeed, given the results to date, any stock market response to FASB Statement 33 on financial reporting and changing prices (which calls for slightly expanded disclosures) should also be undetectable.

While comprehensive data on the effects of Statement 33 will no doubt be forthcoming (see, for example, the June 15, 1981 FASB Invitation to Comment, *Financial Reporting and Changing Prices: The Need for Research*), the preceding conjecture is not universally supported. Noreen and Sepe (1981a), for example, examined monthly unexpected returns of firms subject to Statement 33 in January 1974 (when the general-price-level approach was proposed), November 1975 (when it was withdrawn), and January 1979 (when an "either-or" approach was proposed in an FASB Exposure Draft). Based on a key assumption—that the security price effects (if any) of the 1975 announcement are the reverse of the 1974 and 1979 announcements for all firms—Noreen and Sepe presented results consistent with the contention that all three policy announcements had effects on unexpected returns. The authors, however, do not state why such price changes might have occurred. Moreover, their results have been reanalyzed by Basu (1981), who is critical of their choice of events and research procedures.[10] Nevertheless, Basu also found significant results. Of course, there is the possibility that the results could be due to other events occurring in the same time period.

Although most evidence regarding the impact of required current cost disclosures suggests that there was no market reaction, it is conceivable that investors might still react to certain kinds of revaluation adjustments. This is likely to occur if such adjustments are voluntarily reported by management, with adequate interpretative discussion. Revaluation adjustments are permitted in the

---

[10]For a response to Basu, see Noreen and Sepe (1981b).

United Kingdom and Australia, among other countries. Evidence in Sharpe and Walker (1975) indicates that the share prices of large Australian companies increased abnormally by roughly 10 percent in the month that the (upward) revaluation was publicly announced. The price change was permanent.

It is not clear, however, whether such revaluation effects would occur in the United States, where investors generally have more access to replacement and current cost data. Still, there is intriguing anecdotal evidence to possibly imply that upward revaluations by management could be helpful to stock prices. Palmon and Seidler (1978) note the case of the Monumental Corporation. The firm announced its intention to sell the assets and distribute such proceeds to stockholders as a means of convincing the stockholders of the substance of the undisclosed economic resources in question. The stock price surged more than 20 percent on the day of the announcement. Of course, part of that price change could be due to a change in the timing of cash flows to stockholders, apart from the revaluation effect.

Social Responsibility and Environmental Impact

Beyond financial accounting information, some firms also release data about social responsibility and environmental impact. Is this information useful to investors? Studies of Fortune 500 firms by Ingram (1978) and Anderson and Frankle (1980) are relevant in this regard. Ingram classified certain disclosures about social responsibility according to (1) whether they were stated monetarily and (2) type of expenditure (e.g., pollution control, fair business practice, employee health and safety, etc.). No distinction was made between required and voluntary disclosures. In the first set of tests, no differences in the unexpected returns of portfolios formed on the basis of the above classifications were observed. However, in a second test which controlled for earnings expectations, limited price effects were evident, but only for certain segments of the market in specific years.

Anderson and Frankle also reported evidence of a market reaction for firms that voluntarily reported on social activities in 1972 and 1973, relative to those that did not. But their analysis focused on only one calendar month (March 1973) and, consequently, is likely to be confounded by omitted variables (e.g., impact of annual earnings announcement).

193

Overall, the case for there being a price reaction to social disclosure is a weak one based on the evidence to date. However, there is limited evidence that investors take note of disclosures about the potential illegality or unethical nature of a firm's operations. One issue related to this, sensitive foreign payments, is discussed next.

Sensitive Foreign Payments

The SEC's disclosure program regarding sensitive foreign payments was studied by Griffin (1977) as part of the work of the Commission's Advisory Committee on Corporate Disclosure. Several tests concerning market-adjusted volume and return series were examined in the weeks surrounding a firm's first disclosure of involvement in questionable foreign activities. Transaction volume and the volatility of unexpected return were greater for the disclosing firms relative to a control sample in the weeks surrounding news of the foreign payments. All firms were NYSE listed. Moreover, disclosing firms experienced a small, temporary dip in stock price at the time of announcement. Prices reverted to normal levels within two to three weeks. In short, investors appeared to acknowledge the fact that firms made sensitive foreign payments but made no permanent changes in their assessments of future cash flows based on the disclosures.

SEC Form 8-K Filings

Although many sensitive foreign payment disclosures were contained in the Form 8-K filing, the Griffin study is obviously not a comprehensive examination of the informational content of that document. Pastena (1979) studied the Form 8-K disclosures subject to the SEC's ASR No. 138, *Notice of Adoption of Amendments* . . . , which expanded the scope of required disclosure for reportable events (e.g., unusual events). Relative to a nonreport period, the volatility of unexpected return was greater two days before and on the day of announcement of the 8-K information in *The Wall Street Journal*. However, in a similar test based on the day of official receipt of the 8-K form by the New York Stock Exchange, no unusual price response was observed. Such results are consistent with a market that reacts to a more timely disclosure system. Pastena notes in this regard: ". . . The formal disclosures provide their greatest function by giving management an incentive to be candid and complete in their earlier press release disclosures" (page 783).

194

Audit Qualifications

Do investors take notice of audit qualifications, or do such disclosures simply reflect circumstances and events either well known to the market or of no use in assessing prospective return? The evidence is mixed on this issue. Firth (1978) reported that stock price volatility of companies in the United Kingdom increased and prices declined when investors first learned of a qualified opinion. The strongest effects were observed for the "going concern" and "asset value" categories of audit qualification. That study contrasts with Baskin (1972) and with Ball, Walker, and Whittred (1979), who concluded that the audit qualification had no perceptible impact on investors' decisions. However, the context and the kind of qualification may be important in interpreting these results. Baskin studied U.S. firms with material consistency exceptions, namely, material changes in accounting and reporting practices. Ball et al., on the other hand, evaluated qualifications with respect to depreciation allowances and the value of assets for firms on the Sydney Stock Exchange.

Summary

The studies of the effects of various disclosures lead to few solid conclusions but many interesting possibilities. Research indicates that segmental data is of value to investors and creditors. In addition, there is weak support for the notion that users make a distinction between operating income and extraordinary items in assessing future returns. However, noticeable stock market reactions have not accompanied various reporting standards in areas such as changing prices and inflation, social responsibility, sensitive foreign payments, 8-K reports, and audit qualifications. Thus, the research is not convincing in showing that stock prices have been affected, especially if compared with studies that examine the market's response to announcements of earnings and dividends. In part, that is due to the fact that experimental control is difficult to achieve. While issues of control have been dealt with more completely elsewhere (Foster [1980]), it is worthwhile to underscore the difficulties that researchers encounter in investigating various "other" disclosures: (1) There is often no rationale to predict what kind of security price response one should expect. (2) It is sometimes very difficult to know precisely when the "new" information was made known. (3) Announced changes in regulations and accounting systems may need to be analyzed using different research designs from those used to evaluate the impact of the numbers themselves. (4) Potentially confounding events may be difficult to control for or eliminate due to the self-selected nature of the sample examined or the uniqueness of the event in question. (5) The generic event being studied may be so tied to particular facts and circumstances of each firm that reliance on averages (across firms) may mask the very effects that one is looking for. Most of the studies identified, nonetheless, attempt to combat such problems of research design. Such attempts are in themselves essential so that the "state of the art" may develop further.

Accounting Changes

An accounting change that is proposed or implemented is likely to have certain economic consequences. An important question for researchers to ask is whether those changes produce a reaction in the securities market. While many should have minimal impact on the cash flows of the firm, and are perceived by investors and creditors in this way, others may have noticeable effects on cash flows (e.g., due to tax savings). Such latter accounting changes have the potential to increase or decrease the value of a firm's securities. Unfortunately, except in some fairly trivial situations, accounting researchers can offer little in the way of conceptual guidance that would enable managers, users, and policymakers to predict the timing, direction, and magnitude of the market's response, if any. The result is that most of the "accounting change" studies simply describe what happened to security returns when information about the accounting change was thought to have been conveyed to the market. Such studies seldom provide a plausible explanation of the findings.

In this discussion of research on the impact of accounting changes on security prices, different kinds of accounting changes are examined. One classification is to separate (1) changes made and initiated at the discretion of management and (2) those that are nondiscretionary (e.g., changes mandated by the FASB or the SEC). A second classification is to distinguish (1) accounting changes that are purely cosmetic, (2) those that have direct cash flow effects, and (3) those that have indirect cash flow effects. A third classification, but one that will not be used here, is to concentrate on *why* such changes might have been made. The motivations of the individuals involved in making the changes are important. It has become increasingly popular to view accounting changes as signals about management's integrity and its expectations regarding future cash flows. Unfortunately, there is little security price research that differentiates among management's motivations for accounting changes.

Discretionary versus Nondiscretionary Changes

Discretionary accounting changes occur for a variety of reasons. Factors motivating such changes include tax savings, political or regulatory cost reductions, improved contracting with creditors and employees, reduced costs of preparing information, reduced costs of outside capital, and ability to signal to outsiders. Nondiscretionary or mandated changes are imposed by outside agencies, such as the SEC or the FASB, and affect the financial accounting and reporting process. Unlike the managerial motivations, impetus for change at an agency such as the FASB stems primarily from the needs of investors and creditors for relevant and reliable information for decision making (Chapter 1).

Harrison (1977) examined the security price response to accounting changes classified as discretionary or nondiscretionary. He further classified the changes as income-increasing or income-decreasing. The results show that NYSE firms that voluntarily chose income-increasing alternatives fared worse than the others, while NYSE firms whose income increased due to the required change exhibited favorable stock price effects. One possible implication of the former result is that the market appears to place a premium on management's unfettered selection of conservative accounting standards.

Discretionary: Cosmetic

Rather than focusing on a broad set of accounting changes, Archibald (1967 and 1972), Kaplan and Roll (1972), and Cassidy (1976) studied specific discretionary accounting changes that were largely cosmetic in terms of their effects on cash flows. An efficient market should understand more than the "bottom line" earnings number and thus should not respond to changes in reported earnings induced solely by changes in bookkeeping. The specific test is that there should be no association between unexpected security returns and unexpected earnings changes when such earnings changes are the result of measuring rule changes only.

Archibald reported on the impact on NYSE firms that voluntarily switched from accelerated to straight-line depreciation for external reporting purposes without changing tax accounting treatments. Unexpected returns were not essentially different from normal in the month of announcement of earnings, even though reported earnings increased about nine percent. Kaplan and Roll studied NYSE or AMEX firms that switched from accelerated to straight-line accounting for depreciation and from deferral to flow-through accounting for the investment tax credit. While neither change had an impact on taxes, both increased reported earnings. Kaplan and Roll found that depreciation-switchback firms, though not responding to the change per se, were nevertheless worse performers on the average in the 30 weeks following the earnings announcement. To be sure, the market did not respond in the direction of the earnings change either before, after, or at the time of announcement of the switch.

For the investment credit switch firms, a temporary jump in price apparently occurred at the date of announcement. However, those firms that did not switch (i.e., retained the productive-life method of accounting for the investment tax credit) tended to be better performers on the average in the 30 weeks after announcement. But Cassidy's replication of this result (NYSE only) indicates little postannouncement abnormal return activity for either the switch or nonswitch group. Nonetheless, Cassidy writes: "On the average, firms which changed their method of accounting for the investment [tax] credit experienced negative abnormal returns over the five-year period prior to the change. The firms that continued to account for the investment credit by the more 'conservative' deferral method were firms that outperformed the market" (page 218).

How should the preceding results be interpreted? One view that seems to be gaining acceptance is based on the idea that investors and creditors are apparently willing to pay a premium for more conservative, higher quality methods of computing earnings. The Kaplan-Roll and Harrison results are consistent with this notion, as are other findings. Fabozzi (1978), for instance, reports that accounting changes that reduced earnings quality were associated with below-normal security price performance. Survey research by Hawkins and Campbell (1978) also suggests that earnings manipulation will be recognized and discounted by investors. Thus, managers should be aware not only that investors, creditors, and others recognize that cosmetic changes are just that—cosmetic—but also that when such changes are income-increasing or help produce a smoother time trend, the marketplace is apt to penalize the firm for false signalling by requiring higher rates of return. One possibility is that accounting changes provide substantive signals about management attitudes and behavior, especially in times of less-than-adequate profit performance.

Discretionary: Cash Flow Consequences

An informationally efficient securities market should respond to the effect of the accounting change on future cash flows rather than on reported earnings. If a firm switches to last-in, first-out (LIFO) inventory accounting from a non-LIFO method during inflationary periods, the effect on earnings and the effect on cash flows move in opposite directions. It is thus straightforward to examine on what basis—cash flows or earnings—the market responds, if at all. The earliest studies were by Sunder (1973 and 1975), who reported that NYSE firms adopting LIFO experienced positive unexpected returns in the 12 months before the announcement of the change in the annual report. Of the firms studied, the effect was strongest for firms in the steel industry. On the other hand, a small sample of firms that moved away from the LIFO method showed no sign of unusual behavior, even though they may have lost certain tax benefits. Thus, broadly speaking, the market responded on the basis of cash flows, not reported accounting earnings.

Sunder's analysis left many issues of methodology unresolved, especially issues relating to control of omitted and potentially confounding variables and identification of precisely when the market knew about the change. Three subsequent studies have suggested that factors in addition to tax savings may influence the stock price response to a firm's switch in the method of accounting for inventory. Abdel-khalik and McKeown (1978a) explored the interaction between NYSE-firm market expectations about reported earnings and the adoption of LIFO. Their results: Firms with positive unexpected earnings that switched to LIFO did unusually well relative to control portfolios, but firms with negative unexpected earnings that switched to LIFO performed badly—worse than a control group of firms with similar negative unexpected earnings. The authors offered little explanation for this result.

Ricks' (1980) study of NYSE and AMEX firms changing to LIFO in 1974-1975 concentrated on problems of bias in the selection of firms, evident in the earlier studies. Controlling for the fact that firms adopting LIFO exhibited greater earnings increases in 1974-1975 relative to others, Ricks found that, contrary to the efficient market hypothesis, ". . . [LIFO] change firms experienced significantly lower residual returns in the month of the LIFO change announcement" (page 53). However, problems of methodology remain in this study as well. The author still did not effectively rule out omitted variables (e.g., contemporaneous quarterly earnings or dividend announcements) which, of course, can be damaging if such a short study period is used.

Brown (1980), using weekly instead of monthly returns, observed a market response to the 1974-1975 switch to LIFO that was similar to Ricks' results. Firms (all NYSE) that indicated their intention to switch to LIFO before preliminary earnings announcement did not experience positive unexpected returns (i.e., returns consistent with the tax-saving effect). In short, the Ricks and Brown results stand in contrast to the earlier findings. However, given the weight of evidence in support of the efficient market hypothesis, they must at this stage be regarded as tentative.

Nondiscretionary

It is often argued that nondiscretionary accounting changes should have a negative effect on security returns, since they tend to restrict what would otherwise be a manager's free choice of accounting techniques. But such a prediction is simplistic because it ignores (1) other management reactions that may also be linked to the accounting change, (2) second-order effects of financial data on investors and others (e.g., increased comparability), and (3) other factors (e.g., effects on management incentives) that may affect the market value of the firm. For example, while many opposed Statement 8 on foreign currency translation because it increased earnings volatility, that Statement may well have had salutary ramifications in that it prompted managements to evaluate their foreign exchange risk management practices more closely (Evans, Folks, and Jilling [1978]). Similarly, while Statement 13 on leases may have caused managers to write new leases so as to avoid the ruling, a priori, there is no reason to believe that such activities were necessarily harmful to the future success of the company.

In discussing nondiscretionary accounting changes, the possibility that they are *totally* cosmetic can probably be safely ignored. Such decisions imposed on a firm's management, whether it welcomes or opposes them, alter the measurements on which their performance is based and contractual obligations are monitored. Since changes in the measuring rules inevitably feed back into changes in decisions made, cash flow effects are to be expected. The rule changes themselves may also alter management incentives (e.g., an accounting rule that increases earnings variability may reduce a manager's willingness to take on risky projects). Thus, it becomes extremely difficult to predict when, in what direction, and by how much the market should respond. The discussion below concentrates, therefore, on a description of what happened to firms' stock prices at the time certain new standards or policies were enacted. Recent studies of the effects of FASB standards are emphasized. Included are: Dukes (1976) and Vigeland (1981) on FASB Statement No. 2, *Accounting for Research and Development Costs;* Dukes (1978) and Shank, Dillard, and Murdock (1979) on Statement 8 (foreign currency translation); Abdel-khalik (1981) on Statement 13 (leases); and Collins and Dent (1979), Dyckman (1979), and Lev (1979), among others, on FASB Statement No. 19, *Accounting and Reporting by Oil and Gas Producing Companies.*

Research and Development Costs

Dukes' (1976) analysis of NYSE firms that "expensed" research and development (R&D) costs concluded that the stocks are valued in accordance with the notion that investors employ a model that systematically adjusts reported earnings before they are impounded in security prices. According to the author, earnings were adjusted in a manner that "appears to be directly related to research intensity of the industry" (page 184). In other words, investors' assessments of returns recognized that R&D expenditures do indeed generate future benefits, benefits that are incorporated into earnings projections. One inference of the Dukes study is that security prices were not affected by the FASB-required change in R&D expense recognition (and whatever induced effects the change had on production, investment, and financing decisions of the firm).[11]

Vigeland (1981) essentially confirmed the above conclusion. For NYSE and AMEX firms, Vigeland revealed that surrounding three FASB release dates—that of the Discussion Memorandum, the Exposure Draft, and the final Statement—there was no difference between the common stock returns of firms that switched from deferral to immediate expense accounting and the returns of control firms matched by size, industry, and relative risk (beta). Thus, there is no evidence of a security price effect in response to the required adoption of Statement 2 in 1975.

Foreign Currency Translation

The FASB's Statement 8 is undoubtedly the most controversial rule put into effect so far. Designed to make more compatible the diverse accounting practices of U.S. multinationals, Statement 8 was not well received by management and investors alike, primarily because it assertedly increased the volatility of reported earnings. Many alleged that such increased earnings volatility would damage stock prices.

Studies by Dukes (1978) and Shank et al. (1979), among others, failed to confirm the proposition that security returns were adversely affected at the time of initial implementation of Statement 8. Dukes, however, found that in 1975-1976 NYSE companies with large multinational operations earned lower returns than companies of similar risk having minor overseas operations. He attributes this result to a general weakening of the U.S. dollar, not to the accounting standard per se.

Statement 8's poor reception may have caused some companies to reject acceptable investments and others to reconsider financing and investment policies to avoid perceived excessive earnings fluctuations. But the collective force of their behavior, and investors' understanding thereof, appears to have been rational and generally in accordance with economic considerations. Certainly, the results

---

[11]For evidence on whether Statement 2 "caused" substantive effects on management decision making, see Dukes, Dyckman, and Elliot (1980) who stated that their tests failed to detect an effect attributable to Statement 2; and Horwitz and Kolodny (1980) who concluded, on the contrary, that there was a decline in R&D outlays for small high-technology companies previously using a deferral approach.

do not seem to contradict the efficient-market hypothesis. Additionally, studies of the Statement's impact on management practices could not demonstrate that net cash flows to the typical multinational were augmented or diminished. Contrary to popular opinion, one study reported "that, relative to an earlier survey, respondents showed more interest in cash flow and asset protection than in earnings management as the primary objective of foreign exchange risk management after January 1976 when the standard came into effect" (Evans et al. [1978]).[12]

Leases

The economic and behavioral consequences of accounting for leases under Statement 13 were studied by Abdel-khalik (1981).[13] Included in that study is an examination of the stock and bond price reaction to the requirement that lease obligations satisfying certain criteria be recorded as liabilities rather than disclosed in footnotes. The test period extended from August 1975, when the first Exposure Draft on lease accounting and reporting was issued, to December 1978, when Statement 13 became effective retroactively for all firms (as a result of the SEC's ASR No. 225, *Lease Accounting and Disclosure Rules*).

The results are similar to the studies on Statements 2 and 8. Abdel-khalik posits that while the restructuring of data due to lease capitalization (e.g., increase in ratio of debt to equity) was at first glance a change of form rather than substance, managers may have been induced to make decisions so as to deflect the full impact of the accounting change. For instance, they might have written new leases or renegotiated old leases to avoid satisfying capitalization criteria, acquired assets through purchase rather than lease, or rene-

---

[12]For a more detailed review of the effects of Statement 8 on stock prices, earnings, and hedging behavior, see Griffin (1979).

[13]For studies of the common stock price effects of the SEC's lease disclosure rules, notably ASR No. 147, *Notice of Adoption of Amendments to Regulation S-X Requiring Improved Disclosure of Leases,* see Ro (1978) and Bowman (1980). See also Abdel-khalik, Thompson, and Taylor (1978) for a study of the bond price effects of the SEC's pronouncement. These studies generally support the proposition that SEC lease accounting disclosure rules did not significantly affect market behavior, although Ro reports a decline in stock price associated with firms whose restated pro forma earnings were materially lower than reported.

gotiated agreements with employees, executives, and outside equity holders.

The findings of Abdel-khalik suggest that certain management practices of lessee companies did change (a majority of lessee firms actually wrote new leases to bypass Statement 13), but such induced actions did not manifest themselves in stock or bond price behavior. The authors comment: "The overall tenor of the results of this extensive analysis can be summarized as indicating no significant association between the events leading up to the final implementation of the change in accounting for leases and market-based measures (whether generated from stock or bond prices). With respect to individual samples, some unexpected, but not statistically significant, behavior of market-based systematic risk of common stocks of the samples of retail companies with relatively significant noncapitalized leases was detected during the first half of 1976. We were unable to attribute that behavior to capitalization of leases" (page 26).

Unsuccessful Efforts to Adopt "Successful Efforts" Accounting

There have been two attempts by policymakers to require oil and gas producing companies uniformly to use the successful efforts method of accounting for exploration and drilling costs. The Accounting Principles Board withdrew its proposal in 1971, and the FASB suspended a similar proposal in 1978, nullifying the standards set forth in FASB Statement 19. The FASB action followed the SEC's issuance of a release that permitted the continued application of either method. Hence, in both situations, a standard expected to affect reported earnings but not underlying cash flows—at least directly—was turned down or otherwise overruled by constituents of the accounting-policy process. Managements' consternation stemmed in part from concerns that the security prices of the firms affected (mostly small, independent producers) would potentially be adversely affected.

Were such concerns well founded? Five studies attempted to assess possible economic consequences. First, Patz and Boatsman (1972) conducted tests using unexpected returns over a seven-week period surrounding the announcement of the 1971 APB proposal. There was no difference in the return activity of the full cost versus the successful efforts companies. Four later studies were: Collins and Dent (1979), sponsored by full cost lobbyists; Dyckman (1979), sponsored by the FASB; Haworth, Matthews, and Tuck (1978), conducted at the SEC; and Lev (1979), independently funded. These later investigations assessed the market's reaction to the FASB Exposure Draft proposing the uniform successful efforts rule. Were the security returns of full cost firms adversely affected? Dyckman answered no, except for a transitory effect. Collins and Dent answered affirmatively, reporting that over the test period (35 weeks following the issuance of the Exposure Draft), ". . . the average weekly residual return of the full cost firms was -1.12% while for the successful effort firms the corresponding return was -0.56%" (page 25). Haworth et al. and Lev also reported possible negative reaction. Haworth et al. indicated that full cost firms were initially adversely affected, but there was a subsequent price recovery shortly after the announcement of the Exposure Draft. Similarly, Lev witnessed that ". . . the price of FC [full cost] stocks dropped by about 4.5 percent during the first three days of the announcement period [July 18-20, 1977], while the price of SE [successful efforts] stocks dropped by about one percent" (page 493). The decline in value of stock prices for the full cost firms was apparently permanent.

Overall, the studies' results, especially those that concentrate on specific announcement effects (e.g., Lev [1979]), are somewhat in conflict with findings on other accounting standards that contend that the market reflects cash flow information and understands the implications of cosmetic changes. Nonetheless, the studies' findings mostly confirm what *The Wall Street Journal* reported on July 20, 1977, one day after the Exposure Draft's release: "Share prices of some oil companies, mainly smaller ones, fell in trading yesterday after the FASB disclosed its proposal" (page 8). According to Lev, about 20 percent of the firms sampled were negatively affected.

The oil and gas situation was an important milestone for the kinds of studies discussed so far in this chapter. For the first time, findings based on modern security price research techniques were being introduced in governmental hearings involving reporting practices of U.S. corporations. Would the research withstand the criticism of powerful lobbyists? Whose results would be judged as valid? Or would the techniques be written off, thus damaging many years of academic development? As far as one can tell, the techniques have survived. Indeed, the criticism seems to have led to an increased understanding of the role of empirical analysis in public policy—albeit a fairly limited one. Moreover, the hearings, the criticism, and the attendant publicity seem to have given the research procedures a certain legitimacy that otherwise might have taken years to achieve. Still, it should be emphasized that the findings in such studies discussed above were never considered pivotal in either the FASB's decision to adopt the successful efforts method (December 1977) or the SEC's later decision not to accept one method for all firms (August 1978).

Summary

At this juncture, it is worthwhile to reflect on the research concerning the effects of various FASB-mandated disclosure rules (such as Statements 2, 8, 13, and 19) on prices. (The comments also apply to Statement 33, discussed earlier in this chapter.) Despite many caveats about the present state of research procedures, one general conclusion is that, with the possible exception of the FASB proposal on oil and gas accounting, large-scale and permanent shifts in firms' market values have accompanied neither the proposal nor the implementation of these pronouncements. But this is not to say that for the individual firm, wealth effects have not been experienced due to changes in the standards, and that better research procedures may not be able to detect such effects. The "optimal" set of production, investment, and financing decisions, from management's point of view, will surely change as the choices of accounting and reporting rules change and also as management's incentives and perceptions of the economic environment change.[14] A change in the definition of accounting exposure to foreign exchange risk, for example, seems to have triggered certain management reactions because contracts and less formal arrangements are tied to that definition. Similar reactions have apparently been motivated by changes in lease reporting rules. Nonetheless, precise assessment of the combined, aggregate effects of such induced management responses remains an elusive goal for accounting researchers, hampered not so much by design issues as by lack of an interpretative framework that would explain and predict the relevant relationships.

---

[14]Moreover, when the interactions of many firms are considered simultaneously, one might anticipate that firms not required to change accounting and reporting practices would be affected as well.

206

Alternative Acceptable Methods

The previous section describes research that poses the question of whether accounting changes affected prices in some noticeable way. The focus is on an assessment of short-term announcement effects. The subject of discussion in this section is whether the security returns of firms using one acceptable method differ systematically from those using another acceptable method, given similar facts and circumstances. Assuming that the market has more information than accounting reports alone and is able to analyze rationally all available information, the researcher's prediction is that security returns are independent of the accounting techniques selected. Whether a firm chooses one way of accounting for taxes over another, for example, should not matter as far as security performance is concerned. On the other hand, the ratio of price to reported earnings should be highly dependent on the technique selected. The price-earnings ratio will naturally be different, if reported earnings are calculated using different accounting methods.

Hong, Kaplan, and Mandelker (1978) examined whether a sample of business combinations using the pooling-of-interest method of accounting exhibited return behavior different from the behavior of a sample of firms that used the purchase basis. (All merged businesses involved the issuance of stock; all acquiring firms were NYSE listed.) While firms using the pooling method were generally able to report higher accounting rates of return, there was no statistical difference between their unexpected security returns and those of the group using the purchase method, both in the months surrounding the date that the businesses were combined and in the months surrounding the first earnings announcement (annual or quarterly) following the combination. However, those combined firms that used "the more conservative purchase method [did appear to] have been doing well in the year prior to the merger" (page 41).

Beaver and Dukes (1973) and Good and Meyer (1973) studied whether differences in firms' price-earnings ratios are a direct function of the accounting method adopted. Beaver and Dukes examined NYSE firms that for tax purposes used accelerated depreciation but for reporting purposes used either accelerated or straight-line depreciation. The mean price-earnings ratio of firms using accelerated depreciation for reporting purposes was higher than the mean of firms who used straight-line depreciation. However, the price-earnings ratio of the latter group when based on pro forma earnings with accelerated depreciation was practically identical to the mean ratio of the former group. The two sets of firms, moreover, were no different in terms of relative risk and earnings growth. The finding that the ratio of price to reported earnings recognizes the different accounting methods is essentially equivalent to a securities market that properly allows for such differences in the valuation process. The results reported in Good and Meyer are consistent with Beaver and Dukes' findings. Good and Meyer reveal that the difference between the price-earnings ratios of stocks with high versus average price-earnings ratios diminished when the high and average ratio stocks were adjusted for differences in methods used for depreciation and special items. Thus, accounting methods account for part of the disparity between high and average price-earnings stocks.

A related empirical approach is, for a sample of firms, to recompute reported earnings on a pro forma basis (under the alternative, nonreported method) and then to examine which measure of earnings—reported or pro forma—has the higher correlation with security prices. Such a research approach assumes that the market is easily able to compute earnings under the nonreported alternative. Beaver and Dukes (1972 and 1973) studied deferral versus flow-through tax expense recognition; Foster (1975a) examined statutory versus GAAP-based earnings of OTC-listed insurance companies; and Easman, Falkenstein, and Weil (1979) and Beaver, Griffin, and Landsman (1981) evaluated historical cost versus replacement cost earnings. In general, the results in these studies are consistent with the proposition that the market does not blindly accept or mechanically respond to the reported "bottom line" numbers. The market, instead, seems to adjust the accounting data before decision making. A possible exception, however, is the Beaver et al. study. Here the conclusion is that variables that are described as preholding gain net income, based on the SEC's ASR 190, exhibit a lower correlation with security returns than do historical cost earnings variables. One interpretation of this result is that the SEC-required replacement cost disclosures were unreliable for the purposes of assessing future enterprise cash flows.

Other researchers have used stock price (or stock price deflated in some manner) as the dependent variable, attempting to discover whether stock price variation across firms is better explained by one accounting alternative or another. Dukes' (1976) study on R&D costs (discussed earlier in this chapter) is an example of this approach. Another illustration is provided by Foster (1977b) who found that security prices of OTC-listed insurance companies act as if unrealized gains and losses in marketable securities are an element of earnings, even though such elements are not publicly reported in the financial statements. A similar study by Bowen (1981) is also of interest. Using the ratio of market to book value of common equity as the dependent variable, the author shows that the securities market places a lower price-earnings multiple on the "allowance for funds used during construction" component of earnings than on operating earnings. The sample consisted of electric utility firms. Bowen contends that the statistical analysis provides a means of assessing differences in firms' quality of earnings.

To summarize, the evidence so far reveals that the security returns of firms using one acceptable method of accounting are essentially the same as the returns of firms using other acceptable methods, if the facts and circumstances are similar. Thus, security prices are not influenced by the choice of accounting method. A firm's price-earnings ratio, on the other hand, can be greatly influenced by the selection of accounting method. But the effect is borne directly in the ratio's denominator (i.e., earnings).

Estimating and Predicting Relative Risk

Individuals wishing to obtain benefits from portfolio diversification need to assess prospective security returns, the volatility of security returns, and how those returns are interrelated. Correlations and covariance measures are frequently used to assess those interrelationships. The volatility or variance of return for a well-diversified portfolio depends almost entirely on those interrelationships, as variation not explained by them is diversified away. Therefore, persons holding diversified portfolios would find financial reports useful if such reports were to provide information about covariation in security returns. "The necessity to consider co-movements in security returns," comments Hakansson (1976), "is perhaps the main lesson for accountants from the [research] work done in the last decade."

This section discusses research on the use of financial information for assessing a security's relative risk—a variable that can be derived from return data. For research purposes, relative risk is the dependent variable, to be explained or predicted by accounting and other financial information.

If security returns conform to the market model (Chapter 4), the covariation factor may be captured by beta—the security's estimated relative risk. Beta for a security is calculated as a weighted summation of the security's covariance with all other securities in the market portfolio, divided by the variance of the return on the market portfolio. That weighted summation of security covariances is more conveniently expressed as the covariance of the security's return with the market portfolio. Beta, therefore, expresses the riskiness of a security relative to the variance of return on the market portfolio. Similarly, portfolio beta expresses the riskiness of the portfolio relative to the market variance. If portfolio beta equals one, market risk and portfolio risk are identical. A beta of less than one (or more than one) means that the portfolio of securities is less (more) volatile than the market. The returns on a portfolio that has a beta of zero are thus unaffected by market movements.

Justifications for beta as a measure of risk have extended the above arguments based on portfolio theory and the market model to those that employ the two-parameter capital asset pricing model (Chapter 4). The capital asset pricing model predicts a linear (i.e., additive) relationship between relative risk and expected return for securities and portfolios when the market is at equilibrium, that is, when all investors are satisfied with the securities they hold at current prices.[15]

Strict acceptance of the capital asset pricing model leads to a curious result in accounting: The only object of analysis for portfolio investment decision making is assessment of beta, since the investor can expect no other component of return (in excess of a risk-free premium) to be compensated by the market. The strategy is simple. One selects an overall portfolio beta and then buys and sells securities so as to maintain that desired level as the individual betas change. However, notwithstanding that individual security betas

---

[15]Certain assumptions must hold, however, for equilibrium to exist. These assumptions are restrictive and recently have prompted empirical tests supporting the validity of the model to be questioned (see Roll [1977]). The most crucial assumption appears to be that a market-wide index of security returns constitutes a truly efficient portfolio, that is, a portfolio that yields the highest possible return with least possible risk (i.e., variance of that return).

change from period to period in a way that is unpredictable, portfolio betas will tend to possess a high degree of constancy. The individual changes in beta will tend to cancel each other out. In this situation, firm-specific information about beta is of minimal value. Despite this result, the section proceeds on the assumption that the assessment of relative risk (more fundamentally, the covariation factor) is a relevant parameter in investment decision making. Certainly, billions of dollars are invested in mutual funds, pension funds, and other funds managed in ways cognizant of security beta. Recognition of beta by managers of course can be either direct or indirect (as a component of a more encompassing risk measure).[16]

The remainder of this section discusses the empirical research classified as (1) approaches to the estimation of beta using past stock prices, (2) evidence on the behavior of betas over time, (3) use of accounting information in explaining and predicting beta, and (4) use of beta in evaluating whether one accounting alternative is more informative than another.

Estimation of Beta

Initially, beta was estimated as the slope coefficient in a regression equation relating security returns and market returns for a specified period of time. Sixty months of return data were usually considered as reasonable for obtaining timely and efficient estimates (see Bogue [1973] and Gonedes [1973]). A more recent approach is that of Scholes and Williams (1977), who proposed an estimation technique that uses daily returns. Its chief advantage is that daily returns allow for the use of a much shorter time interval and, consequently, the derivation of estimates that are more sensitive to changing economic conditions. Regression approaches usually assume that beta is constant over the period of time used for estimation. When that assumption is violated (e.g., the beta coefficient is unstable), individual beta estimates are biased and may be inappropriate for purposes of portfolio management.

Behavior of Betas over Time

Is beta stable over time? There are three broad categories of pos-

---

[16]For stimulating criticisms of the usefulness of beta in investment analysis, see Blustein (1980) and Wallace (1980).

sible time-series behavior: (1) security betas might behave in an erratic (random) fashion, (2) betas might remain fairly constant over time, or (3) betas might change slowly over time, reverting to some long-run average value. Evidence in Bogue (1973), Blume (1975 and 1979), and Elgers, Haltiner, and Hawthorne (1979) suggests that the third category—beta behaves as a mean-reverting series—is the most representative. Mean reversion implies that next period's beta should be adjusted toward the long-run mean (often an industry-wide or economy-wide average). The prediction under the mean-reverting assumption is that differences between security beta and the long-run average are forecasted to become smaller over time. Many firms engaged in securities analysis (e.g., Merrill Lynch) have adopted some variant of this adjustment procedure.[17]

Use of Accounting Information in Explaining and Predicting Beta

Knowledge of the behavior of beta is likely to improve its assessment. A logical question is whether such assessments or predictions can be improved with the help of information in financial reports. The early studies (Ball and Brown [1969]; Beaver, Kettler, and Scholes [1970]; Gonedes [1973]; Lev [1974]; Beaver and Manegold [1975]; Bildersee [1975]; Griffin [1976b]; Thompson [1976]) were entirely correlational. They found that various accounting-based measures (e.g., earnings variability, earnings beta, leverage, payout, and size) were associated with estimates of beta derived from stock prices. In other words, accounting data were "relevant" to the assessment of relative risk or beta.

On the predictive side, two trends in the literature have appeared. The first, of lesser relevance for decision makers, compares the forecasting performance of accounting-based predictors of beta

---

[17]Mean reversion has a statistical and an economic interpretation. It may be due to measurement error in that high betas may be "high" primarily because of positive measurement error. Likewise, low betas may be "low" because of negative error. If error in one period is uncorrelated with error in another period, this is sufficient to produce a reversion to the long-run mean. Reversion may also occur if new projects taken on have less extreme characteristics over time, are better integrated into general market influences, or lend themselves to internal diversification. However, mean reversion is not likely to last indefinitely. Periodically, there will be major "shocks" to the system such as oil crises, changes in regulation and management, unexpected inflation, and so forth. A recent study by Williams and Targia (1979) reported major shifts in industry betas, explainable apparently in substantive terms.

with market-based predictors. Beaver, Kettler, and Scholes (1970), Eskew (1979), and Elgers (1980) are examples. Based on the results of these studies, there is little consensus concerning the predictive superiority of one set of information over the other.

The second and more pertinent approach is to combine both data sets in some optimal fashion. Rosenberg and his colleagues have provided the most comprehensive investigations (e.g., Rosenberg and McKibben [1973]; Rosenberg and Marathe [1975], also Welles [1978]). Indeed, a risk-measurement service is now marketed by Barr Rosenberg Associates, based in part on those studies. The system develops short- and long-run predictions of relative risk and residual variance using fundamental (accounting) and market variables. As reported in their background material (Barr Rosenberg Associates [1978]), historical beta adds little relative to fundamental factors in predictions of risk.[18] Nonetheless, the Rosenberg-Marathe results leave little doubt that risk estimates based on market and nonmarket data are better able to predict security returns than those using one set of data alone.

**Use of Beta in Evaluating the Informational
Content of Accounting Alternatives**

Most of the work using beta to evaluate accounting alternatives compares beta determined from market price data and risk estimates derived from accounting data based on alternative accounting methods. The object is to assess whether the choice of accounting method influences the market's assessment of risk as reflected in beta. For example, certain FASB accounting standards (e.g., Statements 2, 5, and 8) have the probable effect of increasing the volatility of reported earnings. An element of their justification is that earnings numbers under the proposed method better reflect the underlying risks faced by the enterprise. But are such earnings numbers more highly associated with beta?

Thus far the research is limited to Derstine and Huefner (1974), who studied the LIFO versus FIFO choice, and Eskew (1975), who

---

[18]The Rosenberg system involves complex estimation procedures. Its chief advantages, relative to earlier works, are that predictive ability is judged in terms of observables (security risk) and that the explanatory variables are allowed to change over time as new financial data become available. Earlier analysis had used estimated future beta based on market data as the predictive criterion.

studied the successful efforts versus full cost choice in the oil and gas industry. In neither case is there evidence to conclude that the choice of accounting alternative makes a difference to the market's assessment of risk. However, risk association tests of the above kind have been criticized by Collins and O'Connor (1978) and refinements in the methodology have been suggested by Thakkar (1978). Another line of research is to examine the extent to which changes in regulation are associated with changes in risk. Abdel-khalik and McKeown (1978b) examined the impact of ASR 190 on relative risk. Horwitz and Kolodny (1977) and Collins and Simonds (1979) report findings regarding the impact of the SEC's line-of-business disclosure program on relative risk.

Unfortunately, there are theoretical shortcomings in both lines of research. Neither is able to predict unambiguously the impact of the disclosure or accounting alternative on market risk before the empirical analysis. In addition, if the market is efficient, it is difficult to pick up market responses to new information in a beta measure, because extensive histories are often needed to obtain relatively efficient estimates of beta before and after the disclosure of the new information.

Newer Methodologies

Use of Option Prices

The emergence of a model that predicts the price of an option on common stock (the "option-pricing model") has created new research possibilities in accounting and finance. The option-pricing approach uses option prices and other data such as common stock prices to estimate a common stock's variance of return from date of the most recent option valuation to date of expiration of the option. Since the current option price depends on the market's assessment of future common stock volatility, the option price should "jump" when the market learns of forthcoming news announcements that will occur before expiration date. The option price responds to the anticipated increased volatility in stock price at the date of earnings announcement. Knowledge of whether the news is good or bad is not vital under this option-pricing approach.

Patell and Wolfson (1979a and 1981) adopted this approach to investigate the price effects of quarterly earnings announcements. Their results are consistent with the earlier research, which concentrated, more simply, on stock price volatility observed directly rather than indirectly via option prices. The earlier research indicated that stock price volatility increases at the time of a major news announcement (e.g., earnings). Whether or not such an option-pricing approach might be practically useful for the analysis of investment strategies or for the evaluation of accounting policy alternatives is too early to say. Many methodological issues must be clarified first.

Use of Intraday Stock Prices

Another new methodology capitalizes on the availability of a complete stock price history, that is, prices and transaction amounts to the hour and second as well as time-stamped news announcements. The Dow Jones Broad Tape is one source of news history. Such news wire revelations are not always the very first public dissemination, although clearly when the news hits the tape, knowledge is instantaneously transmitted to large numbers of potential buyers and sellers of securities. Relative to studies that use monthly, weekly, or daily returns, intraday responses to news announcements allow a precise estimate of the relationship between information and price change. The chances that the information actually *caused* the price response are obviously high when using hourly or transaction-by-transaction price movements.

However, the validity of this approach depends on what one would expect to observe in the absence of major news announcements (i.e., the null hypothesis). Researchers usually posit the existence of a tendency for price changes to reverse themselves over very short intervals. A lack of appearance of that reversal tendency, then, is viewed as consistent with the presence of information flowing to the market.

Based on this idea, Patell and Wolfson (1979b) found that the incorporation of new information into stock prices does not occur instantaneously. Instead, the price response persists for more than a few hours, sometimes extending into the following day. While little more is known about these very short-term price effects, findings could be potentially useful for "speculative" investors, governmental agencies (concerned with the detection of insider trading), standard-setting bodies (wishing to assess short-term effects of regulation changes), and management (hoping to time its news announcements as advantageously as possible).

Concluding Comments

This chapter summarizes recent research on the effects of financial information on security prices. The evidence is reasonably conclusive on several broad issues. First, accounting information and stock price movements are significantly associated, even when the effects of other information (e.g., dividend announcements) are considered. Second, accounting information appears to be able to assist in the assessment of prospective return (e.g., in the prediction of beta). However, it is not clear that investors or creditors are able to capitalize on the predictive value of accounting data by generating excess security returns: profitable investment strategies based on publicly available information are likely to be eliminated quickly due to the efficiency of the capital market. Third, much of the appeal of historical security price analysis for investment decisions and accounting policy is its relevance to future situations. Given a proposed accounting disclosure, change in standard, and so forth, the research findings offer evidence on whether and to what extent the value of the firm as manifested in security prices might be affected. Finally, many results are hampered by the lack of a cogent theoretical framework that would deduce the relationships to be observed before the empirical analysis. As such, most of the studies still tend to be exploratory and in search of regularities that might be replicated or explained subsequently by others.

REFERENCES

Abdel-khalik, A. Rashad. FASB Research Report, *The Economic Effects on Lessees of FASB Statement No. 13, Accounting for Leases.* Stamford, Conn.: FASB, 1981.

Abdel-khalik, A. Rashad, and Ajinkya, Bipin B. "Accounting Information and Efficient Markets." In *Handbook of Accounting and Auditing,* edited by John C. Burton, Russell E. Palmer, and Robert S. Kay, chap. 47. Boston: Warren, Gorham & Lamont, Inc., 1981.

Abdel-khalik, A. Rashad, and McKeown, James C. "Understanding Accounting Changes in an Efficient Market: Evidence of Differential Reaction." *The Accounting Review,* October 1978, pp. 851-68. (1978a)

_____. "Disclosure of Estimates of Holding Gains and the Assessment of Systematic Risk." *Journal of Accounting Research.* Supplement 1978, *Studies on Accounting for Changes in General and Specific Prices: Empirical Research and Public Policy Issues,* pp. 46-77. (1978b)

Abdel-khalik, A. Rashad; Thompson, Robert B.; and Taylor, Robert E. "The Impact of Reporting Leases Off the Balance Sheet on Bond Risk Premiums." In FASB Research Report, *Economic Consequences of Financial Accounting Standards: Selected Papers,* pp. 101-58. Stamford, Conn.: FASB, 1978.

Aharony, Joseph, and Swary, Itzhak. "Quarterly Dividend and Earnings Announcements and Stockholders' Returns: An Empirical Analysis." *The Journal of Finance,* March 1980, pp. 1-12.

Ajinkya, Bipin B. "An Empirical Evaluation of Line-of-Business Reporting." *Journal of Accounting Research,* Autumn 1980, pp. 343-61.

Anderson, John C., and Frankle, Alan W. "Voluntary Social Reporting: An Iso-Beta Portfolio Analysis." *The Accounting Review,* July 1980, pp. 467-79.

Arbel, Avner, and Jaggi, Bikki. "Impact of Replacement Cost Disclosures on Investors' Decisions in the United States." *International Journal of Accounting Education and Research,* Fall 1978, pp. 71-82.

Archibald, T. Ross. "The Return to Straight-Line Depreciation: An Analysis of a Change in Accounting Methods." *Journal of Accounting Research.* Supplement, *Empirical Research in Accounting: Selected Studies, 1967,* pp. 164-80.

_____. "Stock Market Reaction to the Depreciation Switch-Back." *The Accounting Review,* January 1972, pp. 22-30.

Ashley, John W. "Stock Prices and Changes in Earnings and Dividends: Some Empirical Results." *The Journal of Political Economy,* February 1962, pp. 82-85.

Ball, Ray, and Brown, Philip. "An Empirical Evaluation of Accounting Income Numbers." *Journal of Accounting Research,* Autumn 1968, pp. 159-78.

_____. "Portfolio Theory and Accounting." *Journal of Accounting Research,* Autumn 1969, pp. 300-323.

Ball, Ray; Walker, R. G.; and Whittred, G. P. "Audit Qualifications and Share Prices." *Abacus,* June 1979, pp. 23-34.

Barr Rosenberg Associates. "Explanation of the Fundamental Risk Measurement Service Output." Mimeographed. Orinda, Calif.: N.p., 1978.

Baskin, Elba F. "The Communicative Effectiveness of Consistency Exceptions." *The Accounting Review,* January 1972, pp. 38-51.

Basu, S. "Market Reactions to Accounting Policy Deliberations: The Inflation Accounting Case Revisited." *The Accounting Review,* October 1981, pp. 942-54.

Beaver, William H. "The Information Content of Annual Earnings Announcements." *Journal of Accounting Research.* Supplement, *Empirical Research in Accounting: Selected Studies, 1968,* pp. 67-92.

_____. "The Information Content of the Magnitude of Unexpected Earnings." Research paper. Stanford, Calif.: Graduate School of Business, Stanford University, 1974.

_____. *Financial Reporting: An Accounting Revolution.* Prentice-Hall Contemporary Topics in Accounting Series. Englewood Cliffs, N.J.: Prentice-Hall, Inc., 1981.

Beaver, William H.; Christie, Andrew A.; and Griffin, Paul A. "The Information Content of SEC Accounting Series Release No. 190." *Journal of Accounting & Economics,* August 1980, pp. 127-57.

Beaver, William H.; Clarke, Roger; and Wright, William F. "The Association between Unsystematic Security Returns and the Magnitude of the Earnings Forecast Errors." *Journal of Accounting Research,* Autumn 1979, pp. 316-40.

Beaver, William H., and Dukes, Roland E. "Interperiod Tax Allocation, Earnings Expectations, and the Behavior of Security Prices." *The Accounting Review,* April 1972, pp. 320-32.

_____. "Interperiod Tax Allocation and 𝜙 Depreciation Methods: Some Empirical Results." *The Accounting Review,* July 1973, pp. 549-59.

Beaver, William H.; Griffin, Paul A.; and Landsman, Wayne R. "The Correlation of Replacement Cost Earnings with Security Returns." Research paper, revised. Stanford, Calif.: Graduate School of Business, Stanford University, July 1981.

Beaver, William H.; Kettler, Paul; and Scholes, Myron. "The Association between Market Determined and Accounting Determined Risk Measures." *The Accounting Review,* October 1970, pp. 654-82.

Beaver, William H.; Lambert, R.; and Morse, D. "The Information Content of Security Prices." *Journal of Accounting and Economics,* March 1980.

Beaver, William H., and Manegold, James. "The Association between Market-Determined and Accounting-Determined Measures of Systematic Risk: Some Further Evidence." *Journal of Financial and Quantitative Analysis,* June 1975, pp. 231-84.

Benston, George J. "Published Corporate Accounting Data and Stock Prices." *Journal of Accounting Research.* Supplement, *Empirical Research in Accounting: 1967,* p. 1.

_____. "Investors' Use of Financial Accounting Statement Numbers: A Review of Evidence from Stock Market Research." Working paper. Rochester, N.Y.: Graduate School of Management, University of Rochester, 1980.

Bildersee, John S. "The Association between a Market-Determined Measure of Risk and Alternative Measures of Risk." *The Accounting Review,* January 1975, pp. 81-98.

Blume, Marshall E. "Betas and Their Regression Tendencies." *The Journal of Finance,* June 1975, pp. 785-95.

_____. "Betas and Their Regression Tendencies: Some Further Evidence." *The Journal of Finance,* March 1979, pp. 265-67.

Blustein, Paul. "Money Managers' Bedrock Theory of Investing Comes under Attack." *The Wall Street Journal,* September 8, 1980, p. 33.

Bogue, Marcus Cook III. "The Estimation and Behavior of Systematic Risk." Ph.D. dissertation, Stanford University, May 1973.

Bowen, Robert M. "Valuation of Earnings Components in the Electric Utility Industry." *The Accounting Review,* January 1981, pp. 1-22.

Bowman, Robert G. "The Debt Equivalence of Leases: An Empirical Investigation." *The Accounting Review,* April 1980, pp. 237-53.

Brown, Philip. "The Impact of the Annual Net Profit Report on the Stock Market." *The Australian Accountant,* July 1970, pp. 277-83.

Brown, P. R., and Hancock, P. J. "Dividend Rate Changes, Profit Reports, and Share Prices: Some Australian Findings." Extract of Master's thesis, Graduate School of Management, University of Western Australia, February 1975.

Brown, Philip, and Kennelly, John W. "The Informational Content of Quarterly Earnings: An Extension and Some Further Evidence." *The Journal of Business,* July 1972, pp. 403-15.

Brown, Robert Moren. "Short-Range Market Reaction to Changes to LIFO Accounting Using Preliminary Earnings Announcement Dates." *Journal of Accounting Research,* Spring 1980, pp. 38-63.

Brown, Stewart L. "Earnings Changes, Stock Prices, and Market Efficiency." *The Journal of Finance,* March 1978, pp. 17-28.

Cassidy, David B. "Investor Evaluation of Accounting Information: Some Additional Empirical Evidence." *Journal of Accounting Research,* Autumn 1976, pp. 212-29.

Collins, Daniel W. "SEC Product-Line Reporting and Market Efficiency." *Journal of Financial Economics,* June 1975, pp. 125-64.

Collins, Daniel W., and Dent, Warren T. "The Proposed Elimination of Full Cost Accounting in the Extractive Petroleum Industry: An Empirical Assessment of the Market Consequences." *Journal of Accounting & Economics,* March 1979, pp. 3-44

Collins, Daniel W., and O'Connor, Melvin C. "An Examination of the Association between Accounting and Share Price Data in the Extractive Petroleum Industry: A Comment and Extension." *The Accounting Review,* January 1978, pp. 228-39.

Collins, Daniel W., and Simonds, Richard R. "SEC Line-of-Business Disclosure and Market Risk Adjustments." *Journal of Accounting Research,* Autumn 1979, pp. 352-83.

Davis, Darrel W.; Boatsman, James R.; and Baskin, Elba F. "On Generalizing Stock Market Research to a Broader Class of Markets." *The Accounting Review,* January 1978, pp. 1-10.

Deakin, Edward B.; Norwood, Gyles R.; and Smith, Charles H. "The Effect of Published Earnings Information on Tokyo Stock Exchange Trading." *The International Journal of Accounting Education and Research,* Fall 1974, pp. 124-36.

Derstine, Robert P., and Huefner, Ronald J. "LIFO-FIFO, Accounting Ratios and Market Risk." *Journal of Accounting Research,* Autumn 1974, pp. 216-34.

Dukes, Roland E. "An Investigation of the Effects of Expensing Research and Development Costs on Security Prices." In *Proceedings of the Conference on Topical Research in Accounting,* edited by Michael Schiff and George Sorter, pp. 147-93. New York: Ross Institute of Accounting Research, New York University, 1976.

_____. FASB Research Report, *An Empirical Investigation of the Effects of Statement of Financial Accounting Standards No. 8 on Security Return Behavior.* Stamford, Conn.: FASB, 1978.

Dukes, Roland; Dyckman, Thomas; and Elliot, John. "Accounting for Research and Development Costs: The Impact on Research and Development Expenditures." Working paper, no. 80-01. Ithaca, N.Y.: Graduate School of Business and Public Administration, Cornell University, October 15, 1980.

Dyckman, Thomas R. FASB Research Report, *The Effect of the Issuance of the Exposure Draft and FASB Statement No. 19 on the Security Returns of Oil and Gas Producing Companies.* Stamford, Conn.: FASB, 1979.

Dyckman, Thomas R.; Downes, David H.; and Magee, Robert P. *Efficient Capital Markets and Accounting: A Critical Analysis.*

222

Prentice-Hall Contemporary Topics in Accounting Series. Englewood Cliffs, N.J.: Prentice-Hall, Inc., 1975.

Easman, William S.; Falkenstein, Angela; and Weil, Roman. "The Correlation between Sustainable Income and Stock Returns: Changes in Sustainable Income. . . ." *Financial Analysts Journal*, September/October 1979, pp. 44-48.

Elgers, Pieter T. "Accounting-Based Risk Predictions: A Re-examination." *The Accounting Review*, July 1980, pp. 389-408.

Elgers, Pieter T.; Haltiner, James R.; and Hawthorne, William H. "Beta Regression Tendencies: Statistical and Real Causes." *The Journal of Finance*, March 1979, pp. 261-63.

Eskew, Robert K. "An Examination of the Association between Accounting and Share Price Data in the Extractive Petroleum Industry." *The Accounting Review*, April 1975, pp. 316-24.

_____. "The Forecasting Ability of Accounting Risk Measures: Some Additional Evidence." *The Accounting Review*, January 1979, pp. 107-18.

Eskew, Robert K., and Wright, William F. "An Empirical Analysis of Differential Capital Market Reactions to Extraordinary Accounting Items." *The Journal of Finance*, May 1976, pp. 651-74.

Evans, Thomas G.; Folks, William R., Jr.; and Jilling, Michael. FASB Research Report, *The Impact of Statement of Financial Accounting Standards No. 8 on the Foreign Exchange Risk Management Practices of American Multinationals: An Economic Impact Study.* Stamford, Conn.: FASB, 1978.

Fabozzi, Frank J. "Quality of Earnings: A Test of Market Efficiency." *The Journal of Portfolio Management*, Fall 1978, pp. 53-56.

Firth, Michael. "The Impact of Earnings Announcements on the Share Price Behavior of Similar Type Firms." *The Economic Journal*, June 1976, pp. 296-306.

_____. "Qualified Audit Reports: Their Impact on Investment Decisions." *The Accounting Review,* July 1978, pp. 642-50.

Foster, George. "Accounting Earnings and Stock Prices of Insurance Companies." *The Accounting Review,* October 1975, pp. 686-98. (1975a)

_____. "Security Price Revaluation Implications of Sub-Earnings Disclosure." *Journal of Accounting Research,* Autumn 1975, pp. 283-92. (1975b)

_____. "Quarterly Accounting Data: Time-Series Properties and Predictive-Ability Results." *The Accounting Review,* January 1977, pp. 1-21. (1977a)

_____. "Valuation Parameters of Property-Liability Companies." *The Journal of Finance,* June 1977, pp. 823-35. (1977b)

_____. *Financial Statement Analysis.* Englewood Cliffs, N.J.: Prentice-Hall, Inc., 1978.

_____. "Accounting Policy Decisions and Capital Market Research." *Journal of Accounting and Economics,* March 1980, pp. 29-62.

_____. "Intra-Industry Information Transfers Associated with Earnings Releases." *Journal of Accounting and Economics,* in press.

Foster, George, and Olsen, Chris. "Systematic Post Earnings Announcement Drifts in Security Returns: An Hypothesis Discriminating Experiment." Research paper. Stanford, Calif.: Graduate School of Business, Stanford University, September 1980.

Foster, Taylor W. III, and Vickrey, Don. "The Incremental Information Content of the 10-K." *The Accounting Review,* October 1978, pp. 921-34.

Frishkoff, Paul. FASB Research Report, *Financial Reporting and Changing Prices: A Review of Empirical Research.* Stamford, Conn.: FASB, 1982.

Gheyara, Kelly, and Boatsman, James. "Market Reaction to the 1976 Replacement Cost Disclosures." *Journal of Accounting & Economics,* August 1980, pp. 107-25.

Gonedes, Nicholas J. "Evidence on the Information Content of Accounting Numbers: Accounting-Based and Market-Based Estimates of Systematic Risk." *Journal of Financial and Quantitative Analysis,* June 1973, pp. 407-43.

_____. "Capital Market Equilibrium and Annual Accounting Numbers: Empirical Evidence." *Journal of Accounting Research,* Spring 1974, pp. 26-62.

_____. "Risk, Information, and the Effects of Special Accounting Items on Capital Market Equilibrium." *Journal of Accounting Research,* Autumn 1975, pp. 220-56.

_____. "Corporate Signaling, External Accounting, and Capital Market Equilibrium: Evidence on Dividends, Income, and Extraordinary Items." *Journal of Accounting Research,* Spring 1978, pp. 26-79.

Gonedes, Nicholas, and Dopuch, Nicholas. "Capital Market Equilibrium, Information Production, and Selecting Accounting Techniques: Theoretical Framework and Review of Empirical Work." *Journal of Accounting Research.* Supplement, *Studies on Financial Accounting Objectives, 1974,* pp. 48-129.

Good, Walter R., and Meyer, Jack R. "Adjusting the Price-Earnings Ratio Gap." *Financial Analysts Journal,* November/December 1973, p. 42.

Griffin, Paul A. "Competitive Information in the Stock Market: An Empirical Study of Earnings, Dividends and Analysts' Forecasts." *The Journal of Finance,* May 1976, pp. 631-50. (1976a)

_____. "The Association between Relative Risk and Risk Estimates Derived from Quarterly Earnings and Dividends." *The Accounting Review,* July 1976, pp. 499-515. (1976b)

_____. "Sensitive Foreign Payment Disclosures: The Securities Market Impact." In *Report of the Advisory Committee on Corporate Disclosure to the Securities and Exchange Commission.* Washington, D.C.: U.S. Government Printing Office, November 1977, pp. 694-743.

_____. "What Harm Has FASB 8 Actually Done?" *Harvard Business Review,* July-August 1979, pp. 3-6.

Griffin, Paul A., and Ng, David S. "Competitive Information Sources and Capital Market Behavior: Theory and Empirical Tests." In American Institute for Decision Sciences, *Proceedings.* 10th Annual Conference, October 30 - November 1, 1978, pp. 7-9.

Griffin, Paul A., and Nichols, Grosvenor G. "Segmental Disclosure Rules: An Empirical Evaluation." Research paper. Stanford, Calif.: Graduate School of Business, Stanford University, June 1976.

Hagerman, Robert L. "The Efficiency of the Market for Bank Stocks: An Empirical Test." *Journal of Money, Credit and Banking,* August 1973, pp. 846-55.

Hakansson, Nils H. "Information Needs for Portfolio Choice: Some Normative Aspects." In *Financial Information Requirements for Security Analysis,* edited by A. Rashad Abdel-khalik and Thomas F. Keller. Duke Second Accounting Symposium, December 2-3, 1976, pp. 18-46. Durham, N.C.: Graduate School of Business Administration, Duke University, 1976.

Harrison, Tom. "Different Market Reactions to Discretionary and Nondiscretionary Accounting Changes." *Journal of Accounting Research,* Spring 1977, pp. 84-107.

Hawkins, David F., and Campbell, Walter J. *Equity Valuation: Models, Analysis, and Implications.* Research study and report. New York: Financial Executives Research Foundation, 1978.

Haworth, Hugh R.; Matthews, John; and Tuck, Clifford C. "Full Cost vs. Successful Efforts: A Study of a Proposed Accounting Change's Competitive Effect." Research paper. Washington, D.C.: Securities and Exchange Commission, February 1978.

Hong, Hai; Kaplan, Robert S.; and Mandelker, Gershon. "Pooling vs. Purchase: The Effects of Accounting for Mergers on Stock Prices." *The Accounting Review,* January 1978, pp. 31-47.

Horwitz, Bertrand, and Kolodny, Richard. "Line of Business Reporting and Security Prices: An Analysis of an SEC Disclosure Rule." *The Bell Journal of Economics,* Spring 1977, pp. 234-249.

_____. "The Economic Effects of Involuntary Uniformity in the Financial Reporting of R & D Expenditures." *Journal of Accounting Research,* Supplement 1980, pp. 38-74.

Ingram, Robert W. "An Investigation of the Information Content of (Certain) Social Responsibility Disclosures." *Journal of Accounting Research,* Autumn 1978, pp. 270-85.

Jordan, Ronald J. "An Empirical Investigation of the Adjustment of Stock Prices to New Quarterly Earnings Information." *Journal of Financial and Quantitative Analysis,* September 1973, pp. 609-20.

Joy, O. Maurice; Litzenberger, Robert H.; and McEnally, Richard W. "The Adjustment of Stock Prices to Announcements of Unanticipated Changes in Quarterly Earnings." *Journal of Accounting Research,* Autumn 1977, pp. 207-25.

Kaplan, Robert S. "The Information Content of Financial Accounting Numbers: A Survey of Empirical Evidence." In *The Impact of Accounting Research on Practice and Disclosure,* edited by A. Rashad Abdel-khalik and Thomas F. Keller, pp. 134-73. Durham, N.C.: Duke University Press, 1978.

Kaplan, Robert S., and Roll, Richard. "Investor Evaluation of Accounting Information: Some Empirical Evidence." *The Journal of Business,* April 1972, pp. 225-57.

Kochanek, Richard Frank. "Segmental Financial Disclosure by Diversified Firms and Security Prices." *The Accounting Review,* April 1974, pp. 245-58.

Laub, P. Michael. "On the Informational Content of Dividends." *The Journal of Business,* January 1976, pp. 73-80.

Lev, Baruch. *Financial Statement Analysis: A New Approach.* Prentice-Hall Contemporary Topics in Accounting Series. Englewood Cliffs, N.J.: Prentice-Hall, Inc., 1974.

_____. "The Impact of Accounting Regulation on the Stock Market: The Case of Oil and Gas Companies." *The Accounting Review,* July 1979, pp. 485-503.

Manegold, James G. "Time-Series Properties of Earnings: A Comparison of Extrapolative and Component Models." *Journal of Accounting Research,* Autumn 1981, pp. 360-73.

May, Robert G. "The Influence of Quarterly Earnings Announcements on Investor Decisions as Reflected in Common Stock Price Changes." *Journal of Accounting Research.* Supplement, *Empirical Research in Accounting: Selected Studies, 1971,* pp. 119-69.

Morse, Dale. "Price and Trading Volume Reaction Surrounding Announcements: A Closer Examination." *Journal of Accounting Research*, Autumn 1981, pp. 374-83.

Noreen, Eric, and Sepe, James. "Market Reactions to Accounting Policy Deliberations: The Inflation Accounting Case." *The Accounting Review,* April 1981, pp. 253-69. (1981a)

_____. "Market Reactions to Accounting Policy Deliberations: The Inflation Accounting Case Revisited—A Reply." *The Accounting Review,* October 1981, pp. 955-58. (1981b)

Palmon, Dan, and Seidler, Lee J. "Current Value Reporting of Real Estate Companies and a Possible Example of Market Inefficiency." *The Accounting Review,* July 1978, pp. 776-90.

Pastena, Victor. "Some Evidence on the SEC's System of Continuous Disclosure." *The Accounting Review,* October 1979, pp. 776-83.

Patell, James M., and Wolfson, Mark A. "Anticipated Information Releases Reflected in Call Option Prices." *Journal of Accounting & Economics,* August 1979, pp. 117-40. (1979a)

_____. "The Timing of Financial Accounting Disclosures and the Intraday Distribution of Security Price Changes." Research paper. Stanford, Calif.: Graduate School of Business, Stanford University, July 1979. (1979b)

_____. "The *Ex Ante* and *Ex Post* Price Effects of Quarterly Earnings Announcements Reflected in Option and Stock Prices." *Journal of Accounting Research*, Autumn 1981, pp. 434-58.

Patz, Dennis H., and Boatsman, James R. "Accounting Principle Formulation in an Efficient Markets Environment." *Journal of Accounting Research,* Autumn 1972, pp. 392-403.

Penman, Stephen H. "Tests of Dividend-Signaling: A Comparative Analysis." Research paper. Berkeley: School of Business Administration, University of California, September 1981.

Pettit, R. Richardson. "Dividend Announcements, Security Performance, and Capital Market Efficiency." *The Journal of Finance,* December 1972, pp. 993-1007.

_____. "The Impact of Dividend and Earnings Announcements: A Reconciliation." *The Journal of Business,* January 1976, pp. 86-96.

Ricks, William. "The Market's Response to the 1974 LIFO Switch." Research paper. Berkeley: School of Business Administration, University of California, January 1980.

Ro, Byung T. "The Disclosure of Capitalized Lease Information and Stock Prices." *Journal of Accounting Research,* Autumn 1978, pp. 315-40.

_____. "The Adjustment of Security Returns to the Disclosure of Replacement Cost Accounting Information." *Journal of Accounting & Economics,* August 1980, pp. 159-89.

Roche, Peter B. "Successful-Efforts Method for Reporting Oil and Gas Search Costs Backed by Panel." *The Wall Street Journal,* July 20, 1977, p. 8.

Roll, Richard. "A Critique of the Asset Pricing Theory's Tests— Part I: On Past and Potential Testability of the Theory." *Journal of Financial Economics,* March 1977, pp. 129-76.

Rosenberg, Barr, and McKibben, Walt. "The Prediction of Systematic and Specific Risk in Common Stocks." *Journal of Financial and Quantitative Analysis,* March 1973, pp. 317-33.

Rosenberg, Barr, and Marathe, Vinay. "The Prediction of Investment Risk: Systematic and Residual Risk." Paper presented at the Seminar on the Analysis of Security Prices, November 1975, at the Graduate School of Business, University of Chicago.

Scholes, Myron, and Williams, Joseph. "Estimating Betas from Nonsynchronous Data." *Journal of Financial Economics,* December 1977, pp. 309-27.

Shank, John K.; Dillard, Jesse F.; and Murdock, Richard J. *Assessing the Economic Impact of FASB 8.* Research study. New York: Financial Executives Research Foundation, 1979.

Sharpe, I. G., and Walker, R. G. "Asset Revaluations and Stock Market Prices." *Journal of Accounting Research,* Autumn 1975, pp. 293-310.

Sunder, Shyam. "Relationship between Accounting Changes and Stock Prices: Problems of Measurement and Some Empirical Evidence." *Journal of Accounting Research.* Supplement, *Empirical Research in Accounting: Selected Studies, 1973,* pp. 1-45.

_____. "Stock Price and Risk Related to Accounting Changes in Inventory Valuation." *The Accounting Review,* April 1975, pp. 305-15.

Thakkar, Rashmi B. "The Association between Market-Determined and Accounting-Determined Risk Measures: A Note." *Journal of Accounting Research,* Spring 1978, pp. 215-23.

Thompson, Donald J., II. "Sources of Systematic Risk in Common Stocks." *The Journal of Business,* April 1976, pp. 173-88.

Vigeland, Robert L. "The Market Reaction to Statement of Financial Accounting Standards No. 2." *The Accounting Review,* April 1981, pp. 309-25.

Wallace, Anise. "Is Beta Dead?" *Institutional Investor,* July 1980, pp. 23-30.

Watts, Ross. "The Information Content of Dividends." *The Journal of Business,* April 1973, pp. 191-211.

_____. "Comments on 'On the Informational Content of Dividends'." *The Journal of Business,* January 1976, pp. 81-85. (1976a)

_____. "Comments on 'The Impact of Dividend and Earnings Announcements: A Reconciliation.'" *The Journal of Business,* January 1976, pp. 97-106. (1976b)

_____. "Systematic 'Abnormal' Returns after Quarterly Earnings Announcements." *Journal of Financial Economics,* June/September 1978, pp. 127-50.

Watts, Ross L., and Zimmerman, Jerold L. "On the Irrelevance of Replacement Cost Disclosures for Security Prices." *Journal of Accounting & Economics,* August 1980, pp. 95-106.

Welles, Chris. "Who Is Barr Rosenberg? And What the Hell Is He Talking About?" *Institutional Investor,* May 1978, pp. 59-66.

Williams, Arthur III, and Targia, John J. "Stock Market Risk—A Study of the Changing Risk Levels of the 90 Standard & Poor's Industry Groups, 1973-1979." Mimeographed. New York: Merrill Lynch Pierce Fenner & Smith Inc., November 1979.

OTHER REPORTS

Examples of the Use of FASB Statement No. 33, Financial Reporting and Changing Prices

Illustrations of Financial Reporting and Changing Prices: Statement of Financial Accounting Standards No. 33

Financial Reporting and Changing Prices: The Conference

Field Tests of Financial Reporting in Units of General Purchasing Power

See inside front cover for other titles.

For copies of reports and information on applicable prices and discount rates, please contact:

Order Department
Financial Accounting Standards Board
High Ridge Park
Stamford, Connecticut 06905
Telephones: Main Office—(203) 329-8401
                 Order Department—(203) 356-1990

Randall Library – UNCW

HF5681.B2 G79 1982

NXWW

Griffin / Usefulness to investors and creditors of

304900280302V